M000210952

Krzysztof Kieślowski was born in Warsaw on 27 June 1941. His first film was a short documentary for television, *The Tram* (1966), directed while still at the Lodz Film School. More documentaries followed after his graduation in 1969, the most famous of which was *Workers '71*, about the Szczecin strikes of 1971. His first feature for cinema came in 1976 with *The Scar*. *Camera Buff* (1979), won first prize at the Moscow Film festival and established Kieślowski as a leading figure in the Polish cinematic school of 'moral anxiety'. *Blind Chance* (1981) was made during the rise of the solidarity movement, but was banned after the declaration of martial law and stayed on the shelves until 1987. *No End* (1984) was the first film Kieślowski co-scripted with lawyer Krzysztof Piesiewicz. Their next project was *Decalogue*. In 1990 they wrote *The Double Life of Veronica*, filmed by Kieślowski in France and Poland and released in 1991. Their last collaboration was the *Three Colours* trilogy, shot and released between 1992–1994. Kieślowski died on March 13 1996.

Krzysztof Piesiewicz was born in Warsaw on 25 October 1945. After graduating in law from Warsaw University in 1970, he spent three years training for the bar before deciding to specialize in criminal law. The declaration of martial law in 1981 influenced his decision to become more involved in political cases, defending Solidarity activists arrested and put on trial by the authorities. He was also one of the prosecuting lawyers during the trial of the three security policemen accused of the murder of Father Jerzy Popieluszko in 1985. Piesiewicz first met Kieślowski in 1982 while the director was trying to make a documentary about political trials under martial law. Kieślowski later asked him for advice on a film he was planning about his experiences in court: the result was *No End*. It was Piesiewicz's idea to make *Decalogue*, which he says is 'an attempt to return to elementary values destroyed by communism'. He describes himself as a Christian rather than Catholic. Piesiewicz lives in Warsaw with his wife and two children.

DECALOGUE

THE TEN COMMANDMENTS

KRZYSZTOF KIEŚLOWSKI
KRZYSZTOF PIESIEWICZ

Translated by
Phil Cavendish and Suzannah Bluh

With an Introduction by
Krzysztof Kieślowski
and a Foreword by
Stanley Kubrick

faber and faber
LONDON·NEW YORK

First published in English in 1991
by Faber and Faber Limited
3 Queen Square London WC1N 3AU
Published in the United States by Faber and Faber Inc.,
a division of Farrar, Straus and Giroux, Inc., New York

Originally published in Polish in 1990
as *Dekalog*
by Verba Chotomow, Warsaw

Phototypeset by Parker Typesetting Service Leicester
Printed and bound by Antony Rowe Ltd, Eastbourne, England

© Krzysztof Kieślowski and Krzysztof Piesiewicz, 1990
This translation © Phil Cavendish and Suzannah Bluh, 1991
Foreword © Stanley Kubrick, 1991
Introduction © Krzysztof Kieślowski, 1991

Photograph of Krzysztof Piesiewicz by permission of the author.
Photograph of Krzysztof Kieślowski © M. Jeziorowska
All stills from *Decalogue* © Poltel Agency, reprinted courtesy the BBC

Phil Cavendish and Suzannah Bluh are hereby identified
as translators of this work in accordance with Section 77
of the Copyright, Designs and
Patents Act 1988.

A CIP record for this book is available from the
British Library

ISBN 0-571-14498-5

CONTENTS

NOTE

Decalogue V and Decalogue VI were made as feature films for cinematic release, and are called *A Short Film about Killing* and *A Short Film about Love*. They also exist in edited one-hour versions which were made for television transmission. The screenplays published here represent the feature-length films.

Decalogue was made on location in Warsaw during 1988 and 1989.

A Short Film about Killing and *A Short Film about Love* were first released in the UK in 1990.

Decalogue was first broadcast in the UK by BBC2 in May 1990.

FOREWORD

I am always reluctant to single out some particular feature of the work of a major film-maker because it tends inevitably to simplify and reduce the work. But in this book of screenplays by Krzysztof Kieślowski and his co-author, Krzysztof Piesiewicz, it should not be out of place to observe that they have the very rare ability to *dramatize* their ideas rather than just talking about them. By making their points through the dramatic action of the story they gain the added power of allowing the audience to *discover* what's really going on rather than being told. They do this with such dazzling skill, you never see the ideas coming and don't realize until much later how profoundly they have reached your heart.

Stanley Kubrick

January 1991

INTRODUCTION

Of course, the simplest answer to the question why make a series of films about the Ten Commandments would be: 'because they are there'. Such an answer would also perhaps be the most truthful, since essentially it contains all the reasons for our decision to undertake the project. Of course there are other, more complicated reasons. But in order to go into these we would have to analyse why the films are the way they are and not different, and what caused certain choices to be made; in short, the road that we took.

Krzysztof Kieślowski

I believe fate is an important part of life. Of all our lives, my own included. How many twists of fate must there have been for me to be sitting here in Warsaw, writing an introduction to the English-language edition of the *Decalogue*? Naturally, a person may select his or her path through life and so to a certain extent determines what happens along the way. But to understand where you are in the present, it is necessary to retrace the steps of your life and isolate the parts played by necessity, free will and pure chance.

Immediately after completing film school in Lodz, I started making documentary films. I loved the form and believed it was capable of describing the world. I made films about life as it is, not how it might exist in the imagination, and continued to make such films for the next twelve years. It was entirely natural that when martial law was declared in December 1981 I wanted to record the tanks, clandestine news-sheets, and anti-communist slogans daubed on walls. Severe jail sentences went hand in hand with these activities. I was keen to set up my camera in the courts where the sentences were being delivered and hoped to film the faces of both accusers and accused. Getting permission for such a project was difficult, and was eventually granted as late as August 1982.

The camera was received coldly in the court room at first; it was a witness, with an extremely long memory. The judges were never quite certain of my intentions, while the defence lawyers and their clients probably suspected that I was working on behalf

ix

of a completely compromised institution, state-controlled television, and refused to co-operate with me. But this did not last long. After only a few days, the lawyers noticed that whenever the camera was present during the hearings there were either no jail sentences at all, or they were suspended by the judges. There was a simple explanation for this. The judges were afraid that the reels of film recording their faces at the very moment they delivered unjust prison sentences could one day be used as evidence against them. The lawyers then started to tell me in advance of their clients' cases, calculating that they were likely to get off with a shorter sentence. The camera in the court room had become a desirable and welcome presence for them. There were several such cases taking place in military or civilian tribunals every day, and so in order to satisfy all my 'bookings', I had to try to get hold of a second camera. While it was still officially possible, I used to set up the two cameras in the courts without even bothering to check whether they were loaded with film or not.

After a while, unsurprisingly, permission to carry on filming was withdrawn. I never made the film because, although I had been present at several score court cases, I had not managed to record one single jail sentence. But one of the lawyers who had been quick to understand the function of the camera in the court room was Krzysztof Piesiewicz.

Two years later, I was thinking of making a feature film based on my experiences in court. I knew next to nothing about the legal intricacies of political trials, and at that moment thought of Piesiewicz. Together we wrote the screenplay for *No End* and became friends as a result. The film had a rough reception. The authorities were furious because it clearly wasn't sympathetic to them; the Party newspaper *Trybuna Ludu* wrote that it was an 'instruction manual for the underground', and for purely malicious reasons the film was badly distributed. The political opposition regarded the film as compromised and alien; they wanted to be portrayed as triumphant heroes, whereas everyone in this film hangs their heads in shame. The message was that in this war there were no winners. The third powerful force on the Polish political scene, the Catholic Church, criticized the film because there was a suicide and the leading actress was shown on several occasions without a bra, and once without any underwear at all. While all this was going on, I happened to bump into my co-scriptwriter in the street. It was cold. It was raining. I had lost one of my gloves. 'Someone should make a film about the Ten Commandments,' Piesiewicz said to me. 'You should do it.'

It was not a good time. This was a few months before three state security officers were put on trial for the murder of Father Jerzy Popieluszko, with Piesiewicz as one of the prosecuting lawyers in the case, but already there was an ominous sense of foreboding in the air. The country at large had sunk into chaos and disorder; nothing and no one was spared. One could detect a certain tension, a feeling of hopelessness and fear of yet worse to come – indeed, it was glaringly obvious that something was about to happen. By this time I had begun to travel abroad a little and also observed a general uncertainty in the world at large. I am not thinking about politics here, but of normal, everyday life. Behind every polite smile I detected indifference. I had the overwhelming impression that more and more I was seeing people who didn't really have a clear idea of why they were living. I came to the conclusion that perhaps Piesiewicz was right, but realized that the task of filming the Ten Commandments would not be an easy one. I asked him how we should go about it. 'I don't know,' he said.

We still didn't know for quite a long time after that. Should it be one film? Several films? Maybe ten films? A serial, or rather a cycle of ten separate films, based on each of the Commandments? This concept seemed most faithful to the very idea of the Decalogue. Ten propositions, ten one-hour films. Initially, while we were at the stage of writing the screenplays, I wasn't too concerned with the problems of direction. One of the reasons for starting work in the first place was the fact that for several years I had been assistant artistic director to Krzysztof Zanussi in the Tor Film Studio. Since Zanussi was working mostly abroad, he took only general decisions and left the day-to-day running of the studio to me. One of the functions of the studio is to help young directors make their first film. I knew several such directors who deserved to make a breakthrough and I also knew how difficult it was to find the money. For a long time television had been the natural home for a directorial début – TV films are shorter and less expensive, and so there is less risk involved. But the problem was that state television was not interested in one-off films, only serials, although if pushed it sometimes accepted cycles. I thought that if we were to write ten screenplays, we could present them as a cycle based on the Ten Commandments and allocate one each to ten up-and-coming directors. Only much later, when the first screenplay versions were ready, did I realize rather selfishly that I wanted to do the whole lot myself. I had already become quite attached to several of them and was sorry to let them go. I had been keen to direct a few of them anyway and so it seemed logical to do all ten.

From the very beginning, we knew the films would be contemporary. For a while we toyed with the idea of basing them in the world of politics, but the problem of getting them past the censor made this impossible. There was certainly no lack of material in Poland for films about the dramatic, tragic, criminal and often ridiculous mistakes of the authorities; each of the Ten Commandments could have been adequately illustrated. But in reality this was all hypothetical because by the mid-1980s, politics had ceased to interest us. On a day-to-day basis they were tedious and trivial, and, from the historical perspective, hopeless. We didn't believe that politics could change the world, even less so for the better. We also realized that few people were really in a position to understand its subtle twists and turns, and we were not too confident of our own ability to understand them either. So we decided to ignore the world of politics in the films. Also, we began to suspect intuitively that we could market *Decalogue* abroad.

We ignored very Polish specifics, in other words, the daily grind of life around us: queues, meat ration cards, petrol shortages, a bureaucracy which reared its ugly head in even the most trivial of matters, the noisy public on the buses, the price increases as a constant topic of conversation, the ill dying in hospital corridors and so on. Everyday life was unbearably monotonous and terribly uninteresting. We knew then that we had to find extreme, extraordinary situations for our characters, ones in which they would face difficult choices and make decisions which could not be taken lightly. We spent some time deciding what sort of heroes they should be. They had to be credible and recognizable to the extent that the viewer would be able to think: 'I've been in that position. I know exactly how they feel,' or 'Something very similar occurred to me once.' And yet the films could not in any way be an account of ordinary life – on the contrary, they had to take the form of highly compact, streamlined bullets. It very quickly became clear that these would be films about feelings and passions, because we knew that love, or the fear of death, or the pain caused by a needle-prick, are common to all people, irrespective of their political views, the colour of their skin or their standard of living.

I believe the life of every person is worthy of scrutiny, containing its owns secrets and dramas. People don't talk about them because they are embarrassed, because they do not like to scratch old wounds, or are afraid of being judged unfashionably sentimental. Therefore we wanted to start each film in such a way that would suggest that the lead character had been chosen by the camera almost by accident, as if one of many. The idea occurred to us of showing a huge stadium in which, from among the hundred thousand faces, we would focus on one in particular. There was also the idea of the camera picking out one person from a crowded street and then following that person for the rest of the film. Finally we decided to place the action of *Decalogue* in a large housing estate, with thousands of similar windows framed within the establishing shot. Behind each of these windows, we said to ourselves, is a living human being, whose mind, whose heart and, even better, whose stomach is worthy of investigation. This approach had several advantages. The television viewers following the cycle from the beginning would be able to recognize in the individual films people from other parts of the series, encountered only fleetingly in a lift, a corridor, or appearing only with a request to borrow some salt.

The most important problem still remained – how to adapt the action of each film to illustrate the relevant Commandment. We read everything it was possible to read in libraries; a mass of interpretations of the Commandments, discussions and commentaries on the Bible, both Old and New Testaments. But we decided fairly quickly to dispense with all this. Priests draw upon it every day and we weren't here to preach. We didn't want to adopt the tone of those who praise or condemn, handing out a reward here for the doing of Good and a punishment there for the doing of Evil. Rather, we wished to say: 'We know no more than you. But maybe it is worth investigating the unknown, if only because the very feeling of not knowing is a painful one.'

Once this approach had been decided, we found it easier to solve the problem of the relationship between the films and the individual Commandments: a tentative one. The films should be influenced by the individual Commandments to the same degree that the Commandments influence our daily lives. We were aware that no philosophy or ideology had ever challenged the fundamental tenets of the Commandments during their several thousand years of existence, yet they are nevertheless transgressed on a routine basis. Or to put this more simply: everyone knows it is wrong to kill another human being, yet wars continue and police forces the world over find dead bodies in cellars and parks with knives in their throats. One cannot put the question whether it is good or evil to kill without being suspected of naïvety or stupidity. But it seems to me that one can put the question of why one human being may kill another without reason, especially if one voices doubts over whether the law has the right to punish one form of killing with another. We endeavoured to construct the plot of this film so that the viewer would leave the film with the same questions in mind which we had asked ourselves when the screenplay was only an empty page fed into the typewriter.

For a long time we were worried about the dimensions of *Decalogue*, though not in the sense of the work it entailed for us as the scriptwriters and for myself as director. We were afraid of something else. Did we have the right to deal with a subject of such universal significance, a subject which even for many of those who break the Commandments is something deeply sacred? These fears are easy to comprehend in a Catholic country like Poland, where the Church is a powerful force in shaping public opinion. Our fears subsided when we suddenly realized that all writers, painters, playwrights and film-makers indirectly deal with themes which are central to the Commandments – they had done so in the past and would no doubt continue to do so in the future. Doesn't Shakespeare's Richard III covet something which is not rightfully his? The Karamazov brothers had few good reasons for honouring their father, and Raskolnikov had none at all for killing the old woman. Brueghel painted robbers and thieves, and in his films Woody Allen seems unable to stop himself from trying to jump into bed with another woman; it is also not uncommon for someone else to leap into bed with his film-wife. The same applies precisely to second-rate crime films and third-rate melodramas, and it applies also to Beethoven, who praised and at the same time questioned God, sometimes in one and the same symphony. It effects all those who describe a life, a mood or a frame of mind, and we were simply taking our places in the queue.

It took us more than a year to write the scripts, one after the other, in succession. We spent many evenings sitting either in Piesiewicz's kitchen or in my small, smoke-filled room. The next year and two months were taken up with filming. But this was all a long time ago. We are left now with the films themselves, which have been received much better than we could possibly have imagined, although it is not really clear to us why.

Krzysztof Kieślowski, Warsaw, spring 1990

Krzysztof Kieślowski

Krzysztof Piesiewicz

THE TEN COMMANDMENTS

And God spake all these words saying I am the Lord thy God, who brought thee out of the land of Egypt, out of the house of bondage.

ONE
Thou shalt have none other Gods but me.

TWO
Thou shalt not make to thyself any graven image, nor the likeness of any thing that is in heaven above, or in the earth beneath, or in the water under the earth. Thou shalt not bow down to them, nor worship them. For I the Lord thy God am a jealous God, and visit the sins of the fathers upon the children unto the third and fourth generation of them that hate me, and shew mercy unto thousands in them that love me and keep my commandments.

THREE
Thou shalt not take the name of the Lord thy God in vain: for the Lord will not hold him guiltless, that taketh his name in vain.

FOUR
Remember that thou keep holy the Sabbath day.

FIVE
Honour thy father and thy mother; that thy days may be long in the land which the Lord thy God giveth thee.

SIX
Though shalt not kill.

SEVEN
Thou shalt not commit adultery.

EIGHT
Thou shalt not steal.

NINE
Thou shalt not bear false witness against thy neighbour.

TEN
Thou shalt not covet thy neighbour's house, thou shalt not covet thy neighbour's wife, nor his servant, nor his maid, nor his ox, nor his ass, nor anything that is his.

DECALOGUE ONE

The cast and crew of *Decalogue One* included:

KRZYSZTOF	Henryk Baranowski
IRENA	Maja Komorowska
PAWEL	Wojciech Klata

Director of Photography	Wieslaw Zdort
Cameraman	Jerzy Rudzinski
Producer	Ryszard Chutkowski
Composer	Zbigniew Preisner
Artistic Director	Halina Dobrowolska
Sound	Malgorzata Jaworska
Lighting	Jerzy Tomczuk
Film Editor	Ewa Smal
Production Managers	Pawel Mantorski
	Wlodzimierz Bendych
Costume Designers	Malgorzata Obloza
	Hanna Cwiklo
Director	Krzysztof Kieślowski

Still: Henryk Baranowski as Krzysztof and Wojciech Klata as Pawel

It is a grey morning in late autumn. The apartment block, a huge slab of concrete, looks uninviting at this time of year. A mongrel bitch is being chased by several male dogs. Owners of cars parked in the alleyways emerge from the stairwells carrying batteries which they then diligently wire-up to the respective engines. The drivers and dogs startle a small flock of frozen pigeons, who take flight briefly and then start to settle back down again. One of the birds drops from the sky with a swerving, gliding movement and chooses to alight on one of the several hundred window-sills of the huge apartment block. It sits there and looks through the window into the flat.

Silence – perhaps the inhabitants are still asleep, or perhaps they are not at home. Posters, models from Steven Spielberg films, and fashionable red furniture fill a child's bedroom. The bed lies unmade – whoever was in it must have just got up. The large living room has a period wall-clock and a mixture of old and new furniture. Two computer screens stand on a huge, pine table surrounded by loosely tangled wires, extension leads, printers and two keyboards. We move towards one of the computer screens, which has numbers and signs displayed on it. A light, rhythmic clicking of keys being punched out on the keyboard: little PAWEL *is storing something in the computer's memory. He is about ten or twelve years old and is still wearing his pyjamas – evidently he has only just got up, tormented by a mathematical problem which he did not have the time to resolve the previous evening. He smiles: the operation has been brought to a satisfactory conclusion. He gets up from the chair and opens the bedroom door.*

PAWEL: Dad . . .

    (KRZYSZTOF *is sleeping on the large sofa-bed, having fallen asleep in his shirt and wearing his wrist-watch.*)

KRZYSZTOF: Where are your glasses?

PAWEL: Wait, give me some data.

KRZYSZTOF: You did it?

PAWEL: Give me the data, then we'll see.

KRZYSZTOF: You didn't touch mine, did you?

PAWEL: Dad . . .

> (*He is offended: he never touches anything unless they have agreed it beforehand.*)

> Well?

KRZYSZTOF: 79.4 per hour. Journey is four hours and thirteen minutes long.

> (*The boy dashes back to the computer.*)

> Put your glasses on!

> (*He looks at his watch and half-shuts his eyes.* PAWEL *punches the keys, checks the result, and then comes back to his father's room. He tugs his father by the shoulder, keen to tell him the answer and clearly pleased with himself, but* KRZYSZTOF *only pulls up the covers.*)

> I'm not talking to you.

PAWEL: But . . .

KRZYSZTOF: The glasses!

> (PAWEL *goes out of the room. He finds the glasses among the toys and exercise books on a table in his own room. He puts them on and sits sulkily on the bed, listening intently.*)

> Pawel!

> (*The boy gets up from the bed after the second summons and stands reluctantly by the door.*)

> What was the answer?

PAWEL: I don't remember.

KRZYSZTOF: Don't get upset. We agreed you would always wear your glasses. Yes or no?

PAWEL: Yes.

KRZYSZTOF: What was the answer?

> (PAWEL *still in an offended tone.*)

PAWEL: 164,356 kilometres.

> (KRZYSZTOF *narrows his eyes and makes a brief calculation, concentrating hard.*)

KRZYSZTOF: Sounds about right. (*He smiles at his son.*)

> Come here.

(*He holds out his hands.* PAWEL *hesitates for a moment and then quickly goes up to his father and hugs him.* KRZYSZTOF *strokes his hair.*)

I'm sorry, but I have to keep an eye on you. You understand that, don't you?

PAWEL: Yes. You smell of cigarettes. How late were you sitting up?

KRZYSZTOF: Until three.

PAWEL: And?

KRZYSZTOF: I think I cracked it. It should be able to take a huge number of programmes, more than all the ones I've done up until now.

PAWEL: Can I see?

KRZYSZTOF: After lunch. Now get dressed. Everything OK now?

(PAWEL *nods, still clasped to his father: yes, everything is all right now.*)

3

PAWEL *runs out of the block of flats. He walks along to a kiosk, buys a newspaper, and then runs off into the middle of the estate, stopping in front of the nursery school. He looks around and then leaps to one side, pressing himself up against the wall: a* GIRL *of about the same age is taking a heavily wrapped up little child to the school. They go into the building and* PAWEL *waits for a moment before stepping back on to the pavement. He walks past the* GIRL *just as she is coming back through the front gate. Neither betrays any hint of surprise or delight.*

PAWEL: Hi.

GIRL: Hi.

(*They head off in their different directions, but glance back briefly over their shoulders at each other, immediately pretending that they have not actually done so.* PAWEL *hurries along more quickly but stops a few metres further on. A dog which has been knocked over and killed by a car is lying on the estate pathway, its eyes wide-open, yellow, and glazed-over. The little boy slowly stretches out a hand to touch the stiff, frozen animal. He tries to stroke it: the fur is rough and erect, and refuses to yield to his touch.* PAWEL *straightens back up again and walks off slowly towards his own block.*)

4

KRZYSZTOF *is preparing breakfast.* PAWEL *returns with the newspaper.*
PAWEL: Below zero for five days running.
> (*He gives his father the newspaper, his ears still red from the cold outside. He wipes his steamed-up glasses and takes off his coat.*)
KRZYSZTOF: Did you see her then?
> (PAWEL *smiles.*)
PAWEL: Well . . .
KRZYSZTOF: And? Did you say anything to her?
PAWEL: Yes. Hi.
KRZYSZTOF: What did she say to that?
PAWEL: She said, Hi back.
KRZYSZTOF: Did she look at you?
PAWEL: She looked back over her shoulder.
KRZYSZTOF: Well, there you are then.
PAWEL: You know what, Dad?
> (KRZYSZTOF *looks at his son.*)
Her nose was red.
KRZYSZTOF: These things happen, even to girls.
> (*He takes the newspaper and sits down to breakfast.* PAWEL *pours himself some milk, gets up and looks for something on top of the fridge and the kitchen surfaces. He finds an ashtray with a stubbed-out cigarette.*)
PAWEL: You've been smoking.
KRZYSZTOF: It's yesterday's.
PAWEL: We agreed you wouldn't smoke before breakfast, right?
KRZYSZTOF: It's one of yesterday's, honestly.
> (*They finish breakfast.* KRZYSZTOF *is now smoking a cigarette with his cup of coffee and has the newspaper spread out in front of him.* PAWEL *is trying to read something – it is the page with the obituary columns.*)
PAWEL: If . . . someone died abroad, would there be an announcement as well?

[6]

KRZYSZTOF: If someone was prepared to pay for it.

PAWEL: Dad . . .

(*Something in* PAWEL's *voice makes* KRZYSZTOF *put down the newspaper.*)

Why do people die?

KRZYSZTOF: It varies. Sometimes because of heart attacks, or accidents, or old age . . .

PAWEL: No, I mean, why do people have to die at all?

KRZYSZTOF: See what it says under 'death' in the encyclopaedia.

(PAWEL *gets up and takes down the relevant tome from a shelf crammed full of various kinds of encyclopaedias. He flicks through the pages, evidently accustomed to looking things up in it, and reads out aloud.*)

PAWEL: ' . . .a phenomenon caused by the irreversible cessation of all functions of the bodily organism, the heart, the central nervous system . . .' What's the central nervous system?

KRZYSZTOF: Look it up – there's an entry under the heading.

(PAWEL *reaches for another tome and reads the complicated explanation. He closes the book with a thump and comes back.*)

Know now?

PAWEL: It didn't have anything.

KRZYSZTOF: It must have. It's got everything that can be described and understood. Man is a machine. The heart is like a pump and the brain is like a computer. They get exhausted and then stop working – that's all there is to it. What's up? Is something wrong?

PAWEL: Nothing, only (*He points to the newspaper*) they say something here about 'a service for the peace of her soul'. There's nothing about the soul in the encyclopaedia.

KRZYSZTOF: It's just a term. It doesn't really exist.

PAWEL: Auntie thinks it does.

KRZYSZTOF: Some people find life easier to cope with if they think it does.

PAWEL: Do you?

KRZYSZTOF: Me? No. Is anything the matter?

PAWEL: No, nothing.

KRZYSZTOF: Well?

PAWEL: I saw a dead dog today. As I was coming back with the

[7]

papers. The one with the yellow eyes. It was always cold and hungry and hung around the dustbins. Know the one I mean?

KRZYSZTOF: Yes.

PAWEL: Right. Well I was so pleased I got the answer right this morning . . . and it was just lying there and its eyes were completely glazed over.

5

A television crew on a shoot during the school playbreak. A reporter is interviewing the headmaster and a teacher, possibly about the quality of the school milk. A dinner-lady in a white apron is ladling out milk from a large saucepan nearby and one by one the children come forward to receive their glassful. PAWEL *glances away from the scene which is at the centre of attention.* OLA, *the little girl whom we met by the nursery school, is standing alone by the window with a small cardboard box in her arms.* PAWEL *nervously walks over to her.*

PAWEL: What have you got in there?

(OLA *opens the box: a little guinea-pig looks around in surprise.*) What's that for?

OLA: Biology. But the teacher's afraid of it and won't let me take him out.

(PAWEL *delicately strokes the guinea-pig's head.*)

Look at its teeth.

(*She draws back the skin on its snout. The teeth are surprisingly long and yellow, and totally alter the animal's expression – it looks now like a wild, carnivorous beast.*)

Don't be afraid.

(PAWEL *gives it his finger, which the guinea-pig gently nibbles.* OLA *smiles.* PAWEL *smiles as well. The television editor loudly asks all the children to amuse themselves in front of the cameras, and* PAWEL *is called over by his friends. He runs off, leaving* OLA *by the window. Holding the guinea-pig in one hand, she watches the others playing.*)

[8]

6

It is freezing cold. Some young boys have made a skating track out of the frozen puddles. They run up to it and slide along, jumping off unsteadily when the ice runs up against the pavement or some grass. Like the others, PAWEL *is running up to it as fast as he can.* IRENA, *Krzysztof's sister and Pawel's aunt, is standing by the fence around the playground. She watches* PAWEL *affectionately for a while and then calls over to him.* PAWEL *takes a tumble as he skips off the frozen track, brushes himself down, and then waves to his aunt with a smile.*

PAWEL: One more time!

> (IRENA *nods her head.* PAWEL *elegantly skips off the skating track, picks up his satchel, and runs over to her. It is clear that they are both very fond of each other.*
> What's for lunch?

IRENA: Soup and a second course. OK?

PAWEL: Great. There was a TV crew at school today.

IRENA: Why?

PAWEL: Something to do with the milk. When's Dad coming to pick me up?

IRENA: In the evening.

PAWEL: He's working on this really great computer, you know.

7

IRENA *lives in the same old house her parents used to live in. She and* PAWEL *are finishing their lunch in the cosy, but slightly untidy kitchen.*

PAWEL: Shall I do the washing up?

IRENA: No, it's all right. Do you want to see something? It's in a white envelope under the lamp in the sitting room.

> (PAWEL *goes into the sitting room, switches on the lamp and opens the white envelope. Inside are several colour-print enlargements. The pictures are of a Polish excursion to the Vatican and show a festive, smiling group standing around a figure dressed in white.* PAWEL *recognizes* IRENA *among the*

group – she is in all the three or four pictures.)
Recognize me?
(*She stands in the doorway with a washing-up cloth in her hands.*)

PAWEL: Was that from the time you brought me the pink pencil-case?

IRENA: That's right. I got the prints back today.

PAWEL: That's him, isn't it – is he a good man?

IRENA: Yes – he's a very good man.

PAWEL: Is he intelligent?

IRENA: Oh yes, very intelligent.

PAWEL: Do you think he knows –
(*Dish-cloth in hand,* IRENA *goes over to* PAWEL *and sits down beside him without interrupting his train of thought.*)
– what life is for?

IRENA: Yes, he does.

PAWEL: Dad says we have to do things which make life easier for those who come after us. He says that's what life is for. But it doesn't always work out like that.

IRENA: Yes – but maybe that's not the only reason.

PAWEL: Dad's . . . your brother, isn't he?

IRENA: But you know that.

PAWEL: Why doesn't he go to church and visit the Pope like you do?

IRENA: Even when he wasn't much older than you, he used to say that Man was so intelligent he could do everything by himself. That he can rely on himself for everything.

PAWEL: And that's not true?

IRENA: Man is capable of a great deal – take your father, for instance. But he could have achieved much more if he hadn't turned his back on something else. Does that make sense?

8

KRZYSZTOF *and* PAWEL *climb into the lift.* KRZYSZTOF *looks at his digital watch.*

KRZYSZTOF: Are we timing it?

PAWEL: Start.
> (KRZYSZTOF *presses the stop-watch function. The lift goes up.*)
> Dad, Irena's put me in for religious classes.
KRZYSZTOF: When for?
PAWEL: Tuesdays.
KRZYSZTOF: Fine. As long as it doesn't clash with your English.
> (*The lift stops.*)
PAWEL: Stop!
KRZYSZTOF: I forgot. You distracted me by talking so much.
PAWEL: Fff–iddlesticks.
> (KRZYSZTOF *laughs.*)
KRZYSZTOF: You swear and still want to go to religious classes?

9

Frozen to the bone, the two of them take off their coats and scarves. The telephone rings. PAWEL *is at the age when he likes to answer the telephone himself. He runs over to it with only one shoe on.*
PAWEL: Hello?
IRENA: (*Voice over*) Well? Did you ask him?
PAWEL: Aha. (*To his father.*) It's Auntie.
> (KRZYSZTOF *is still in the hallway.*)
KRZYSZTOF: What does she want?
PAWEL: She wants to know if you agreed.
KRZYSZTOF: To what?
PAWEL: To religious classes.
> (KRZYSZTOF *goes over to the telephone.*)
KRZYSZTOF: Don't be silly, Irena. Of course he can if he wants
> to. It's his affair. (*He puts down the receiver.*)
PAWEL: I'm making some tea!
KRZYSZTOF: Make some for me as well.
> (*He glances towards the new computer. He is astonished to see
> that the screen is switched on and emanating a green glow which
> floods out over on to the table and shelves, and the whole
> assortment of hi-tech gadgets lying spread out on the table; the
> leads, the printers and the gauges.*)
Pawel! Did you turn this on?

PAWEL: No – I never touched it.

(*He looks with amazement at the large screen. Both stand rooted to the spot and simply stare at the screen. Lines have begun to flicker across the screen, eventually forming themselves into two words in English: 'I'm ready.'*)

KRZYSZTOF: I must have forgotten to switch it off. (*He switches off the computer. The screen fades.*)

PAWEL: Let me –

KRZYSZTOF: It's not ready yet. (*He switches it on again. The screen glows with the same green light.*)

PAWEL: What can it do?

KRZYSZTOF: A lot. You can even ask it questions in different languages. Polish too.

(PAWEL *types out a question on the keyboard.*)

PAWEL: What is the date today?

(*The answer flashes up almost immediately.*)

COMPUTER:(*In English*) 3 December 1986, Wednesday 337.

KRZYSZTOF: Its calendar is programmed up to the year 3000. What for, I don't know.

(PAWEL *types out another question.*)

PAWEL: Can you play chess?

COMPUTER: (*In English*) Yes.

(*The answer appears immediately.*)

PAWEL: What lessons have I got tomorrow?

COMPUTER:(*In English*) I don't understand.

KRZYSZTOF: You have to put in your name. It still hasn't learnt to recognize people. Not yet, anyway.

(PAWEL *alters the command.*)

PAWEL: What lessons does Pawel have tomorrow?

(*The answer again appears immediately.*)

COMPUTER: Polish, Polish, mathematics, history, PE, PE, 8.45–13.30.

(PAWEL *turns to his father.*)

PAWEL: That's amazing.

KRZYSZTOF: We'll see. The kettle's boiling.

(*We can indeed hear the kettle whistling in the kitchen.*)

PAWEL *is already in bed.* KRZYSZTOF *opens the bedroom door.*

KRZYSZTOF: Time to go to sleep. It's already half-past nine.

(PAWEL *looks up from his book.*)

PAWEL: Have you looked at the thermometer?

KRZYSZTOF: It's minus 14.

PAWEL: Dad –

KRZYSZTOF: We'll see. Be patient. We'll see tomorrow.

(*He switches off the light. The little boy's voice comes out of the darkness just as he is about to close the door.*)

PAWEL: Do you think Mum will ring before Christmas?

KRZYSZTOF: I should think so. Sleep well.

10

A university lecture hall filled with dozens of students. KRZYSZTOF *is finishing a complicated equation on the blackboard and the students are taking notes.* PAWEL *is sitting in the corner and drawing something: Big Chief Sitting Bull and his squaw are sitting around a fire.* KRZYSZTOF *is bringing the lecture to a close.*

KRZYSZTOF: This is more or less how it would look. Of course, we could have solved it earlier (*He underlines a position in a long row of figures written on the blackboard*) but it would have been a shame. The second half of the equation is far more interesting. Thank you.

(*He goes over to* PAWEL.)

Let's go.

(*He looks at the drawings.* PAWEL *puts them in his satchel. A* JUNIOR LECTURER *walks over to them.*)

Yes, Karol.

JUNIOR LECTURER: I've been invited to take part in a discussion group – I just wanted to let you know – in church.

KRZYSZTOF: What's the topic?

JUNIOR LECTURER: Science and religion.

KRZYSZTOF: Interesting.

JUNIOR LECTURER: I just thought, seeing as how I'm your assistant and you're responsible for the department . . .

KRZYSZTOF: But not for the views of my colleagues, thank God.

(PAWEL *points to his watch.* KRZYSZTOF *says goodbye to his assistant.*)

[13]

11

A game of simultaneous chess is underway in a large hall. A MASTER, *or Grandmaster, is walking around a room full of about a dozen chessboards.* KRZYSZTOF *is sitting behind one of them, with* PAWEL *standing beside him. The* MASTER *is taking very little time over his moves and swiftly progresses from board to board.* PAWEL *is closely observing his moves and behaviour. Without much reflection, the* MASTER *makes a move on Krzysztof's chessboard and goes on to the next one.* PAWEL *leans over and whispers something in his father's ear.*

PAWEL: Castle. Then you can check him with the queen.

KRZYSZTOF: That's too simple. He's won eight games already.

PAWEL: Nine. You'll see I'm right – he'll protect his king with the rook and then the game's yours.

(Their turn is getting nearer again. KRZYSZTOF *castles as the* MASTER *is just about to come over. He looks at the father and son in astonishment. Gently supporting himself on the table with his fingers, he thinks for a while and then moves his rook over to protect the king. He moves on to the next board.)*

I told you. He's on automatic pilot. He's lost.

*(*KRZYSZTOF *analyses the position again.)*

KRZYSZTOF: You're right.

(They wait calmly for the MASTER *to come round again, and as he turns to them,* KRZYSZTOF *moves his bishop off the eighth rank of the board.)*

PAWEL: Checkmate.

MASTER: So it is.

*(*PAWEL *happily hugs his father for all he's worth.)*

12

PAWEL *opens the doors on to the balcony. A milk-bottle full of water which has turned into ice is standing outside, the glass having cracked in several places.* PAWEL *picks up the frozen bottle and triumphantly takes it back into the room.*

PAWEL: Look! After only one hour!

(*He prises the pieces of glass off without too much difficulty and throws them into a bucket. He now has a bottle-shaped piece of ice in his hand. He goes over to his father.*)

Feel that.

(KRZYSZTOF *feels the ice: it is cold, but the shape is attractive and smooth to the touch.*)

Nice.

KRZYSZTOF: It is, isn't it. Put it in the bath.

PAWEL: No, let's put it back on the balcony. Then we'll see what happens to it.

KRZYSZTOF: Nothing will happen. It'll just melt when there's a thaw.

(PAWEL *takes the bottle back out on to the balcony and puts it back in exactly the same place as before. He calls out from the balcony.*)

PAWEL: Would tea freeze as well?

KRZYSZTOF: Yes.

PAWEL: Then I'll make a yellow one from the tea and a red one. I'll put in some paint.

KRZYSZTOF: Fine.

(PAWEL *comes back and stands over his father as he works on the computer.*)

PAWEL: Can we do a calculation now? Yesterday you said we could do it today.

KRZYSZTOF: OK.

PAWEL: On this one?

KRZYSZTOF: No, on the usual one. I'm not sure this one's quite up to it yet.

(*They move over to the small computer.*)

We can't assume it will be below freezing the whole time. Let's say for ten hours, mostly during the nights. But we'll have to find out exactly.

PAWEL: How?

KRZYSZTOF: From the Meteorology Institute. Give them a ring and ask them the ground temperature for today, yesterday and the day before yesterday.

(PAWEL *looks up the number in the phone book and picks up the receiver.*)

PAWEL: Hello, could you give me today's ground temperature, please? Thank you. And yesterday's and the day before's? Thank you very much. Yes, here in Warsaw. Thank you.
(*He notes down the information and goes back to his father. KRZYSZTOF covers the screen with his hand.*)

KRZYSZTOF: What's the equation for pressure?
(PAWEL *instantly recites the equation from memory.* KRZYSZTOF *moves his hand away: it tallies with the figures on the screen.*)
How many degrees was it?
(PAWEL *reads from the piece of paper.*)

PAWEL: After 7 p.m., it was minus 17.4 degrees. Yesterday it was minus 16.8, and the day before that minus 13.4.
(KRZYSZTOF *feeds the information into the computer. He quickly punches the keys and the computer makes the calculation. A few moments later the answer flashes up on the screen.*)
Well?

KRZYSZTOF: This is the resistance per centimetre square of ice. It means someone three times your weight can walk on it safely.

PAWEL: The boys have been sliding on it for several days already. They've been making fun of me.

KRZYSZTOF: Well, tomorrow you'll be able to go as well.
(PAWEL *runs over to the balcony door, opens it, and shouts out loudly.*)

PAWEL: Tomorrow I can come skating!

KRZYSZTOF: Pawel!

PAWEL: Why shouldn't they know! Tomorrow I can go skating! Are you going to give them to me now?

KRZYSZTOF: What?

PAWEL: Don't pretend. The present I'm getting for Christmas. From you and Mum.

KRZYSZTOF: What is it then?

PAWEL: But I already know . . .

KRZYSZTOF: Where are they then?

PAWEL: Under your bed.
(KRZYSZTOF *smiles. He checks the figures again while glancing at the piece of paper on which* PAWEL *has written all the temperatures. He does the calculation again – the result is*

[16]

identical. PAWEL *enters the room at the same moment, several inches higher as a result of a pair of splendid, Western-made skates. He moves with difficulty around the floor.*)

KRZYSZTOF: Are they all right?

PAWEL: They're fantastic.

KRZYSZTOF: Good, now off to bed. I'm going for a jog and I want you asleep by the time I get back.

13

KRZYSZTOF *jogs along the lamp-lit pathways between the apartment blocks in his track-suit and training shoes. The pathways slope away towards an area which is less well lit and this is the direction* KRZYSZTOF *takes. Only a solitary lamp-post stands there throwing light on to a small lake.* KRZYSZTOF *slips down a low bank and steps gingerly on to the ice – it is firm. He stands more confidently now and then jumps up and down. He runs into the middle of the lake, stamping his feet as he goes. The ice seems safe. He gathers speed and slides: his Adidas training shoes are not the best sort of thing for this kind of activity, but he manages to slide for several yards nevertheless. One side of the lake narrows into a stream which is flowing either into or out of the lake. It is not frozen over. The ice begins to creak –* KRZYSZTOF *steps off the lake by the bank and returns with a stick to check the depth of the water. He plunges the stick several inches deep into the water and then repeats the experiment in several places elsewhere – it is shallow everywhere. He bangs the ice with the stick and tries to break it over as large an area as possible, but the ice is solid and can be broken only near the stream.* KRZYSZTOF *finally throws the stick away and turns back. He can see a small bonfire on the higher bank which runs along the opposite side of the lake. A man wearing a fur coat is sitting beside it. He has a young face and is smiling, despite being deep in thought. They look at each other for a while, after which* KRZYSZTOF *turns back and heads for home.*

14

It is now dark in Pawel's room.
KRZYSZTOF: Are you asleep?
    (*He speaks softly and hears a soft reply.*)
PAWEL: No. Look how shiny they are.
    (KRZYSZTOF *goes into the bedroom.* PAWEL *has hung his new
    skates right above the bed. The street-lamp outside is reflected in
    the blades and narrow streaks of light dance along the wall when
    *PAWEL *lightly nudges them. They are speaking softly to one
    another.*)
KRZYSZTOF: I've checked the ice.
PAWEL: That's why I was waiting.
KRZYSZTOF: It's safe. Only promise you won't go near the
    stream. It doesn't freeze over. You can go fifteen metres, but
    no closer.
PAWEL: Fifteen metres. OK.
KRZYSZTOF: It's shallow, but why get wet? Where's your teddy?
    (PAWEL *pulls back the covers. The teddy-bear is lying next to
    him on the pillow.*)
PAWEL: He's already asleep.

15

*Bright, sunny weather and gleaming ice. Pawel's new skates slide in
slow motion on to the ice followed by* PAWEL *himself. He glides
smoothly over the surface. It is clearly a dream because he is moving to
the accompaniment of music.* PAWEL *skates several times around the
small lake, his circles getting smaller and smaller around the figure of*
OLA, *who is standing in the middle. The skating, the sun, the skates
cutting into the clear ice, and the faces of* PAWEL *and* OLA, *are all
beautiful and surreal.*

16

KRZYSZTOF is sitting at a desk strewn with papers, deep in thought.
The bars of music from the previous scene can be heard fading gradually
in the background. An early winter dusk is beginning to descend outside
the window. KRZYSZTOF *switches on a light. He notices that the papers*
spread out in front of him are slowly turning a navy-blue colour. He
watches in astonishment as entire pages of letters and numbers he has
noted down drown in a lake of blue. Only after a while does he realize
the rational reason for their vanishing. He swiftly gathers up the various
papers and picks up a bottle of ink which has been standing on the desk;
the bottle has cracked and the navy-blue fluid is escaping from it in a
thin, dark stream. KRZYSZTOF *saves what he can. The ink-bottle*
leaves a navy-blue trail along the floor as it is taken away to the
waste-bin. KRZYSZTOF *is covered in ink. He hears a soft knocking at*
the door and walks over to it: a little girl of about four years old is
standing in the doorway, clearly embarrassed.
GIRL: Mum wants to know if Pawel is at home.
    (KRZYSZTOF *smiles.*)
KRZYSZTOF: No, he isn't. Why?
GIRL: Mum's asking. I don't know.
    (*Embarrassed, she runs off.*)

17

KRZYSZTOF watches her disappear around a corner at the far end of the
corridor. He tries to wash off the ink in the bathroom. There is a dark
stain on the bridge of his nose where, clearly without thinking, he has
touched his face with his inky fingers. Through the gurgling of the
tap-water he can detect the wailing siren of an emergency vehicle. A
fire-engine with its blue, flashing warning light turns into the estate,
followed by a police car and an ambulance. KRZYSZTOF *stares blankly*
at his soapy, ink-stained hands. The telephone rings, jolting him out of a
trance in which there is perhaps a sense of impending doom.
KRZYSZTOF: Hello.
VOICE: (*Over*) Good evening, it's Ewa Jezierska here.

KRZYSZTOF: Good evening.

VOICE: (*Over*) Is Pawel home? Marek still hasn't come back yet.

KRZYSZTOF: Ah, hello, I'm sorry, I didn't know who it was for a moment. No, he's still not back yet. He should be . . . They should be at their English class. What time is it?

VOICE: (*Over*) It's after five. They ought to be back by now.

KRZYSZTOF: They'll be back any minute.

(KRZYSZTOF *is now completely calm.*)

VOICE: (*Over*) I ask because something's happened.

KRZYSZTOF: What?

VOICE: (*Over*) I don't really know. Something's happened on the estate. I'll go over and fetch them.

KRZYSZTOF: Please tell Pawel to come home at once.

(*But there is no reply – Ewa Jezierska has evidently put the phone down.* KRZYSZTOF *stands motionless for a second, then runs to the bathroom and rinses his hands. He puts the stained sheets of paper and the newspapers which he used to wipe the ink off the desk into a plastic bag.*)

18

KRZYSZTOF *breaks into a run for the last few metres to the neighbouring block. He has forgotten about the plastic bag and is still clutching it uselessly in one hand. People are running in various directions. Another police car turns into the estate, its siren wailing.*

19

KRZYSZTOF *runs several steps at a time up the stairs to the second floor. He finds the flat, rings on the doorbell, and then knocks with increasing agitation. The door is opened by a good-looking, dishevelled* YOUNG WOMAN *in a dressing-gown.*

KRZYSZTOF: Sorry – is Pawel there?

(*The* YOUNG WOMAN *smiles apologetically.*)

YOUNG WOMAN: I've got flu. We didn't have lessons today. I sent them home.

KRZYSZTOF: When?

YOUNG WOMAN: As soon as they arrived, at four o'clock.

>(*Ewa* JEZIERSKA *is standing downstairs by the lift. She is an elegant woman of about forty years old. She presses the call-button, but is impatient for the lift to arrive and starts to thump on the door with her fist.* KRZYSZTOF *walks up to her.*)

KRZYSZTOF: They're not there. She's ill.

>(*Mrs* JEZIERSKA *goes pale and slumps down against the lift-door, beads of perspiration on her forehead.* KRZYSZTOF *wants to help her up, but is surprised to find that he is still clutching the plastic bag. Ewa* JEZIERSKA *stares blankly at the plastic bag and almost half addresses it.*)

JEZIERSKA: The ice on the lake has given way.

KRZYSZTOF: That's impossible.

JEZIERSKA: It has. It has.

KRZYSZTOF: I'm sorry, but it couldn't have done.

JEZIERSKA:It has, it has – it's broken.

>(*The lift-doors open.* OLA *is standing inside.*)

KRZYSZTOF: You haven't seen Pawel have you?

OLA: At school . . . I saw him at school. He told me all about his dream.

20

KRZYSZTOF *runs into the stairwell of his own block: no one is there. He closes his eyes and silently counts to twenty, then slowly presses the call-button for the lift and waits patiently for it to arrive, as if nothing untoward has happened. He waits in the lift for a while holding the doors open, having noticed an old man slowly shuffling towards him. The old man presses the first-floor button and gazes sternly at him. He slowly shuffles out again after the lift has stopped at the first floor.* KRZYSZTOF *waits equally calmly and then presses the button to his own floor. The lift moves upwards. It is clear that he has decided to behave rationally.*

KRZYSZTOF *opens the front door and calls out at once.*
KRZYSZTOF: Pawel? Pawel!
> (*His voice betrays the hope that this nightmare will soon be over,
> but the flat is silent.* KRZYSZTOF *realizes for the second time that
> he is still clutching the absurd plastic bag in his hands. He throws
> it into a corner with a sudden burst of anger, but then again
> regains his composure. He goes over to his son's room: the skates
> are hanging by the bed. This is exactly what he was hoping to see
> and he breathes a sigh of relief. He goes over to the phone and
> dials a number.*)
KRZYSZTOF: Irena?
IRENA: (*Voice over*) Yes?
KRZYSZTOF: Has Pawel rung?
IRENA: (*Voice over*) When?
KRZYSZTOF: Just now.
IRENA: (*Voice over*) He rang after school, around two. I wanted
> him to come over for lunch, but he said he had English.
KRZYSZTOF: That's just it – he didn't.
IRENA: (*Voice over*) Where is he?
KRZYSZTOF: I don't know. He's not here.
IRENA: (*Voice over*) Has something happened?
KRZYSZTOF: I don't know. Some ink spilt, that's all.
IRENA: (*Voice over*) What?
KRZYSZTOF: It's nothing. My bottle of ink suddenly cracked. It
> spilt all over the table.
IRENA: (*Voice over*) But what about Pawel?
KRZYSZTOF: He's not here. People are saying the ice has given
> way. Here, on the lake.
IRENA: (*Voice over*) I'm coming right over.
> (*He puts down the receiver. He finds a walkie-talkie on the table
> in Pawel's room and puts it in his pocket. In the small room full
> of sporting equipment – dumb-bells, small weights, a Bullworker,
> etc. –* KRZYSZTOF *takes a bicycle off the wall, finds the pump
> and starts to pump up a tyre.*)

It is now starting to get dark. KRZYSZTOF *looks odd on a bicycle against a background of nearly full winter. He cycles slowly along the estate, stopping from time to time to take out the walkie-talkie and repeat quietly:*

KRZYSZTOF: Pawel, over.

> (*There is no reply.* KRZYSZTOF *gets back on the bicycle and shouts out, this time without the walkie-talkie.*)
> Pawel!
> (*He cycles systematically around the apartment blocks, stopping every so often to transmit his quiet, technical appeals. His calls when he is not using the walkie-talkie are becoming louder and louder. A* MAN *appears on the balcony of one of the blocks.*)

MAN: Are you calling me?

> (KRZYSZTOF *stops and locates the cheerful* MAN *only with difficulty.*)

KRZYSZTOF: No.

MAN: Because my name's Pawel.

> (*The* MAN *leaning out over the railings looks quite happy to continue his jovial remarks further, but* KRZYSZTOF *rides off towards a nearby wood of thinly planted trees. The pathways are deserted and leafless. He rides towards a Red Indian village which has been built as a children's playground and comes across a wigwam made out of branches. He goes inside: it is dark and empty. He finds a can of tinned food standing upright on a log: it is full of stubbed-out cigarettes. He touches it to see if it is still warm and then holds it up against the sky; wisps of smoke float out of the opening.* KRZYSZTOF *sits on the table and transmits a message on his walkie-talkie.*)

KRZYSZTOF: Pawel, over. Pawel, answer me! Pawel, I know you're there!

23

On the bed in Pawel's room, hidden behind the teddy-bear, is the second walkie-talkie. KRZYSZTOF's *mechanical voice can be heard appealing over the air-waves.*
KRZYSZTOF: Pawel, answer me! Pawel, I know you're there!
    (*His voice echoes eerily in the empty apartment.*)

24

KRZYSZTOF *rides towards the lake, which is now bathed in light from the fire-brigade's search lights. Several firemen are standing on what is left of the ice and attempt to probe the water with long poles. The water is deep where the ice has given away and the poles are easily plunged in up to their hilts. More firemen are trying to do the same on the other side of the lake where the bank is higher. There, the ice has broken right up to the very edge of the lake. A crowd of people watches their efforts in silence. A large vehicle drives up pulling a boat on a trailer and several men help to unhitch it. Everyone watches anxiously each time the poles are pulled out of the water. Several policemen try to push the crowd away so that the firemen can get through to the boat. A* WOMAN *in an apron fails to react to their appeals and stares at the rods as they are pulled out of the water as if she is hypnotized. A* MAN *standing next to* KRZYSZTOF *turns around just as he is putting his bicycle down to one side.*
MAN: The bastards released some hot water.
KRZYSZTOF: What did you say?
MAN: From the power station.
KRZYSZTOF: What?
MAN: They released some hot water into the lake from the power
    station during the night. The bastards.
KRZYSZTOF: The bastards.
    (*He is not really conscious of what he is saying, but understands
    what has happened and why his calculations have failed.*)
    I worked out the resistance of the ice. According to the
    equation. The pressure per square centimetre —

[24]

MAN: You can't beat them, you know.

KRZYSZTOF: Yes. A chance in a million. He couldn't have foreseen it.

MAN: Who?

(KRZYSZTOF *whispers something to himself and the* MAN *cannot catch his reply. A small boy goes up to the* WOMAN *in the apron who is standing by the lake-side. She does not notice him. The boy slips his hand into hers but the* WOMAN *is so anxious that she still fails to respond. The boy starts pulling her away. She resists, but in doing so gradually becomes aware that somebody is holding her hand and checks to see if she is right. As if blind, she runs her other hand over his face. She finds it incredible, but recognizes the familiar contours.*)

WOMAN: Jacek?

JACEK: Yes, Mum.

WOMAN: Jacek.

(*The* WOMAN *clasps the boy to her and hugs him desperately.*)
Jacek. My little boy. Jacek, my baby. Where have you been?

JACEK: We've been playing Red Indians.

(*The* WOMAN *straightens up again with the boy in her arms and starts to walk away. Her husband follows a few steps behind carrying her coat. The firemen in the boat continue their thorough search of the lake, metre by metre, shouting out to their colleagues guiding the boat along with search-lights. The cars standing on the banks also switch on their headlamps. The lake now resembles a theatre-stage.* KRZYSZTOF *looks around: he sees the fire burning in the same place as before and the young man still sitting beside it as if he has not moved since the previous evening.* KRZYSZTOF *has a feeling the man is looking at him, but he could be imagining it. He hears a voice beside him.*)

OLA: Excuse me . . .

(KRZYSZTOF *turns around.* OLA *is standing next to him, her face solemn and wracked with concentration.*)
Pawel was supposed to call me this evening. Do you remember me?

KRZYSZTOF: Yes.

OLA: Maybe that boy knows something.

KRZYSZTOF: Which boy?

[25]

OLA: The little one – Jacek.

(KRZYSZTOF *finally understands what she is trying to tell him and runs off towards the blocks of flats. He catches up with all three of them, the* WOMAN *with* JACEK *in her arms and the man walking behind them, just in front of the stairwell entrance. He touches the boy's shoulder – he turns around. The* WOMAN, *sensing that something is happening, stops. The boy looks for a moment at* KRZYSZTOF *and than eventually replies to the unasked question.*)

JACEK: Pawel wasn't playing with us.

25

KRZYSZTOF *can see* JACEK *slowly disappearing between the gap of the closing lift-doors, evidently with something he still wants to say.*

JACEK: Pawel —

(*The doors close and the lift moves up without* KRZYSZTOF *finding out. He dashes up the stairs and reaches his floor just as the family are getting out of the lift. The* WOMAN *is walking along the top of the landing by the stairs with* JACEK *in her arms, but the little boy manages to catch hold of a bannister railing and clings on with all his might. His face is now roughly level with* KRZYSZTOF's *as he stands on the stairs.*)

JACEK: He was sliding on the lake. With Marek and another boy. They were skating together. The three of them.

(KRZYSZTOF's *hand unconsciously and rhythmically taps on the railing which* JACEK *had been holding on to only a moment ago, his face slowly assuming a mask-like expression. A door slams shut somewhere in the distance and sounds reach his ears of a dog barking and music being played on a radio.* KRZYSZTOF *does not move.*)

26

KRZYSZTOF *is sitting in the large living room. Here, all is quiet. After a while, one side of his face starts to become illuminated by a greenish glow.* KRZYSZTOF *does not pay any attention to it. The glow becomes more and more intense. He finally becomes aware of this source of light and turns his head. The huge screen of his computer is glowing in the dark with a bright, green glare.* KRZYSZTOF *stares at it blankly; a line flashes up across the screen. After a while, a sentence appears.*

COMPUTER: (*In English*) I'm ready.

(KRZYSZTOF *has been sitting with his hands tightly clenched, but now unclenches his fingers and moves them towards the keyboard. Slowly, letter by letter, he types out a sentence.*)

KRZYSZTOF: Are you there?

(*Despite the fact that* KRZYSZTOF *has pressed the reply command button, the computer thinks for a moment, and then a sentence appears.*)

COMPUTER: (*In English*) Repeat again.

KRZYSZTOF: I asked if you were there.

(*The computer is silent.* KRZYSZTOF *presses the key with the request for a response, but the screen merely glows with the same bright, green light. After a while* KRZYSZTOF *again taps out some more letters, one after the other.*)

What can I do?

(*The question remains on screen for a moment, then the screen goes green again and the letters disappear.* KRZYSZTOF *types out a further question.*)

Why?

(*As before, the letters dissolve into greenness.* KRZYSZTOF's *hands continue to punch out the keys on the keyboard.*)

Why take a small boy?

(*The sentence lingers.* KRZYSZTOF *adds another one.*)

Listen to me. Why take a small boy? I want to understand . . .

(*He presses the reply key – the letters disappear. He continues to write.*)

If you are there, give me a sign.

(*The sentence lingers.* KRZYSZTOF *deletes the first letters of the sentence. They disappear one after the other, leaving only one word remaining: 'Sign'.* KRZYSZTOF *presses the ×2 key. The word is doubled in size. He presses the key several times again, and finally the word occupies the whole screen: 'Sign'. He presses*

[27]

the command key 'answer'. The computer quickly responds.)
COMPUTER: Manifestation. Omen. Mark. Symbol.
(KRZYSZTOF *writes.*)
KRZYSZTOF: Illumination.
COMPUTER: Light. Fire. Beam. Candle.
(*The computer is now responding swiftly.* KRZYSZTOF *writes.*)
KRZYSZTOF: Candle.
COMPUTER: Symbol. Church. Cross.
(KRZYSZTOF *writes on.*)
KRZYSZTOF: Sense. Hope.
(*The computer falls silent for a moment. Then letters start to appear.*)
COMPUTER: (*In English*) Terminology unrecognized.
(KRZYSZTOF *switches it off. The green light fades from the screen. There remains only a small dot.*)
KRZYSZTOF: (*In English*) Terminology unrecognized. (*In Polish*) Terminology unrecognized.

27

A new church – a huge, dark mass – is being erected at one end of the estate. KRZYSZTOF *hesitates for a moment before deciding to enter. Architecturally, the church is modern and one might almost say extravagant.* KRZYSZTOF *finds his way to the crypt, which has been completed and where the services are temporarily being held.*

28

The walls of the crypt are coarse and bear traces of timber work. The interior is lit with small, working-men's lanterns. The provisional altar is also crude, the painting of the Virgin Mary on the altar surrounded by planks of wood on top of which stand flowers and candles. The priest looks up as KRZYSZTOF *enters. He is sitting in the confessional, his face criss-crossed with little squares of light and shade by the light falling through the mesh.* KRZYSZTOF *has forgotten how to behave in church; he walks towards the altar. Halfway there he moves as if to kneel, but then changes his mind. The crude plank, which is evidently the place where people receive Communion, does not completely divide the altar from the rest of the church.*

KRZYSZTOF sees several unlit candles in a large holder and takes one of them. The priest calmly looks on as KRZYSZTOF searches in his pockets for some matches, and discovers he does not have any. He stands with the candle in one hand. Then, sensing another presence, he turns, goes over to the confessional, and opens the little window. The priest is holding some matches in his hand. He gives them to KRZYSZTOF without saying a word, after which KRZYSZTOF returns to the altar. He lights the candle, tilts it at an angle and watches the burning wax drip on to the unplaned wood to form a little blob. He sticks the candle to the plank of wood and waits for the wax to set. The little flame darts and flickers – perhaps someone somewhere has opened a door. KRZYSZTOF protects it with the palm of his hand and waits until the flame is burning more strongly. Then, still with his palms outstretched to protect the burning flame, he starts to retreat, ready to go back if the flame shows any sign of going out. He drops his hands to his sides only after he has reached the doorway and can see that the candle is still burning with a bright, clear flame.

29

Even at a distance KRZYSZTOF can hear the sound of wailing women and one hysterical shriek in particular which rises up above the general commotion. The boat is being rowed back from the middle of the lake, stretchers already waiting on the bank. KRZYSZTOF passes Ewa JEZIERSKA, who turns her head away, her mouth wide open but incapable of sound. He moves nearer the lake. The tumult and shouting is dying away. The boat draws level with the bank, the small, wet bodies of three young boys lying inside, looking even smaller than when they had been alive. KRZYSZTOF stumbles over something; his bicycle is lying trampled in the mud, both wheels bent. The firemen carry the three bodies over to the stretchers. KRZYSZTOF stares at the peaceful face of his son, his glasses still intact over closed eyes. As the firemen put PAWEL's body on to the stretcher, IRENA bends over and pulls up the half-undone zip on his jacket before making a quick, small

[29]

sign of the cross over his forehead. The young man in the fur coat whom KRZYSZTOF *twice saw sitting by the fire now crosses in front of him. He passes the stretchers and* IRENA *kneeling down beside them, steps out of the circle of light, and slowly vanishes into the dark.*

30

KRZYSZTOF *runs back into the church. The candle is still burning with a bright, even flame in front of the altar.* KRZYSZTOF *walks over to the crude plank which divides it from the altar. He stares intensely at the painting of the Virgin Mary for a moment, then raises his fist and smashes it down with all his strength against the burning candle. The muffled thud echoes throughout the concrete interior. The altar and all the crude, surrounding woodwork shudder. The candles in front of the altar topple over, dripping wax all over the face in the painting. The priest leaves the confessional, kneels on the concrete floor and clasps his hands together in prayer.* KRZYSZTOF *goes over to the font with the holy water, which like everything else in the church is cast in concrete. He puts his hand into it but encounters only a block of ice – a holy block of ice. He pulls it out and holds it to his face. A small trickle of water (melted ice? tears?) escapes through his fingers. The remains of the wax from the extinguished candles continue to drip along the face in the painting. The priest is deeply engrossed in prayer.*
    KRZYSZTOF *mumbles something, the words initially indistinct. Only after a while are we able to make out what he is saying.*
KRZYSZTOF: . . . who . . . who is . . . is there . . . who is there to
  . . . who is there to turn to? . . . who is there to turn to? . . .
  who . . .

DECALOGUE TWO

The cast and crew of *Decalogue Two* included:

DOROTA	Krystyna Janda
CONSULTANT	Aleksander Bardini
ANDRZEJ	Olgierd Lukasiewicz
Director of Photography and Cameraman	Edward Klosinski
Producer	Ryszard Chutkowski
Composer	Zbigniew Preisner
Artistic Director	Halina Dobrowolska
Sound	Malgorzata Jaworska
Lighting	Jerzy Tomczuk
Film Editor	Ewa Smal
Production Managers	Pawel Mantorski
	Wlodzimierz Bendych
Costume Designers	Malgorzata Obloza
	Hanna Cwiklo
Director	Krzysztof Kieślowski

Stills: Aleksander Bardini as the consultant
Krystyna Janda as Dorota

I

All is white. Flat snow caps have formed along the tops of car roofs. A CARETAKER *is briskly sweeping away the snow from the pathways which run between the apartment blocks. Two men in the distance walk towards the camera. One is pulling a toboggan, while the other supports a refrigerator which has been precariously balanced on top. The* CARETAKER *briefly pauses from his work on catching sight of the two men, but resumes almost immediately and with his next stroke uncovers a frozen rabbit from beneath the thick layers of snow. It has presumably fallen from one of the windows or balconies.* The* CARETAKER *cranes his neck upwards, his gaze finally coming to rest on a small balcony which is slightly different from all the others: entirely glazed over with small, bright yellow panes of glass, it serves as a household conservatory.*

2

The conservatory is full of cacti and the temperature is maintained by a small electric fan heater. The plants are luxuriant and a deep shade of green.
    The balcony belongs to a modestly sized flat. Several pre-war portraits hang on the walls and a small cup-shaped trophy holding several pipes with well-chewed mouthpieces stands on a table. Some small colour photographs have been slipped into the corners of the picture frames, one of which depicts a young man and a woman with two smiling children gazing straight into the camera. A canary cage hangs from an old, traditional stand, its bars covered with a napkin, as is the usual practice. The cage is uncovered by a hand which belongs to a hospital CONSULTANT: *the canary immediately launches itself into song and its singing will be heard throughout this sequence. The*

---

* In the days leading up to Christmas, it is not unusual for Polish households to hang meat which they cannot fit into their fridges outside their balcony windows. The weather is usually cold enough to keep the meat from going off.

CONSULTANT, *in socks and slippers, warmly wrapped up in a scarf and wearing a jumper on top of his pyjamas, methodically lights all the rings on the gas stove and puts a large saucepan of water on each one.*

The CONSULTANT *is sixty-five years old and has the face of a man who is exacting in his judgements of others, as well as of himself. He walks out on to the balcony to inspect the cacti. One of them presumably requires extra special attention, since he examines it exceptionally thoroughly. He is interrupted by the ringing of an alarm-clock. He switches it off and immediately turns on the radio, listening first to the news round-up and then, with a practised movement, altering the wavelength and listening to the news in English while sprinkling bird-seed into the canary's cage. There is a ring at the front-door bell. The* CONSULTANT *is surprised: he had not been expecting anyone. He turns the three locks and opens the door to find the* CARETAKER *standing in the doorway with the frozen rabbit in his hand.*

CARETAKER: This didn't fall off your balcony by any chance did it, doctor?

(*The* CONSULTANT *looks at it in surprise.*)

CARETAKER: Sorry . . . it must belong to someone else then.

(*The* CONSULTANT *smiles. He turns back the three locks, carries the four saucepans of boiling water from the kitchen into the bathroom, pours them into the bath, and adds some cold water. He wipes the steam from the bathroom mirror.*

Now dressed in a thick, autumn overcoat, he puts some empty milk and mineral water bottles into a shopping-bag. Piles of neatly stacked bank notes are lying in a kitchen cupboard. He counts out several hundred zloty, marks down the sum on a small piece of paper stuck to the cupboard door, walks to the front door, and again opens the three locks . . .)

3

A woman is standing by the window in the stairwell. She lives in the same block, is wearing a dress and smoking a cigarette. She makes a move as if to say something to the CONSULTANT *as he walks past, but then changes her mind and turns back to face the window. Her*

[34]

shoulders are slender and delicate. She crushes her cigarette out with quite unnecessary brutality.

4

The CONSULTANT *lengthily and distastefully examines the bread rolls in the local grocery store before finally putting some bread, cheese and two bottles of milk into the bag. He walks over to the cash-register with a wry grin on his face.*

CONSULTANT: I see the rolls are stale again, as usual.

CASHIER: You can always make a complaint.

CONSULTANT: I'd be only too pleased.

(*There are few people in the shop at this time of day. The* CASHIER *pulls out the complaints book and a pen attached to it by a piece of string. The* CONSULTANT *meticulously notes down yet another observation – several of the previous pages are taken up with his hand-writing – while the* CASHIER *takes the empty bottles out of the bag. The* CONSULTANT *returns the book.*)

CASHIER: Thank you, doctor. Two bottles of milk and two mineral waters, is it?

CONSULTANT: That's right.

(*He takes out his old wallet, which has had to be patched up in several places.*)

5

He climbs out of the lift. DOROTA – *the woman with the delicate shoulders – has lit another cigarette and is still standing in the same position by the window. The* CONSULTANT *walks past her, repeats the ritual with the three locks, then puts his shopping bag down and quietly tiptoes over to the peep-hole in the front door.* DOROTA *is standing on the other side. The* CONSULTANT *opens the door.*

CONSULTANT: You want something from me. I'm listening.

DOROTA: I live on the top floor. I hope you remember me.

CONSULTANT: Yes, I do. You ran over my dog two years ago.

(*He pulls the door ajar and lets her through into the hallway.*)

DOROTA: My name is Dorota Geller. My husband is currently in your ward at the hospital.

CONSULTANT: You want to know how he's progressing?

DOROTA: Yes.

CONSULTANT: Patients' families are received between three and five o'clock on Wednesday afternoons.

DOROTA: But that's in two days' time.

CONSULTANT: That is correct. Today is Monday.

(*He closes the door behind his visitor.* DOROTA *swivels around to face the peep-hole.*)

DOROTA: (*Under her breath*) Pity I didn't run you over instead.

(*A ring at the door-bell interrupts the* CONSULTANT *from his routine scanning of the advertisements in the daily newspaper. It is a special code: two short rings followed by two long ones.* MRS B., *the home-help, is standing at the door.*)

MRS B.: It's cold today, doctor.

CONSULTANT: It certainly is.

(*He leads her straightaway out on to the balcony and shows her the cactus which he had been inspecting earlier in the morning.*)

CONSULTANT: It's not well, is it?

(MRS B. *leans over the cactus like a doctor.*)

MRS B.: It's dying . . .

CONSULTANT: Do you think so?

(*The woman confirms her diagnosis with a sad nod of the head: she knows all about plants. They go back into the apartment. The* CONSULTANT *takes the boiling kettle off the gas in the kitchen, sprinkles several large spoonfuls of coffee into two glasses and pours in the water.* MRS B. *sits down at the table. The two of them clearly enjoy this particular part of the day.*)

CONSULTANT: You know something, Mrs B., it wasn't a cold after all: he was teething. He cried all night and when I put my finger in his mouth in the morning, I could feel this tiny, sharp ridge across his lower gums. It was a tooth.

MRS B.: So you didn't sleep then?

CONSULTANT: Well, he didn't drop off until dawn. I stayed at his side and didn't sleep, while she – well, she didn't sleep either because she was anxious about the two of us. Come morning my father appears from his own room and opens his mouth

[36]

wide. Ahhh, he says, and points with a huge smile on his face
to a gap where there's a tooth missing.

MRS B.: So he'd been to the dentist's then?

CONSULTANT: No, he never went to the dentist. He had perfect
teeth, even though he must have been over fifty. Except for
this one – and he'd pulled it out himself. Anyway, I tell him
all about the little boy's first tooth and he laughs and says: of
course, it all makes sense, it all fits.

(MRS B *smiles. It might seem indelicate to draw attention to the
fact, but her entire front row of teeth is missing. Their absence,
however, does not seem to concern her greatly.*)

CONSULTANT: Father's got the tooth wrapped up in a
handkerchief and shows it to the boy. Clean and white,
almost good as new. Then he takes his grand-daughter on to
his knees and shows her as well. Well, Mrs B., I put on my
scarf and can see through the gap in the door that the little
boy is sleeping soundly. Father's sitting in the living room
with the little girl, who's giggling and trying to fit the tooth
into her mouth. The wife is standing in the corridor with
rings around her eyes from lack of sleep. There are too many
teeth in this house for my liking, she says. It's a bad omen –
look after yourself, won't you. Get some rest, I say to her on
my way out. Father doesn't have to go out today. She
solemnly nods her head: fine, she says.

(*The* CONSULTANT'*s eyes are half-closed and it is clear from the
tone of his voice that he has finished.* MRS B. *drinks up the
remains of her coffee and there is a moment of silence.* MRS B.
*realizes this is all for today and in any case has finished her
coffee.*)

MRS B.: I've finished . . . May I?

(*She clears the coffee glasses from the table and leaves them in the
sink. She takes a soft rag from a roll of dish-cloths and starts
dusting the shelves in the living room. The* CONSULTANT *gets up
from the table in the kitchen and puts on his overcoat with the fur
collar. He remembers the advertisement he has ringed in* Zycie
Warszawy *and gives* MRS B. *the copy of the newspaper.*)

CONSULTANT: I ringed three today . . . Make sure you lock the
door properly when you go, Mrs B.

[37]

(*He walks out of the flat and notices* DOROTA *smoking a cigarette at the far end of the corridor. She has not moved from the window since leaving his flat.*)

CONSULTANT: Look . . .

(*He is speaking to her back.* DOROTA *has not turned around.*)

CONSULTANT: If you're really worried, you can come and see me this afternoon.

(*He walks away and climbs into the lift.*)

6

DOROTA *is an attractive woman of about thirty, but one who looks as if she has aged slightly before her time. She walks over to a letter lying on a small table. We are able to read the first few words – 'My Love, it is winter here and freezing cold. I cannot forget . . .' – and would perhaps be able to make out the rest, but* DOROTA's *hands are now tearing the sheet of paper into little pieces. She switches on the telephone-answering machine. It responds with a voice on tape.*

VOICE: (*Over*) Dorota, are you there? . . . Pick up the receiver if you're there . . . OK, you're not there. I'm going skiing in a week's time. Love and kisses.

(*There is a moment of silence, followed by an electronic bleep and a second voice.*)

VOICE: (*Over*) Janusz Wierzbicki here. There's something I need to talk to you about. I'll drop by this evening.

(*There are no more messages, only silence.* DOROTA *sets the answering machine again and goes over to the window. The* CONSULTANT *is tramping across the square between the apartment blocks in the direction of the nursery school.*

The POSTMAN *rings at the doorbell. He is a small man with a disproportionately large head and a hearing-aid in his ear which is obviously not particularly effective, since he finds it necessary to raise his voice almost at once.*)

POSTMAN: Some money for you, Mrs Geller. Sickness benefit for your husband. Identification, please.

(*The* POSTMAN *bends the ear with the hearing-aid towards her.*)

DOROTA: I've only got a passport.

[38]

(*The* POSTMAN *fills in the receipt and gives her the money.*)
Nothing else?
(*The* POSTMAN *throws his bag over his shoulder and shakes his head.*)

7

The CONSULTANT *is completing his examination of a little boy in the headmistress's office at the nursery school, which on this occasion is being used as a doctor's surgery. He sends the little boy on his way with a playful smack on his behind and then makes a note on his health card. His next patient is a little girl.*
CONSULTANT: Don't you go to the dentist?
    (*The little girl shakes her head: no, she doesn't. The*
    CONSULTANT *makes some more notes.*)
HEADMISTRESS: That's everyone, doctor.
CONSULTANT: Their teeth are in very bad shape.
HEADMISTRESS: Their diet isn't what it should be.
CONSULTANT: Too true.
HEADMISTRESS: Same time as usual, then? Monday?

8

The CONSULTANT *enters the hospital and the porter touches the peak of his cap in greeting.*

9

The nurses and other doctors bow to the CONSULTANT *in greeting as he walks through the ward. Patients on the mezzanines take their cigarettes out of their mouths and wish him good morning. In the corridor of his own ward, the* CONSULTANT *pulls aside a* JUNIOR DOCTOR.
CONSULTANT: Which room is Geller in?
    (*The* JUNIOR DOCTOR *thinks for a moment.*)

JUNIOR DOCTOR: The one who's just had the operation? He's in room twelve.

CONSULTANT: Could you bring me his medical records?

(*He walks over to room twelve and is about to enter when he notices* DOROTA *through the pane of glass in the door: she is standing at the bedside of one of the sick patients. He studies them both and then walks away.*

Dorota's husband ANDRZEJ *is a few years older than she is.* DOROTA *is looking at him with the sense of pained stupefaction which overcomes us all at the sight of life slowly abandoning someone dear to us. She has brought her husband a jam-jar full of stewed fruit, but realizes the futility of her gesture and puts it back into her shoulder-bag. She tries to adjust his pillow and smooth down the quilt, and then finally leaves.* ANDRZEJ *cautiously opens his eyes after she has gone; perhaps he has just woken up, or perhaps he had not been asleep at all but simply could not face the prospect of speaking to his wife. A spasm of pain ripples across his face. He surveys the world around him from beneath his half-closed eyelids. The white paint is peeling on the bed-rail, struck repeatedly by drops of water from a source somewhere up above. The dripping is intermittent, slow at first, with long intervals between each drop, then one, two, three in quick succession. He can see small rivulets of water at the point where the wall and ceiling meet. Leaves lie scattered on the window-ledge outside.* ANDRZEJ *narrows his eyes – this dismal scene is not what he wanted to see at all. Water is also dripping from the radiator into a bucket which has been placed underneath, to the same rhythm as the water dripping on to the bed-rail.* ANDZREJ's *face again contorts with agony.*

10

SECRETARY: There's some woman here to see you, doctor. Calls herself Geller.

CONSULTANT: Is it the afternoon already?

(*The* SECRETARY *checks on her watch.*)

SECRETARY: Three minutes past twelve.

(*The* CONSULTANT *drags himself away from his papers and motions with his hand as* DOROTA *enters his office.*)

CONSULTANT: Please, take a seat.

(DOROTA *takes out a packet of cigarettes and a box of matches.*)

DOROTA: May I?

CONSULTANT: I don't smoke myself, but if you really must . . .

(DOROTA *puts the cigarettes and matches away. The* CONSULTANT *is examining an X-ray from the patient's records against a light.*)

Diagnosis, treatment, operation – all a bit too late, I'm afraid.

DOROTA: What do you mean?

(*The* CONSULTANT *turns to face her.*)

CONSULTANT: It's looking bad.

(*He tidies up his papers, considering the conversation at a close.*)

DOROTA: Will he live?

CONSULTANT: I'm afraid I don't know.

(DOROTA *gets to her feet and stands over him.*)

DOROTA: I have to know, doctor. And you must –

CONSULTANT: My only 'must' is to treat your husband to the best of my ability. I can only be certain of one thing – that nothing is certain.

II

Early dusk. The porter sees the CONSULTANT *on his way out of the hospital and touches his cap. The* CONSULTANT *turns down a side-street.* DOROTA *draws up alongside him in her Volkswagen.*

DOROTA: I'll give you a lift.

CONSULTANT: Thank you, but I prefer walking.

(DOROTA *waits until he has walked off and then slowly drives after him.*

The Volkswagen turns into the estate at a safe distance behind him. The CONSULTANT *disappears around the corner of one of the apartment blocks.* DOROTA *speeds up, but loses sight of him. She reverses, drives up to the block where they both live and parks where she shouldn't, right in front of the stairwell entrance, so that the* CONSULTANT *cannot enter without her seeing him.*)

12

The CONSULTANT *is sitting in a large room packed full of makeshift shelves and parcels full of phials, bottles and colourful packets of pills. Two young men are assisting him as he checks the various names of the drugs and their Polish equivalents in the books laid out in front of him. He puts his glasses on and then takes them off again as he tries to read the use-by date. A man dressed in black with a white dog-collar around his neck enters the room. It is the* PRIEST *whom we may remember from the first story. The* CONSULTANT *raises his glasses.*
CONSULTANT: There's a whole week's work here.
PRIEST: I'm very sorry, but we're having our class in here in a
    minute.
    (*The* CONSULTANT *smiles sourly.*)
CONSULTANT: Make that a month.

13

DOROTA *is half-frozen by now, despite having switched on the car-engine and warming her hands on the blow-heater. On seeing the Volkswagen from a distance, the* CONSULTANT *retreats and enters another stairwell instead.*

14

The CONSULTANT *presses the top button on the lift panel. By walking along the corridor on the top floor which runs the entire length of the building, he can reach his own stairwell. He calls the lift for the second time and rides down to his own floor. He takes out his keys, unlocks the three locks, and so on.*
    DOROTA *is surprised to see the light being switched on in his conservatory.*

15

Still in his overcoat, the CONSULTANT *reads the message left for him by Mrs B.: 'Your soup is in the fridge. I have repotted the cactus and propped it up with a stake. Please try not to touch it. I rang up about the adverts. I will tell you all about them on Wednesday, Mrs B.' The door-bell rings. The* CONSULTANT *holds his breath. The ringing is repeated, this time insistently.*

CONSULTANT: Hold on a second!

(*He lights the gas, puts the four saucepans with water which Mrs B. has prepared on the rings, and goes to open the door.* DOROTA *enters the room without bothering to take off her sheepskin coat.*)
I came in through another entrance. You can smoke if you want!

(DOROTA'*s hands are trembling as she reaches for a cigarette. She gets up to fetch an ash-tray but finds nothing on the desk except a framed photograph. It shows several men standing next to a plane with propellers.*)
How are you managing to have baths?

DOROTA: I heat the water on the stove.

CONSULTANT: Listen, I'm afraid I really don't know the answer to your question.

(DOROTA *inhales on her cigarette and flicks the ash into the palm of her hand.*)

DOROTA: I really . . . My husband and I . . . I really do love him.

CONSULTANT: I've seen you both on several occasions. It certainly seemed that way.

(DOROTA *looks at the ash in the palm of her hand.*)
Medical science knows nothing about the causes of your husband's illness, little about the after effects, and is even less able to predict survival rates –

(DOROTA *interrupts him.*)

DOROTA: Americans inform their patients.

CONSULTANT: Yes, they do. When it comes to saying they're going to die, they are sometimes correct. Not so often when it's the other way around.

DOROTA: I can take it. Why don't you just tell me: he's going to

die. At least I'll know. I'll do everything I can for him . . .
(*The ash from her cigarette falls to the floor.*)

CONSULTANT: There's nothing you can do. All you can do is
wait.

(*The* CONSULTANT's *terse, rational replies are beginning to upset*
DOROTA, *but she has come here for a purpose and must carry it*
through to the end. She succeeds this time in flicking the cigarette
ash into the palm of her hand. She regains her composure.)

DOROTA: If you can spare me another minute, I will explain why I
have to know.

CONSULTANT: I'm listening.

DOROTA: I was never able to have children. But now I'm three
months pregnant and it's not my husband's child. If I have
an abortion now, I may never have another chance again. But
if my husband lives, I don't want the child. The man who I
am referring to is very special to me. I don't know if you
believe it is possible to love two people at the same time . . .

CONSULTANT: The chances of a full recovery are minimal. He has
a greater chance of surviving and spending the rest of his life
a vegetable. So much for medical science. As for me, I've
seen too many people defy the odds and survive when
medical science had given up on them, and too many who've
died virtually without rhyme or reason.

(*Taking her time,* DOROTA *methodically stubs out her cigarette in*
the box of matches. The violently lighted sulphur flares into a
brief, strong flame.)

Does he have to know the child is not his?

(DOROTA's *face assumes what novelists sometimes describe as a*
'*wry smile*'.)

DOROTA: I see you prefer to scheme rather than –

CONSULTANT: I know that people will agree to anything.
Sometimes –

DOROTA: There are some things you simply cannot do to another
person, especially if you love them. And especially if they're
dying. Do you believe in God?

CONSULTANT: Yes.

DOROTA: Well, I have no one to ask.

(DOROTA *walks out without saying goodbye. The* CONSULTANT

[44]

looks up, watched by the children eating ice-cream in the photograph. He gets to his feet and covers the canary cage with the napkin, just as the bird begins to sing.)

16

A man wearing a windcheater is sitting on a bulging rucksack in the corridor by Dorota's front door.

JANEK: I rang several times. Didn't you listen to the answering machine?

DOROTA: Yes, I did.

(She opens the door and looks at the rucksack.)

Is that Andrzej's?

JANEK: We're leaving in a week. Straight to Delhi, then walking to base camp with the porters.

(They enter the flat. JANEK puts the heavy rucksack down in the hallway.)

DOROTA: What did you bring that thing here for?

JANEK: Why leave it around for someone to poke their noses into when no one's going to be around.

DOROTA: Isn't it a bit early to be talking about funerals?

(JANEK takes out a card from his pocket.)

JANEK: I'm leaving him a note . . . We'll miss him in the mountains.

DOROTA: Take it. Take it away!

(She opens the door with a loud clatter and tries to drag the rucksack out into the corridor by herself.)

Is he a member of the club or isn't he?! Does he have the right to keep his rucksack in the locker or doesn't he?!

JANEK: He does, but . . .

DOROTA: Well, it can bloody well stay there then. At least until he's dead!

(She throws the rucksack out into the corridor and slams the door shut. JANEK remains in the hallway.)

JANEK: Look, I'm sorry. We didn't mean to . . . You must be feeling dreadful.

DOROTA: No, I'm all right now. It wasn't all that stupid of you.

[45]

JANEK: What wasn't?

DOROTA: Bringing that bloody rucksack here.

JANEK: How is he?

> (DOROTA *is silent.*
>
> *She is sitting in the kitchen, staring vacantly at a glass of steaming-hot tea. She touches it with her finger and then slowly nudges it, millimetre by millimetre, towards the edge of the table. It takes a while for the glass to get there but* DOROTA *does not stop pushing: it topples over the edge and falls with a clatter to the floor.* DOROTA *does not react, almost as if she had been completely unaware of what she was doing. She can hear the telephone ringing in the next room, and waits. After two rings, her voice sounds out from the outgoing message on the answering machine.*)

DOROTA: This is the answering machine for Andrzej and Dorota Geller. This is a recording. If you would like to leave a short message, please do so after the tone. The recording lasts for half a minute.

> (*There is a brief, electronic bleep followed by a distinctive, male voice.*)

MAN: (*Voice over*) It's me, it's afternoon over here, but evening with you. I've just come back from a rehearsal. It was packed out. I'm feeling completely lonely. I've been waiting for you every day. I'll ring again tomorrow evening my time, night-time your time. The tape's probably about to run . . .

> (*The machine hums softly before switching itself off.*)

17

It is still early in the morning and the CONSULTANT *is examining something under a microscope in an empty laboratory. His inspection lasts some time.*

CONSULTANT: The previous plate, please.

> (*The* JUNIOR DOCTOR *swaps the sample under the extended lens. The* CONSULTANT *leans over the microscope again.*)
> And the one before that.
> (*The operation is repeated.*)

And the most recent.
(*The* JUNIOR DOCTOR *again swaps the preparation.*)
Take a look yourself.
(*It is now the* JUNIOR DOCTOR's *turn to peer into the lens. The* CONSULTANT *changes the plates and informs him which one is which.*)
That one's from two weeks ago. This is from one week ago. And this is the most recent.
(*The* JUNIOR DOCTOR *lifts his eyes from the microscope: the lens has left a small circular impression around his eye.*)
JUNIOR DOCTOR: You always used to teach us . . .
CONSULTANT: Never mind all that for now. What's your opinion?
JUNIOR DOCTOR: Progress.
(*The* CONSULTANT *nods in agreement – his opinion precisely.*)

18

The GYNAECOLOGIST *looks the sort of man who has seen a great many women in his life, and not all of them in a professional capacity. He completes his examination and looks towards* DOROTA.
GYNAECOLOGIST: Coming along nicely. You can get down now.
(DOROTA *does not move.*)
DOROTA: I have to have an abortion, doctor. I came to arrange an appointment.
GYNAECOLOGIST: What, a beauty like this?
DOROTA: Yes, even a beauty like this.
(*The* GYNAECOLOGIST *opens his notebook and looks for a free appointment.*)
GYNAECOLOGIST: Have you been here before?
DOROTA: No, it's my first time.
GYNAECOLOGIST: How about the day after tomorrow? Name?
DOROTA: Geller. Dorota Geller.
GYNAECOLOGIST: Dorota . . . beautiful name.

19

DOROTA *looks around the Europejski Hotel lobby. A* MAN *in his early thirties wearing glasses looks up from his cup of coffee.*
DOROTA: Are you the person?
MAN: Yes . . . Hello. Witek told me all about you.
    (*He takes out an envelope and a colourfully wrapped parcel.*)
DOROTA: When did you fly in?
MAN: During the night. Witek asked me to tell you all his news.
DOROTA: I'm listening.
MAN: He's already done the concert. He had trouble getting
    through to you on the phone. He asked me to tell you . . . He'll
    try again tonight . . . the concert was packed . . .
DOROTA: I know.
    (*The conversation is limping somewhat.*)
MAN: That's about it really. You have the keys to his flat . . .
DOROTA: Yes.
MAN: He asked if you could bring some scores with you. They're
    lying on the piano, several sheets in a green cover. That's
    about it really.

20

DOROTA *opens the piano-lid in Witek's flat and delicately presses the keys with her fingers. She removes them from the keyboard, but the music she had started to play will continue to be heard throughout the whole sequence. The apartment consists of one large room in which the dividing walls have been knocked down. Witek must have left in a hurry: his bed is unmade and his things lie scattered everywhere.* DOROTA *goes over to a jacket on a hanger. She slides her hand into one of the sleeves and presses it against her body. She then goes into the bathroom and switches on the light. There is a message daubed with lipstick on the mirror: 'Got up earlier. Nine at the Philharmonic. Dorota.' The letter 'o' in the middle of the word 'Dorota' is written in the shape of a Smiley.* DOROTA *also smiles, returns to the piano, and puts the letter and the colourfully wrapped parcel on top of the scores with the green cover.*

[48]

21

MRS B. *is smiling differently from usual as she stands in the doorway.*
CONSULTANT: Good morning, Mrs B.
　　(*He studies her intently.*)
　　Has anything happened, Mrs B.?
MRS B.: I bought it.
CONSULTANT: You bought it!
MRS B.: Yes, I answered the ad. The one you put a ring round in
　　the newspaper.
CONSULTANT: So why haven't you put it on to show me?
MRS B.: It's too beautiful . . . I don't think I could wear it ever.
　　It's such a shame . . . You know what people are like these
　　days. They'd steal from the blind.
CONSULTANT: Tell me all about it.
　　(MRS B. *puts on the dress to show him.*)
MRS B.: It's long and black with tassels. It fits perfectly, just as if
　　it was made especially. And with the collar I've always
　　dreamed about.
CONSULTANT: How much did you pay for it? Are you going to
　　tell me?
　　(MRS B. *is smiling openly and happily.*)
MRS B.: It cost me all I have, doctor. Every last penny I've saved
　　over the last thirty years.
　　(*She has already changed back into her normal clothes and taken
　　a screwdriver out of her bag. She is now standing by the balcony
　　doors and is unscrewing the windows in order to clean them.*
　　*Some X-ray photographs have been pinned up against one of the
　　panes of glass. She walks over to the window and studies them
　　intently.*)
　　So you've started working from home?
CONSULTANT: Yes. People keep asking me how long they've got
　　left to live.
MRS B.: And you tell them?
CONSULTANT: No, I don't. Anyway, I'm never really able to say.
　　(MRS B. *breaks off from her work and confesses in a half-whisper
　　as if it was one of her deepest secrets.*)

[49]

MRS B.: I'd want to go quickly and have it all over and done with.
(*The* CONSULTANT *assumes her grave and conspiratorial tone of voice.*)

CONSULTANT: Are you afraid of dying?

MRS B.: Who isn't, doctor? But there'll always be a gleam in my windows while I'm still on this earth.
(*The* CONSULTANT *takes down the X-rays and puts them in his briefcase. He sprinkles some coffee into the two glasses in the kitchen and pours in some boiling water.* MRS B. *stands at the entrance wiping her hands on her apron. They both sit down and drink their coffee, as is their usual habit, trying not to scald their tongues. After a moment's silence,* MRS B. *reminds him.*)
You got to the bit where you were leaving the house with your scarf on.

CONSULTANT: Ah yes, the scarf. Not long to go, Mrs B. So, I go off to the hospital. Someone comes up to me and says there's going to be a pick-up to England during the night. I ring home – the wife is asleep. Father picks up the phone and speaks in a low voice so as not to wake her up. How are the children? I ask. Oh, they're fine, he says. I've been playing with them – your little girl got so excited she wet herself. The little boy was hungry when he woke up so I fed him, and he's quite happy now gurgling to himself in baby talk. I laugh: what's he saying? Presumably he's handed over the receiver by this stage because all I can hear is this goo-goo, gah-gah noise on the other end of the line. That was around eleven. I left the hospital at twelve, but when I got home there was nothing there any more.
(MRS B. *is sitting stock still, the glass held to her lips.*)

MRS B.: That was the time . . .?

CONSULTANT: Yes, Mrs B. Instead of the house there was only a huge crater in the ground. It was a couple of minutes after midnight, the very same day.

22

DOROTA: (*Voice over*) This is the answering machine for Andrzej and Dorota Geller. This is a recording. If you would like to leave a short message, please do so after the tone. The recording lasts for half a minute.

(*As usual, there is a short electronic bleep. Although* WITEK *is ringing long-distance, his voice is as clear as if he was calling across from the other side of the room.*)

WITEK: (*Voice over*) Dorota, pick up the phone. You're there, aren't you?

(DOROTA *picks up the receiver. It is night-time.*)

Dorota, I've been trying to get hold of you for days.

DOROTA: I've not been in.

WITEK: (*Voice over*) Did they grant you a passport?

DOROTA: Yes. But I won't be needing it.

WITEK: (*Voice over*) Why not?

(DOROTA *is silent.*)

Dorota! Why not? How's Andrzej?

DOROTA: It's looking bad. Very bad.

WITEK: (*Voice over*) Why won't you be needing the passport?

DOROTA: I'm going to have an abortion.

WITEK: (*Voice over*) What did you say?

DOROTA: I'm going to have an abortion. Tomorrow.

(*Now* WITEK *falls silent.*)

Do you understand what I'm saying?

WITEK: (*Voice over*) Yes. Dorota, if you go ahead with it and Andrzej dies, then it's over between us.

DOROTA: I know.

(*Again there is silence.*)

This conversation must be costing you a small fortune.

WITEK: (*Voice over*) You're the only person I want to be with.

DOROTA: You'll have to ask someone else to bring the scores.

WITEK: (*Voice over*) Yes. I want . . . I love you.

(DOROTA *puts down the receiver and disconnects the telephone from the plug-point at the wall. She clutches her pillow and holds it to her chest.*)

23

A middle-aged blonde woman is in charge of the room crammed full of files.

DOROTA: I want to hand back my passport.

OFFICIAL: Name please?

DOROTA: Dorota Geller.

> (*The female* OFFICIAL *pulls out one of the files, finds the identity card without too much difficulty and looks in astonishment at a piece of paper which is clipped on to it.*)

OFFICIAL: But you only picked this passport up a few days ago.

DOROTA: That's right.

OFFICIAL: You don't have to hand it back straightaway, even if the journey is postponed.

DOROTA: It hasn't been postponed. I've decided not to go at all.

24

The CONSULTANT *is holding a meeting in his office.*

CONSULTANT: . . . as far as this matter is concerned, I'm afraid the news is not good. To get rid of all the bugs and cockroaches would mean emptying the hospital for several days, and we are simply not in a position to do this. I'm afraid we will have to grin and bear it for another year at the very least.

> (*His* SECRETARY *appears at the door to his office and whispers to him.*)

SECRETARY: That woman, the one who was here before . . . Geller . . .

CONSULTANT: Please show her in.

> (*The* SECRETARY *leaves the office and the* CONSULTANT *returns to his interrupted monologue on bugs and cockroaches.*)

25

SECRETARY: The consultant says he will make a special exception. (*She opens the glass doors which lead from the corridor to the ward and lets* DOROTA *in. We may recall that the door to room twelve has a glass panel.* DOROTA *looks through it.* ANDRZEJ'*s hair is matted with sweat and his cheeks are even more sunken than before. A plastic tube leading to a kidney-shaped plastic basin is hanging from his mouth; he spits through it every now and then without opening his eyes. A young man in a white doctor's coat is standing slightly behind* DOROTA *but she has not noticed him. He is staring intently at both her and her husband. His face is one we have seen somewhere before, perhaps in this cycle of stories, perhaps elsewhere. Perhaps it is a face we have all seen at one time or another . . .* DOROTA *sits down beside* ANDRZEJ *and leans towards him.*)

DOROTA: Andrzej. Can you hear me?
(ANDRZEJ'*s face is contorted with agony but relaxes slightly. This is the only indication that he has heard his wife speaking to him.*)
Can you hear me?
(*She now speaks softly but distinctly, careful to punctuate the individual words.*)
I . . . love . . . you . . . very . . . much.
(*It is difficult to say whether* ANDRZEJ *has understood. His face again crumples into a painful grimace.* DOROTA *strokes his wet hair, wanting him to know that she is there and that she cares about him, even if he cannot hear her. The young man in the white coat is still watching them both through the door-glass window. He looks at* ANDRZEJ, *whose face gives the impression of someone hovering between this world and the next.* DOROTA *cuts a little lock of her husband's hair from his forehead and leaves the room.* ANDRZEJ *surveys the world around him; the bed-rail with its peeling paint, and the water dripping down on it from its unknown source. The rivulet seems to have swollen into a thick, mercurial-like solution and the drops of water are now striking the railing with a surprising force.*)

[53]

26

DOROTA *marches forcefully through the secretary's office and violently opens the door to the consultant's office. He is caught in mid-sentence. His* SECRETARY *rises to her feet, recognizing that she has failed in her duty to defend the territory under her responsibility. The* CONSULTANT *turns to her first.*

CONSULTANT: Leave us, please.

DOROTA: That won't be necessary. This will only take a second.
(*She looks him squarely in the eyes.*)
You refused to pass sentence on my husband, but don't think you can get away with an easy conscience. You've signed a death warrant on my child instead.
(*The* CONSULTANT *turns again to his* SECRETARY.)

CONSULTANT: I asked you to leave us.

DOROTA: I have an appointment at the abortion clinic in an hour's time.

CONSULTANT: You mustn't go ahead with it.
(DOROTA *stops suddenly.*)

DOROTA: What?

CONSULTANT: You mustn't go ahead with it. (*He has difficulty finding the words for what he has decided to tell her.*) He's going to die.

DOROTA: How do you know?

CONSULTANT: The complications are more and more rapid. He doesn't stand a chance.

DOROTA: Swear to it in God's name.
(*The* CONSULTANT *is silent.*)
Swear to it in God's name!

CONSULTANT: As God is my witness.
(*The tension drains from* DOROTA's *face and is substituted by an expression of calm. She moves back towards the door without a trace of her former determination. The* CONSULTANT *stops her just in front of the door.*)
Is it true you play in the philharmonic orchestra?
(DOROTA *turns to face him.*)

DOROTA: That's right.

CONSULTANT: It would be nice to hear you some time.
(DOROTA *studies him intently and then slowly closes the door behind her.*)

27

It is dusk. DOROTA *stands by the window of her flat and looks out into the dark expanse of unlit estate beyond the glass.*

The CONSULTANT *like* DOROTA, *is also looking out of the window but this time it is the window of his glasshouse and his face is illuminated by the red glow of the electric fan-heater which keeps the room warm.*

ANDRZEJ's *face is pale. Is that a faint buzzing he can hear? A slight humming, perhaps? Or is it a droning? He raises his eyelids. A bee is swimming round and round in circles in the jar of stewed fruit. At a certain moment the buzzing stops. The bee clambers slowly up the side of the glass and on to the lip. It stands on the edge, brushes its wings briefly, and then flies off.*

28

A concert hall. DOROTA *is sitting among the violinists, concentrating totally on her playing. The* CONSULTANT *is among the audience and stares at* DOROTA, *completely absorbed by the fine, beautifully played music, with its light and harmonious notes. Nothing else is happening. The music saturates the hall and then stops.* DOROTA *lifts her bow from the violin.*

29

At night the consultant's room loses its dry, official character. Light from a small lamp on the desk plucks out only the barest details. The CONSULTANT *is dozing, his head tilted back against the armchair. The papers spread out in front of him, some test-results and health-cards, indicate that he has fallen asleep while working. He is woken up by a soft knocking at the door.*

[55]

CONSULTANT: Come in.
(*The door opens to reveal* ANDRZEJ, *still pale and thin, but very much alive. For the first time we hear his deep masculine voice.*)
ANDRZEJ: May I?
CONSULTANT: Please.
ANDRZEJ: You were asleep.
CONSULTANT: I was only dozing. Please.
(ANDRZEJ *still feels a little unsteady: he walks over hesitantly and holds the back of the chair for support.*)
ANDRZEJ: I couldn't sleep.
CONSULTANT: Please, sit down.
ANDRZEJ: I wanted to thank you.
CONSULTANT: There is nothing to thank me for. In your case especially.
ANDRZEJ: I never thought . . .
CONSULTANT: Neither did I. The test-results, the analyses, the X-rays, all pointed to . . . Proof once again, you see, that we shouldn't be trying to cure X-ray pictures.
ANDRZEJ: I've returned from the land of the dead, haven't I?
CONSULTANT: You have.
ANDRZEJ: The whole world seemed to be collapsing all around me. Everything so squalid and filthy, as if someone was deliberately trying to help me on my way. So I'd have no regrets about leaving it all behind.
CONSULTANT: And are things looking a little brighter now?
ANDRZEJ: Not really. But at least I can touch a table. It seems more solid than before, more real somehow.
(ANDRZEJ *touches the table, which has certainly seen better days: it is badly cracked and chipped, and only someone in a very special frame of mind would have described it as 'more solid'. Almost as if now embarrassed about having said so,* ANDRZEJ *folds his hands, twiddles his fingers and peers at them.*)
And on top of all this . . .
(*The* CONSULTANT *waits patiently.*)
We're going to have a baby.
(*He lifts his smiling eyes. The* CONSULTANT *accepts his expression of joy.*)
CONSULTANT: I am pleased, Mr Geller, very pleased.

[56]

DECALOGUE THREE

The cast and crew of *Decalogue Three* included:

EWA	Maria Pakulnis
JANUSZ	Daniel Olbrychski
JANUSZ'S WIFE	Joanna Szczepkowska
Director of Photography	Piotr Sobocinski
Cameraman	Dariusz Panas
Producer	Ryszard Chutkowski
Composer	Zbigniew Preisner
Artistic Director	Halina Dobrowolska
Sound	Nikodem Wolk-Laniewski
Lighting	Jerzy Tomczuk
Film Editor	Ewa Smal
Production Managers	Pawel Mantorski
	Wlodzimierz Bendych
Costume Designers	Malgorzata Obloza
	Hanna Cwiklo
Director	Krzysztof Kieślowski

Still: Daniel Olbrychski as Janusz and Maria Pakulnis as Ewa

A snow-covered, winter evening. A spruce tree rising from the ground in front of the apartment block has been decorated with Christmas lights. Christmas carols can be heard issuing from church loudspeakers and individual apartments in the distance. Windows glow in the dark, lit up by Christmas trees visible behind their net curtains. A drunk is dragging a Christmas tree along the snow-covered street – he is obviously late and shows great determination to get it home on time. He staggers past a car which has a light burning on the roof: it is a white Fiat* with the taxi-cab's usual corona. Forty-year-old JANUSZ *is sticking a false beard of cotton wool to his chin. He climbs out of the car, turns the fleece lining of his large, light-coloured fur coat inside out, ties a belt around his waist, and puts a red cap on his head. He slams the door shut, opens the boot, takes out a large sack presumably full of presents, throws it over his shoulder, and moves off towards the tall block of flats which is home for all our acquaintances, past, present and future.*

2

JANUSZ, *disguised as Father Christmas, has difficulty reaching over to press the lift call button. The lift arrives quickly – evidently it had not been far away.* KRYZSZTOF (*the scientist from the first story*) *climbs out and holds the doors open.*

JANUSZ: Merry Christmas.

KRZYSZTOF: Merry Christmas. I'm sorry, I didn't recognize you.

(*He looks at* JANUSZ: *those who remember the recent tragedy on*

---

* There are two types of Polish Fiat, both manufactured in the 1970s under Italian licence. The larger version, which Janusz drives, is quite commonly used by taxi-drivers, along with the more luxurious Polonez, which is driven by the taxi-driver in Decalogue Five. Ewa drives the smaller version of the Fiat in this story. As in other countries, cars in Poland are useful indicators of status. Foreign cars, like the Volkswagen driven by Dorota in Decalogue Two, and the Mazda driven by Roman in Decalogue Nine, are the top end of the scale.

the lake involving his son will understand his expression. JANUSZ
does not notice this expression and does not remember the tragedy.
He adjusts his beard and rings the doorbell to his own flat. After
the 'who's there?' from the other side of the door, he replies in a
gruff voice.)
JANUSZ: Father Christmas.

3

Excited and frightened at the same time, the children take refuge
behind their mother. Janusz's mother-in-law, a genteel woman of
sixty, regards the spectacle with a hint of disapproval. Janusz's WIFE
is thirty-five years old and has the pale expression of a woman worn
out by the demands of life in general. Or perhaps just life with her
husband in particular. JANUSZ/*Father Christmas sits in the chair*
which has been especially left vacant for him.
JANUSZ: Do any children live in this house? I've been told there's
    a little girl called Kasia and a little boy called Antos. Kasia is
    supposed to be a brave little girl . . .
    (*The three-year-old girl slips out from behind her mother.*)
    Are you Kasia? I understand you have a little rhyme for me.
KASIA: Saint Nicholas, Saint Nicholas, we want you to tickle us.
    (*Everybody laughs. Father Christmas also booms out good-*
    naturedly in his strange and unreal voice.)
JANUSZ: And what about Antos? Have you been a good little boy
    today?
    (*The little boy's mother leans over and whispers something into*
    his ear. ANTOS *listens, but is staring intently at the watch which*
    has popped out from underneath the sleeve of Father Christmas's
    fur coat and which of course he recognizes. Without tearing his
    eyes away from the watch, he says quickly:)
ANTOS: I helped Mummy with the cake.
    (JANUSZ *opens the sack and pulls out the presents. He celebrates*
    this moment, reading out the little gift-tags which have been
    Sellotaped to the various parcels. There are a number of small
    and slightly larger presents for everyone. The gift tag with the
    words 'For Mum' is attached to a longish, almost metre-long,

thin, leather holder. JANUSZ *reads it out before giving the present to his* WIFE. *Everybody starts to unwrap their presents. Taking advantage of the general commotion,* JANUSZ *slips across into the bathroom and removes his beard. Only now do we see his real face: it is sweaty, thoughtful, and sad, like a clown's with his mask removed. There is a soft knock at the door: his* WIFE *is standing there holding a pair of top-quality ski poles, a disbelieving smile on her face.*)

WIFE: Thank you. Do you really think we'll be able to go?

JANUSZ: We can always try.

(*His* WIFE *comes into the bathroom and uses the pretext of wiping the remains of the sweat and cotton wool from her husband's face in order to be near him.*)

WIFE: It's very kind of you. Really.

(JANUSZ *does not succumb to his wife's brief caresses, neither recoiling from her touch, nor drawing closer.*)

Thank you.

(JANUSZ *is left by himself. He looks in the mirror and his gaze is met by the face of a man who has seen his fair share of suffering.*)

4

The family is singing carols. Janusz's WIFE *is lighting the sparklers hanging from the Christmas tree and* JANUSZ's *voice can be heard from the kitchen trying to sing along with the family choir. He is slowly washing his way through a pile of dirty dishes. His* WIFE *comes in.*

WIFE: Kasia's falling asleep.

JANUSZ: We promised . . .

(*He puts the dishes aside, walks to her room, leans over the small girl, and delicately touches her cheek with his hand.*)

Are you asleep?

KASIA: No. You promised we could go to midnight Mass.

JANUSZ: You can.

KASIA: Are you going to carry me?

JANUSZ: Come on, let's do the dishes first.

(KASIA *raises herself with an enormous effort of will and slips into her father's arms.*)

[61]

KASIA: You know I can't sing, don't you?

(*JANUSZ gives her a drying-up cloth and several dripping spoons, and demonstrates how to wipe the large, silver cutlery, which is only brought out on special occasions.*)

5

Midnight Mass: Christmas trees, the crib, small lamps, a large congregation of calm, festive faces, and JANUSZ, *his daughter in his arms and his family around him.*

PRIEST: . . . these days of happiness and joy which we will be spending with our nearest and dearest should be the occasion for the drawing together of the family. It is so difficult in this day and age to find fulfilment in the field of public endeavour, which is why even more so we should seek love and affection among those who are dearest to us . . .

(*JANUSZ's concentration is being distracted. He has noticed the silhouette and profile of a woman's face several rows ahead, and is staring in her direction. She turns her head away from him, perhaps sensing someone's eyes on her. Or perhaps purely by accident.*)

PRIEST: On each and every day, but on this day especially, we should think about others with love and a sense of responsibility for their well-being. The spare seat at the table which we leave especially for the unexpected guest should not be just a symbolic gesture. We should also celebrate as a community and try to find a place in our hearts for all those who suffer, all those who are abandoned, and all those who are alone . . .

(*JANUSZ is again staring ahead towards the place where only a few moments ago he had glimpsed the face of the dark-haired woman, but she is no longer there. There is a pillar next to the empty space – perhaps she is standing behind it. JANUSZ leans forward, trying to decide whether he had really seen someone he knew, or whether he had merely imagined it.*)

6

JANUSZ *and his family are among the people returning from midnight*
Mass. He is carrying the sleeping KASIA *in his arms.* ANTOS *is*
bounding along, sliding boisterously along the frozen puddles. JANUSZ
races him, despite having KASIA *in his arms, and manages to slide*
further. His WIFE *is carefully guiding her mother along the slippery*
pavement. Just as they are about to enter the block, JANUSZ *suddenly*
realizes he has forgotten something.

JANUSZ: The champagne! Hold her for a second, will you?
> (*He gives the little girl to his* WIFE *and runs over to the white*
> *Fiat minicab.*)
> It's frozen!
> (*He returns with the bottle and they all disappear into the*
> *stairwell entrance.*

7

They climb into the lift and JANUSZ *tenses for a second. He has*
noticed the profile of the dark-haired woman he saw earlier in church
through the glass of the stairwell doors.

8

JANUSZ *arranges the glasses on a tray and sets about opening the*
champagne. As soon as he hears the front door being closed, he
quickly unplugs the telephone from the wall and does the same with
the extension lead into the kitchen. Feeling more relaxed now,
he tilts the neck of the bottle at the appropriate angle (forty-five
degrees) and carries the tray with the filled glasses into the living room.
He distributes the glasses, kisses first his mother-in-law, and
then his WIFE.

JANUSZ: Merry Christmas once again.
> (*This merry domestic scene is interrupted by the shrill,*
> *disagreeable ringing of the block intercom bell.* JANUSZ *tenses,*

but his expression alters almost immediately: who could it be? He lifts the receiver.)
Hello.
(His WIFE *stands a little uneasily in the doorway.* JANUSZ *puts the receiver back on its hook and says nothing, trying to collect his thoughts.)*
I couldn't catch what they were saying . . . something about someone hanging around the taxi . . .
(He dashes out of the apartment.)

9

JANUSZ *runs out of the building and looks around: no one is there. Shivering from cold, he is on his way back when he hears the sound of a match being struck behind him. It is the same woman he had seen earlier in church. She has dark hair, black, expressive eyes and a large mouth. Her features seem even more sharply defined in the glow of the match. They exchange glances for a moment before the match burns out.*

EWA: That's the second time you haven't wished me Happy Christmas.

JANUSZ: *(With controlled anger)* What do you want?
*(*EWA *is silent.)*
It's Christmas Eve. Tell me what you want.
(Tears roll slowly down EWA*'s cheeks. She does not bury her face in her hands and is not crying, but the tears are there, trickling down her face one after the other.)*
This is emotional blackmail . . .

EWA: Edward's gone missing.

JANUSZ: Edward?
*(*EWA *nods. Tears are still streaming down her face.)*
Don't cry . . .
(He takes her face into his hands, but EWA *does not succumb to his touch, evidently uninterested in this display of sentiment. She closes her eyes and says quickly:)*

EWA: He went out this morning and didn't come back. I've got to find him.

JANUSZ: But it's Christmas Eve.

EWA: I know, I'm sorry.

> (*She frees herself from his embrace, steps around him and walks off.*)

JANUSZ: Wait Ewa! I'll go with you.

EWA: What did you tell them at home?

JANUSZ: I said someone suspicious was hanging around the cars.

EWA: Give me the keys.

> (*The tears have vanished. She takes the keys.*)
> I'll be waiting around the corner.
> (*She walks over to Janusz's taxi, starts the engine and drives off.*)

10

JANUSZ *stops for a second outside his front door. He briefly prepares himself for the entrance, wanting to look like someone who has just had his car stolen. He forcefully opens the door and runs briskly into the flat.*

JANUSZ: The car's been stolen. They were seen making off along the Embankment.

> (*His* WIFE *and mother-in-law look up at him from the table.*)
> Maybe I'll be able to catch a taxi. In the meantime give the police a ring.

WIFE: Maybe it's not worth it . . .

JANUSZ: It's our living.

11

JANUSZ *runs across the square in front of the block.* EWA *is waiting for him around the corner in the passenger seat of his Fiat.*

JANUSZ: Were you at midnight Mass?

EWA: No.

JANUSZ: But I saw you.

EWA: I looked for him at friends and then went to the police.

> (JANUSZ *wants to stroke her face, but* EWA *draws back.*)

[65]

Don't touch me. I need your help, not your pity.

JANUSZ: Where do we go first?

EWA: Where would you go if your wife went missing?

JANUSZ: The hospital.

EWA: There's one on emergency call on Bracka Street.

12

They drive across an intersection and JANUSZ *is forced to slow down. A cavalcade is blocking the road, a single car drawing several sledges along in its wake, accompanied by people waving balloons and torches at the cars which have stopped to let them across.*

JANUSZ: I've been drinking champagne.

(EWA *takes several coffee beans out of her handbag.*)

EWA: Chew on these. Come on, let's go. You can chew them while you're driving.

13

The hospital reception area is deserted. The corridors are poorly lit and all the doors along them are locked. JANUSZ *twists each door-handle in succession, but to no avail.*

JANUSZ: Is this called being on emergency duty?

EWA: If you want to help, then stop asking stupid questions. If you don't, then go back to bed.

(*She goes past* JANUSZ *and walks up the stairs. A streak of light is visible from one of the rooms in the first-floor corridor. A small Christmas tree stands on the doctor's table and a radio is playing. The* DOCTOR *himself is asleep, his head lolling backwards.* JANUSZ *knocks on the door embrasure.*)

JANUSZ: Are you on duty here?

(*The* DOCTOR *opens his tired eyes without altering his position.*)

DOCTOR: No, that was yesterday.

EWA: I must have made a mistake.

JANUSZ: What about today?

(*The* DOCTOR *reaches for the telephone without saying a word.*

[66]

He looks at JANUSZ *while waiting for the voice at the other end.*)
DOCTOR: Who's gone missing?
JANUSZ: A husband.
DOCTOR: (*Looks at* JANUSZ) Yours?
EWA: Mine.
DOCTOR: Husbands have a habit of going missing – especially at
  Christmas time. (*Into the receiver*) Jurek? (*Speaking to* EWA)
  Name?
EWA: Garus.
DOCTOR: (*Into the receiver*) Garus . . . Age?
EWA: Thirty-eight.
DOCTOR: Garus, thirty-eight years of age . . . There's a little lady
  over here who's lost her husband. What time did they bring
  him in? (*To* EWA) How long's he been missing?
EWA: Since noon.
DOCTOR: It's not him, then. Bye. (*He puts down the receiver.*)
  They brought a guy in this morning who'd lost both his legs
  in a car accident. Just before eleven.
EWA: Come on, let's go.
  (JANUSZ *turns around in the doorway.*)
JANUSZ: Shall I switch the light off?
  (*The* DOCTOR *does not reply: he is already asleep in the same
  position as before.*)
EWA: Everybody's drunk.
JANUSZ: He's just exhausted. Are you sure he left at midday?
EWA: I went out in the morning to buy something. When I got
  back at noon he wasn't there.
JANUSZ: We'd better go to the other hospital then.

14

*The car turns into Aleja Ujazdowska from Piekna Street. As they
drive past the Actor's Club,* EWA *recognizes something through the
side-window.*
EWA: Stop.
  (*She directs* JANUSZ *towards a small Fiat parked just outside the
  club. She peers inside.*)

[67]

It's his car.

JANUSZ: Have you got your own set of keys?

(EWA *takes the keys out of her handbag. They open the car-door. A scarf is lying on the front seat.* EWA *holds it uncertainly in her hand.*)

Leave it. He might be cold when he gets back.

EWA: Difficult to see how if he's lost both his legs.

(JANUSZ *slams the door as hard as he can.*)

JANUSZ: Lock it.

EWA: Let's leave him a sandwich. He might be hungry as well.

JANUSZ: Very funny.

EWA: It could be even funnier. We could find a hotel room and go to bed together, and then you could ring him up and tell him which room we're in, so he could . . .

JANUSZ: It wasn't me who rang him.

EWA: Don't try and deny it. You were the one who wanted to end it all. Go back to your family and have a quiet life. Of course it was you.

JANUSZ: It wasn't!

EWA: He told me. You didn't say who you were, that's true.

JANUSZ: For fuck's sake, Ewa, it wasn't me!

EWA: No? Perhaps not. The hospital in Praga, please.

15

The white Fiat taxi draws up outside the hospital in the Praga district.

16

A DOCTOR *leads them down along a long, empty, curving corridor. An elderly* MAN *pops his head out of a small window.*

DOCTOR II: Looking for the guy without the legs?

EWA: You go. I don't think I can bear it.

(JANUSZ *enters the room behind the elderly* MAN. *They stop by one of the metal tables and his 'guide' draws back the sheet covering the dead man's body. His face is covered in gashes and*

[68]

his teeth are jutting out of his mouth in a rictus grin.)

ELDERLY MAN: Is it him?

JANUSZ: I don't know.

ELDERLY MAN: Aren't you the one who did that story on us the
time I was still working on the railways? I looked out for
your stuff after that but never saw anything. Were you –

JANUSZ: Yes.

ELDERLY MAN: What is the world coming to . . .

(JANUSZ *goes to fetch* EWA. *They come back together: again the
room with the metal tables, again the elderly* MAN *draws back the
sheet . . .* EWA *watches as if hypnotized and draws closer.*
JANUSZ *and the elderly* MAN *exchange glances.* EWA *suddenly
turns and buries her head in his coat.*)

JANUSZ: Ewa . . .

(*The elderly* MAN *discreetly leaves the room.* JANUSZ *attempts to
cover up the dead body, but there is no need:* EWA *looks up at
him, her face composed and tearless.*)

EWA: Don't bother. It's not him. I wanted it to be him. Or you. I
wanted it to be your face and your teeth.

(*She takes out a cigarette and lights it – neither hand is
trembling.*)

I dreamt once that you'd broken your neck – your tongue
was hanging out – it was a wonderful dream.

(*She turns back towards the man lying on the table.*)

I wonder who he'll have made a happy person.

JANUSZ: Do you want to carry on looking?

EWA: Yes.

JANUSZ: Maybe he'll be back by now.

EWA: Maybe he will.

17

*We are back in the street again. A police car is controlling an East
German Trabant in the distance.*

EWA: Police. You're in a stolen car, remember.

(JANUSZ *slows but slams down hard on the accelerator as soon as
the Trabant and the police car are behind him.*)

JANUSZ: Hold tight.

(*A blue flashing light appears behind them. The car takes the Marszalkowska roundabout at great speed, barely keeping its grip on the road. Gaily decorated Christmas trees flash past. The Polonez is still behind them with its flashing blue light.* JANUSZ *turns downhill. The Polonez follows.*)

EWA: Have you got your documents? Slow down.

(*The police car catches up with them in a tunnel. Two policemen run over to the front doors of the Fiat.*)

POLICEMAN: Out, please. Hands on the roof.

(JANUSZ *climbs slowly out of the car.* EWA *places her hands on the car roof with a smile. The officers frisk them quickly and efficiently before allowing them to take their hands off the roof.*) Is this your car, sir?

(JANUSZ *takes out his documents. The* POLICEMAN *reads them and glances over, first at* JANUSZ, *then at* EWA, *before handing them over to his colleague, who also reads them carefully.*) This car was reported stolen.

EWA: We found it. They had abandoned it on the Embankment.

(*The* POLICEMAN *hands back the documents.*)

POLICEMAN: Had anything to drink?

JANUSZ: I didn't make it home in time.

POLICEMAN: Drive a little more slowly in future, sir. Merry Christmas.

(*They touch the peaks of their caps and then drive off.* EWA *smiles at* JANUSZ.)

EWA: Very cool . . . Shall we try again? Do you want to?

JANUSZ: With the seat-belts on?

(EWA *shakes her head.* JANUSZ *starts the engine, settles back into the driving seat and slowly steers the car off the pavement. They start to pick up speed. By the time he takes the bridge over the Vistula river, he must be doing a ton at least. A tram is travelling in the opposite direction away from the east bank and is already halfway across the bridge.* JANUSZ *swings the hurtling vehicle on to the tram-lines. The car is now screaming along at full pelt and the tram headlights seem to be approaching at terrific speed.* EWA *stares soundlessly ahead, her eyes wide open and composed. A pale-looking young man with a face which would be difficult to*

forget is at the controls of the tram. He drives calmly, illuminated by the car headlights flying headlong towards him. The car gets nearer and nearer and the tram-driver smiles quietly to himself, his face glowing whiter and whiter in the intensifying glare of the approaching headlights. JANUSZ *swerves away only at the very last second. The Fiat virtually grazes the side of the oncoming tram and after a long, clumsy skid which sends clouds of powdered, white snow flying in all directions finally comes to rest sideways-on opposite a tram-stop.*)
Had enough?
(EWA *slowly shakes her head: no, she hasn't.*)

18

Ewa's apartment is on a low-built housing estate. The car-park is crammed full and JANUSZ *only finds a free space after a long search. He climbs out first and takes a look around.*
JANUSZ: Your car's not here.
(EWA *gets out without saying a word.* JANUSZ *looks around once more and is suddenly struck by a thought.*)
He couldn't have left his car in front of the club in the morning. It was snowing in the afternoon and yet his car was clean.
(EWA *looks at him questioningly.*)
There was no snow on the car roof. Yet it began to snow again around five o'clock.
EWA: Maybe he arrived later on.
JANUSZ: But the club shuts after two.
EWA: Well, I don't know. If he's at home, it wouldn't be a good idea to be seen coming in together. Wait here. If he's not there, I'll come out on to the balcony. If I don't come out after a few minutes, you might as well go.
(EWA *walks off.* JANUSZ *calls after her.*)
JANUSZ: Ewa! Goodbye, just in case.
(EWA *raises her hand and waves goodbye with her fingers.* JANUSZ *gets into the car and holds his head in his hands as if to say: what on earth am I doing here?*)

[71]

19

EWA *enters the apartment and walks straight over to the telephone.*
She crouches on the floor so that JANUSZ *is unable to see her from*
outside in the street below. She dials a short, three-digit number.
WOMAN: (*Voice over*) Hello, hospital.
EWA: There's been an accident. A man's passed out and is lying at
  a bus-stop.
WOMAN: (*Voice over*) Address?
EWA: On the corner of Walbrzyska and Pulawska street, as the
  bus goes towards the city centre.
WOMAN: (*Voice over*) Is he drunk?
EWA: No. We took his documents.
WOMAN: (*Voice over*) Name?
EWA: Edward Garus. Born 1949.
WOMAN: (*Voice over*) Your name?
  (EWA *glances at a copy of a newspaper,* Polityka, *which is lying*
  on a stool. She reads out the by-line at the bottom of one of the
  articles.
EWA: Anna Tatarkiewicz.
WOMAN: (*Voice over*) The details have been logged.
  (EWA *replaces the receiver and only then switches on the lights in*
  the room. There are two napkins, a bottle of wine, and a small
  Christmas tree branch in a vase on the table. She goes out on to
  the balcony and watches as JANUSZ *gets out of the car and walks*
  towards the building. She casts an eye over the apartment, then
  moves quickly over to a cupboard, takes out a suitcase which has
  her husband's raincoat inside and hangs it up on a peg in the
  hallway. She adds another toothbrush to the one already standing
  in a mug by the mirror in the bathroom. She takes out a razor and
  an old, moulting shaving brush from a washbag, dips the brush in
  soap and rinses it with water from the tap. The doorbell rings just
  at this moment. EWA *opens the door.* JANUSZ *walks uncertainly*
  into the flat without taking his coat off. EWA *studies him with*
  curiosity.)
EWA: Aren't you going to take your coat off?
JANUSZ: I'm frozen.

[72]

EWA: How about some tea?

JANUSZ: Lovely.

(EWA *puts on the kettle, sits down and looks at* JANUSZ *in expectation, while cupping her face in the palms of her hands.*)

Listen – it wasn't me who rang – Three years ago – It wasn't me – that's rubbish.

(*If* JANUSZ *had glanced towards* EWA *at that moment he would have noticed the faint trace of a smile. But he is not looking in her direction.*)

Our relationship meant a lot to me. If you really want to know the truth, you were . . . I loved you. I was hoping to change everything.

(*It would be unfair to interpret the smile on* EWA's *face as an expression of slight cynicism, but who knows whether this isn't indeed the case.*)

He stood there with his back to us as we got dressed. It wasn't particularly pleasant. You didn't even look at me. I took your hand but you pulled it away. Then he gave you the choice: either you go with him or stay with me – and you went with him. You probably don't remember what actually happened, that's why I'm telling you.

EWA: Is that what happened? Did I leave with him?

JANUSZ: Well, not exactly. He said he would let you come along with him only if you agreed never to see me again.

EWA: Is that how it was?

JANUSZ: And you said: 'I don't intend to.' I said something like 'Fine.' That's what really happened.

(EWA *lowers her hands from under her chin and holds them out to* JANUSZ.)

EWA: Give me your hand, you poor darling . . .

(JANUSZ *lets her take his hand.* EWA *strokes it delicately.* JANUSZ *strokes her hand back.*)

Unloved, unblameworthy, he wanted to change everything.

(JANUSZ *detects the faint note of mockery in her voice and wants to retract his hand, but* EWA *grips it with unexpected determination.*)

And now you love your wife, right?

JANUSZ: I love the children.

[73]

EWA: And you tried so hard to make up for what you'd done. So caring and considerate, always remembering to collect the laundry from the cleaners . . .

(EWA *digs her nails into the palm of his hand.*)

JANUSZ: Let go.

EWA: I suppose you think driving like a maniac makes you a real man. And that you only need to touch me and I'll immediately draw the curtains and leap into bed with you . . .

(EWA *has been digging her nails harder and harder into his hand throughout this brief monologue.*)

JANUSZ: Let go.

EWA: Gladly. You reek of petrol anyway.

(JANUSZ *massages the palm of his hand and involuntarily raises it to his nostrils. He goes out to the bathroom.* EWA *hurries after him.*)

And I don't suppose you ever stopped to think about what I had to go through? The look he gave me as we walked out? How he treated me in bed? Did that ever occur to you?

(*All this is spoken through the closed door to the bathroom. Inside,* JANUSZ *is examining the two toothbrushes, the shaving brush and the razor. He unscrews the razorhead and sees an old, rusty blade inside which has not beeen used for years.* EWA's *shouting reaches him from the other side of the door.*)

In bed! Do you hear?!

(JANUSZ *tries the blade: it is blunt and unable to cut through skin even when pressed hard. He screws up the razorhead again and places it back on the shelf.* EWA *knocks on the door, falls silent for a moment, then resumes her monologue in a calm, equable voice.*)

I never slept with him from that night onwards, not once. Do you hear?

(JANUSZ *is silent: he does not know what to do next.* EWA *is also silent. They stand for the few moments like this, then* EWA *asks in a normal, neutral tone of voice.*)

What are you doing in there?

(JANUSZ *opens the door.*)

JANUSZ: Nothing. I was washing my hands.

[74]

(EWA *returns to the living room and reaches for a piece of wafer.*)

EWA: It's Christmas Eve. One shouldn't tell lies, I'm sorry.
Everything is completely normal between Edward and
myself. Merry Christmas . . .

(*She breaks off a piece of the wafer, hands it to* JANUSZ, *breaks
off a smaller piece for herself as he holds it in his fingers and puts
it into her mouth.* JANUSZ *does the same and then remembers the
razor-blade.*)

JANUSZ: Has Edward grown a beard?

EWA: No, of course not.

(EWA *looks at him intently.*)
We're sharing a wafer, and we've clean forgotten why we
came here in the first place. We ought to get going.

JANUSZ: Where to?

EWA: The hospital, the police, then the station.

(EWA *puts on her overcoat, wraps herself up in a scarf, goes into
the bathroom, and takes the razor off the shelf. She unscrews the
blade exactly as* JANUSZ *did a few minutes ago. The blade is still
as blunt as it was before. She screws it back up again and flushes
the toilet. After the sound of the gushing water has subsided, she
hears* JANUSZ's *voice on the telephone.*)

JANUSZ: (*Out of shot*) Is that the hospital? I want to check if
anybody by the name of Garus, Edward Garus, has been
brought in today.

(EWA *waits anxiously for the response.*)
(*Out of shot*) He's thirty-eight . . . born in 1949.

(JANUSZ *is silent for a moment.* EWA *places her ear against the
door in order to catch everything he is saying.*)
(*Out of shot*) Do you cover the whole Warsaw area?

(EWA *realizes that* JANUSZ *has not found out what she wanted
and is about to leave the bathroom when she hears his voice
again, this time speaking more loudly.*)
(*Out of shot*) Somebody rang in? And?

(EWA *now waits calmly. She hears a violent knocking on the
bathroom door and flushes the toilet again before opening the
door.*)
I rang the hospital. They've had a call.

EWA: And?

[75]

JANUSZ: He was seen lying at a bus-stop on Pulawska Street but
by the time they got there he'd gone.

EWA: How come?

JANUSZ: They didn't know. Apparently that's often the case with
drunks. They suggested trying the drying-out centre.

20

The battery is weak and reluctant to start the engine. JANUSZ *notices
two young lads waiting at a nearby taxi-stop.*

JANUSZ: Can you give us a push?

BOYS: Will you give us a lift? To Praga?

JANUSZ: I'm in a hurry.

BOYS: Well, push it yourself then.

(JANUSZ *pushes the Fiat. The oil is frozen and it is hard going,
but the car finally picks up momentum on a gentle slope.* EWA
releases the clutch, the engine splutters into life and JANUSZ *hops
into the moving vehicle.* EWA *wants to change places, but*
JANUSZ *simply waves his hand.*)

JANUSZ: You can drive.

(EWA *puts her foot down on the accelerator.*)

Why did you mention the railway station?

EWA: He used to hang around there a lot. Or at the airport. He'd
ring up in the middle of the night and say he was leaving. But
he'd always turn up the next morning.

21

*The front entrance of the drying-out centre is shut, but a light is
burning in the small barred window around the back. They peer in: the
bodies of two grown men lie limply in a stream of hose-pipe water. The
hose-pipe is being held by a powerfully built* MAN *in a white overall.*
JANUSZ *taps at the window. The* MAN *turns off the water and lets
them in. Everything in the small room is neatly arranged. He pulls a
file with the letter 'G' in large type on the cover from a metal filing
cabinet, expertly fingers through the pages, and then looks up.*)

MAN: Jew?

EWA: No . . .

MAN: We had a Garus here in '79. He was a Jew.

(JANUSZ *leans over to have a look at the file.*)

JANUSZ: Does everyone have a file like that?

(*The* MAN *smiles – Janusz's question has clearly given him satisfaction.*)

MAN: Got to keep everything ship-shape. Some of them won't tell me who they are, but while they're under the hose I take down the details. One of them hasn't got his papers with him – maybe he's the guy you're looking for.

(*He leads them into a tiled room which is fitted with the hose-pipe. His two frozen guests are lying curled up on the floor. The* MAN *tut-tuts and shakes his head. It is indeed difficult to recognize the naked bodies lying against the wall.*)

They've fallen asleep on me.

(*He turns on the hose and directs the water straight at them. They get to their feet and try to protect themselves from the cold, sharp shower.*)

Look at 'em dance . . . Maybe he's the one you want? Or perhaps the other one?

(*He directs the stream of water so that the two men are forced to turn and face* JANUSZ *and* EWA.)

JANUSZ: Stop that . . . Stop it! (JANUSZ *turns off the water.*) Can't you see they're frozen?

(*The* MAN *takes a step towards him.*)

MAN: Look, shithead, if you want to be chucked in there with them as well, then . . .

JANUSZ: Try it. Just try it.

(JANUSZ *speaks calmly, but with authority. Sensing his superiority, he rips the hose-pipe out of the tap.*)

Come on then. Let's see you dance.

(*The* MAN *looks at him for a moment, then throws a small pile of clothing towards the two drunks.*)

MAN: Time to get dressed, methylates.

(*In order to release some of his aggression, he kicks a boot in their direction which had not quite reached the cell bars when he had thrown them the clothes earlier.*)

[77]

22

Early dawn. Both EWA *and* JANUSZ *are walking towards the car.*
EWA *takes his hand and would perhaps like to cuddle up to him, but*
JANUSZ's *pace does not slacken. They get into the car and* JANUSZ
puts the key in the ignition.
JANUSZ: I'm going home. This is ridiculous.
  (EWA *places her palm on his hand as he moves to shift the car into*
  gear. JANUSZ *does not react and merely shifts the car into gear*
  before putting his hand on the steering wheel. EWA's *hand follows*
  and never leaves it.)
Can I drop you off somewhere?
  (EWA *looks at him fondly.* JANUSZ *drives off and turns into a*
  broad street. EWA *suddenly leans over, grabs the steering-wheel*
  with both hands, and hangs on to it for grim life. JANUSZ *is*
  unable to straighten the car and brakes sharply while trying to
  pull her hands off the wheel. The car is not travelling at great
  speed but careers inevitably towards a lamp-post. Collision.
  JANUSZ *smashes his head against the mirror and blood starts to*
  seep from the cut in his forehead. EWA *releases the steering-wheel.*
  A headlamp is smashed, the bumper and fender are badly dented,
  but the engine is running normally. JANUSZ *gets out and tries to*
  stem the flow of blood with a handful of snow. The snow is dirty
  and his face is now streaked with blood and dirt. EWA *watches*
  him from the passenger seat, then gets out, unbuttons her
  overcoat, pulls out her blouse from beneath her skirt and rips off a
  piece of material. She wipes the dirt and melted snow from
  JANUSZ's *face and tries to stop the bleeding. The cut is not deep*
  and the blood clots as EWA *holds the make-shift bandage against*
  his forehead.)
EWA: I've smashed up your car.
  (JANUSZ *does not respond.*)
I've ruined your Christmas Eve.
JANUSZ: No, why? It's been great fun.
EWA: Drive with me to the station.

23

A Christmas tree with fairy-lights stands in the middle of the empty ticket-hall. EWA *and* JANUSZ *walk through the empty waiting-rooms and along the platforms.* EWA *goes up to two men asleep on a bench and takes a good look at them, completely unnecessarily as it later turns out. They hear a strange noise and turn to try and trace where it is coming from. They reach a long, sloping walkway which leads down on to one of the platforms. A young, unattractive* WOMAN *wearing a railway worker's uniform is speeding down the slope on a skate-board. They catch up with her just by the platform.*

JANUSZ: Are you on duty by the close-circuit TV?

WOMAN: Yes.

JANUSZ: We're looking . . . Have there been any accidents?

WOMAN: No. I've been skating a little to stop me falling asleep.

EWA: There's a man who comes here quite often. Wears a short, white, sheepskin jacket. He comes here a lot, but never gets on any of the trains.

(The WOMAN *tries to recall who it might be, or is perhaps only able to picture him in her mind's eye.* EWA *reaches for her handbag, takes out a passport-sized photograph, and hands it to the* WOMAN. *She looks at the photo for a long time and then gives it back to* EWA *without saying a word: she does not know him. She gets off the skate-board and walks off.* EWA *now gives the photo to* JANUSZ. *It is of a man in a white, sheepskin jacket with a woman standing beside him. He has a small child on his back in a comfortable baby-carrier and a larger, older child in his arms. The three of them are smiling at the camera.)*

JANUSZ: Who's that?

EWA: Edward.

JANUSZ: And her . . .

EWA: His wife. They're his children. They've been living in Krakow for the past three years.

(JANUSZ does not understand. EWA *has a grave expression on her face, the gravest she has had all night.)*

JANUSZ: For the past three years?

EWA: Virtually. I've told you quite a few lies tonight.

[79]

JANUSZ: But what did you want? Revenge?

EWA: No. Do you know that game where if a man appears around a corner it's good luck, and if it's a woman, it's bad luck?

JANUSZ: Yes. I close my eyes and put my foot down on the pavement. If it lands in the middle of the paving stone I'll have a good day, and if it lands on the line, I'll have a bad day.

EWA: I've been playing it today. I told myself that if I managed to stay with you for a whole night until seven in the morning, however it was done . . .

(A train draws up to the platform: nobody gets on or off. The conductor, whose face we know from somewhere, raises his hand in the air and gives the signal for the train to pull off.)

JANUSZ: Well?

EWA: I would carry on my life as normal.

JANUSZ: And if not?

(EWA folds her hands. The conductor watches them for a second, perhaps because they are the only people on the platform.)

EWA: I had everything prepared. I live on my own . . .

(She pulls a small bottle of tablets out of her pocket, but does not show them to JANUSZ. Only we see this movement. She puts the little dispenser back in her pocket. The conductor, again looking in their direction, gets back into his carriage and the train begins to pull away.)

It's difficult being on your own. On a day like this. People –

(JANUSZ nods understandingly.)

JANUSZ: Close up . . . draw the curtains.

EWA: Exactly.

24

JANUSZ *is treating* EWA *more tenderly than before – something difficult to describe in words but easy for an actor to express. He opens the car door for her and they move off. The wound on his forehead is still a little bloody and he wipes it from time to time. As they are driving along, they notice two young teenagers in hot pursuit of a third. It is clearly a matter of some seriousness, since they are pelting hard after him. The fugitive has about fifteen metres' advantage.* JANUSZ *accelerates without a word, overtakes the pursuers and, as they are neck and neck with the* YOUTH *making his escape,* EWA *throws open the rear door.*

EWA: Jump in!

> (*The* YOUTH *makes a grab for the doors and loses his footing for a second on the icy roadway, but with a great effort, and helped by* EWA, *he manages to pull himself inside. He is gulping for air and drops of saliva are visible in the corners of his mouth.*)

Where to?

> (*His pursuers turn back and run towards their own car.* EWA *repeats the question. The* YOUTH *seems not to know: perhaps he does not want to go anywhere in particular, or perhaps does not want anything at all.*)

YOUTH: They'll catch up with me sooner or later anyway.

EWA: So why are you running away?

YOUTH: I don't know. It doesn't make any sense.

25

The YOUTH *asks to be dropped off on the Aleja Jerozolimska roundabout. The car in pursuit is nowhere to be seen.* JANUSZ *stops the car, and the* YOUTH *jumps out and disappears into an underground subway.* JANUSZ *turns right by the Metropol Hotel and watches the empty roundabout. The other car is roaring up the road from the station. It screeches to a halt and drives up on to the pavement. The pursuers jump out and run into the subway without bothering to shut the car doors. The subway is completely empty. Nobody emerges from the other side.* JANUSZ *makes a move as if to get out of the car.*

EWA: There's nothing you can do.

> (JANUSZ *changes his mind.*)

JANUSZ: You're right.

> (*The roundabout is still empty.*)

EWA: You've done your good deed for the day.

JANUSZ: Yes.

26

The white Fiat taxi with its dented bumper drives slowly to the Actors'
Club. JANUSZ *crosses over into the left hand lane without bothering to*
check what is coming in the opposite direction and pulls up alongside
the pavement.

EWA: I know it wasn't you who rang him. See you around.

> (EWA *climbs out and transfers to her own car.* JANUSZ *waits for*
> *her car engine to start and warm up before walking back to his*
> *own white Fiat. The two cars now stand opposite each other,*
> *about twenty metres apart. The small Fiat's headlamps light up*
> *and flash several times.* JANUSZ *flashes back in reply.* EWA
> *repeats the gesture – perhaps it is merely accidental, but the short*
> *and long bursts of light seem to establish a pattern of*
> *communication, like a conversation which neither partner is able*
> *to complete. The small Fiat finally emits one long and*
> *uninterrupted beam of light, and slowly drives off.*)

27

JANUSZ *softly opens the front door to his apartment. The kitchen is*
empty. He walks on tiptoes into the living room. His WIFE *is sitting in*
an armchair.

JANUSZ: Everyone's asleep . . .

> (*His* WIFE *confirms with a nod of the head.*)

The car's been found.

WIFE: I know. They rang during the night.

> (*Silence.*)

Ewa?

JANUSZ: Ewa.

WIFE: Does this mean you'll be wandering off at all hours of the
night again?

JANUSZ: No. No, it doesn't.

DECALOGUE FOUR

The cast and crew of *Decalogue Four* included:

ANKA	Adrianna Biedrzynska
MICHAL	Janusz Gajos
Director of Photography and Cameraman	Krzysztof Pakulski
Producer	Ryszard Chutkowski
Composer	Zbigniew Preisner
Artistic Director	Halina Dobrowolska
Sound	Malgorzata Jaworska
Lighting	Jerzy Tomczuk
Film Editor	Ewa Smal
Production Managers	Pawel Mantorski
	Wlodzimierz Bendych
Costume Designers	Malgorzata Obloza
	Hanna Cwiklo
Director	Krzysztof Kieślowski

Still: Adrianna Biedrzynska as Anka and Janusz Gajos as Michal

I

Early spring. The first, delicate leaves have blossomed on the branches of young trees. A Great Dane on its early morning walk cocks a leg up against one of these trees and stays frozen in this pose for an improbably long time, like a sculpture – 'Dog Relieving Itself'. TOMEK, *whom we will meet in one of the following stories, unhooks his little milk-cart from its chain. The sun has already risen, its red glow reflected in the glass of the balcony doors and apartment windows. One of these red-tinged windows is opened from the inside. A young woman deeply inhales the fresh, spring air.*

2

ANKA *is twenty years old. She is of medium height and has regular features, except perhaps for her breasts, which are a little too large for her stature. When she smiles, her upper lip lifts just a little too high and dimples appear in her cheeks. She is the sort of person whom people will be describing as a 'girl' well after she is into womanhood.* ANKA *closes the window, having had her fill of morning air. A large rucksack stands in the middle of the room – obviously someone is about to go off travelling.* ANKA *shifts it to one side. Still in her night-shirt, she fills a glass jug with water and creeps towards a door marked 'Man's Room!' Various objects can be seen lying inside: a drawing-board, some graphic designs on tracing paper, an ashtray heaped with cigarette ends, also a wallet and a plane ticket.* ANKA *puts the jug of water down and unbunches a pair of socks lying on top of a suit. Just as she thought: one is longer than the other. She puts the socks down again and walks over with the jug of water to the bed.* MICHAL *sleeps without pyjamas and is only covered up to the waist by the sheets. His feet protrude from under the covers and one hand is held nestled beneath his head. The sight of* MICHAL *sleeping always moves* ANKA. *Perhaps she is similarly moved by the sight of him when he is wide awake. She crouches down by the bedside and studies his face intently, holding the jug of water high above his sleeping head.* MICHAL *opens*

[85]

his eyes and looks at her for a second without really properly gaining consciousness. ANKA *smiles and tips the jug, a stream of water splashing straight down on to his face.* MICHAL *yells, pulls the covers over his head, and then cautiously pokes his head out. Just as he makes a move to get up,* ANKA *pours the rest of the water all over him.* MICHAL *is soaked.* ANKA *flees to the bathroom. He finds a pot in the kitchen, fills it with water, and walks over to the bathroom door. It is locked. Silence.*

MICHAL: Anka, I'm in a hurry.

ANKA: Dad, no!

(MICHAL *adopts a more serious tone of voice.*)

MICHAL: I'm in a real hurry. Let me in.

ANKA: Do you promise?

MICHAL: Let me in!

(ANKA *detects a genuine note of grievance and slowly opens the door.* MICHAL *stands in the doorway with a grave expression on his face. He is a slim, cheerful-looking man with affable eyes – no hint of the middle-aged philanderer or dried-out has-been. He brings the pot out from behind his back and bursts into the bathroom.*)

Easter Monday* is it?

ANKA: Daddy, no . . .

MICHAL: Easter?

ANKA: I won't dry in time. You won't make it to the air –

(MICHAL *swings the pot forcefully and throws the whole lot over her.* ANKA *switches on the hairdrier – it stops working almost instantly. She presses the on–off switch several times and checks the plug-point. The light is still working, so she brings it into the kitchen. The drier still won't work. She stands helplessly with her broken hairdrier and wet hair.*)

MICHAL: If Adam happens to drop by, give him those drawings.

ANKA: I'm all wet.

MICHAL: Well, don't come then.

(ANKA *tries to arrange her hair. She is now in trousers and a grey blouse without a bra.*)

---

* It used to be a time-honoured Polish tradition for people to pour water over each other on Easter Monday. The Polish term 'Lany Poniedzialek' means literally 'Pouring Monday'.

Is that how you go around these days?

ANKA: Everyone looks like this nowadays, Dad. No one wears
bras anymore.

(MICHAL *puts away his documents and then reaches over to the
drawers of an old dresser. The objects lying inside could not
possibly be of any interest to a woman: old, unworn watches,
broken set-squares, and compasses. But underneath all of these
objects lies a faded yellow envelope with some sort of inscription
on the side.* MICHAL *hesitates for a second, leaves the envelope in
its place, and then hides it again beneath the various other
paraphernalia.*)

Oh fuck it, Dad!

MICHAL: We agreed you wouldn't swear, especially at home.

ANKA: But I can't find my keys!

MICHAL: Take mine instead. I didn't let you in yesterday, did I?
You must have got in by yourself.

ANKA: Yes. Maybe I left them in the lock and someone took
them.

MICHAL: Maybe.

ANKA: Now I'm really frightened to be left on my own.

MICHAL: Where did you get undressed?

(*He pulls aside a chair standing next to the bed and finds a bra,
which he casually throws to her in passing.*)

ANKA: I'm going to be frightened all on my own!

MICHAL: I'm looking for them, aren't I? Anyway you won't be
here on your own for most of the time.

ANKA: What do you mean?

MICHAL: I mean that someone can come and stay, like Jarek, or
someone. There's nothing to get all agitated about.

ANKA: I'm not sure I want him to.

(*They put their coats on.*)

MICHAL: Hang on, what did we have to eat yesterday? We'd run
out of bread.

ANKA: I went out to buy some rolls.

(*With the huge rucksack now on his back,* MICHAL *goes back
into the kitchen and with satisfaction takes the bunch of keys out
of the bread-bin.*)

[87]

3

ANKA *and* MICHAL *get off at the the bus-stop outside the entrance to the international airport.*

4

Check-in point in the departure lounge.
ANKA: Aren't you ever scared?
MICHAL: Yes, but with luck maybe I'll fall asleep.
 (*They fall silent for a moment – the usual awkwardness before parting.*)
ANKA: I don't like it when you go away. Won't you be too warm in that jacket?
 (MICHAL *pulls her towards him and strokes her still wet hair.*)
 I forget to tell you. I copied a few things out for you from the encyclopaedias. Literature, painting, history, population, major towns – damn, I forgot to check who governs –
MICHAL: It's all right, sweetheart. I know.
ANKA: Bye, Dad.
MICHAL: Look after yourself.

5

A sympathetic-looking young lad is waiting in a small Fiat parked outside the airport. On seeing ANKA, *he gets out of the car, calls over to her and offers his cheek for a greeting kiss. But to no avail.*
JAREK: Don't I get a kiss? I've been waiting half an hour.
ANKA: Hi.
 (JAREK *is a thick-set, energetic lad with a dark complexion. He grins a lot; too often, arguably.*)
JAREK: I saw you both. You forgot to wave Daddy goodbye with your little handkerchief.
ANKA: You're right.
 (*She swiftly gets out of the car and runs over to the visitors' terrace*

[88]

which overlooks the boarding-gate area. JAREK *follows after her.*)

No, wait there.

JAREK: Doesn't he like me or something?

ANKA: He does, but just wait there.

JAREK: Are we going back to your place later?

ANKA: No.

JAREK: Not this time?

ANKA: No, not this time.

(ANKA *catches sight of her father about to board the bus which takes the passengers to the plane. The bald patch in the middle of his head is more visible from her present vantage point than when she is at home.*)

Daddy!

(*The bald patch stops: her father waves back and indicates that he has to get on the bus. The bus pulls away.*)

OLDER MAN: Your fiancé?

(ANKA *makes no reply. The plane taxis towards the take-off point.*)

Excuse me, but I have the impression we have met before somewhere.

ANKA: Yes. It was in the bogs.

OLDER MAN: I beg your pardon?

ANKA: I said, yes, we have met somewhere before. In a shit-house in Koluszki.

OLDER MAN: Please excuse me.

ANKA: By all means.

6

The OPTICIAN *is a typical example of a masculine-looking female, her hair short, her manner brisk, her voice deep and manly.*

OPTICIAN: First name?

ANKA: Anna.*

---

* The name 'Anka' is the diminutive, or less formal, version of 'Anna'. The Polish language contains various diminutive possibilities of first names, several of which

OPTICIAN: Age?

ANKA: Twenty.

OPTICIAN: Student?

ANKA: At the Theatre School, final year.

(*The optician's pen stops.*)

OPTICIAN: What entry exams did you have to pass? My son wants to apply.

ANKA: Literature, poetry, prose, music . . .

OPTICIAN: I know. Which poet did you recite?

ANKA: Herbert.

OPTICIAN: Herbert. Well, there's no hope then. You're very attractive. Are you having trouble with your eyes?

ANKA: Yes. Yesterday I was watching a plane take-off from a long way away. I should have been able to see it clearly, but it was just a blurred dot. Then I remembered I was having trouble making out bus-numbers. I can only see them in focus when they're quite close.

(*The* OPTICIAN *places a metal spectacle frame with one side covered over her eyes. She walks over to the letter-board hanging on the far wall.*)

OPTICIAN: Read them out, please

ANKA: (*In English*) F-A-T-H-E-R – 'Father'.

OPTICIAN: You were guessing towards the end.

ANKA: Yes.

OPTICIAN: And you understand English?

ANKA: Yes. Why did you pick those letters?

OPTICIAN: I also like to test intelligence.

ANKA: The plane I couldn't see clearly yesterday had my father in it.

(*The* OPTICIAN *points to the letters on the bottom row.*)
I don't know.

OPTICIAN: Indeed, you do seem to have a problem.

---

are used regularly by characters in the screenplays. For simplicity's sake we have restricted them to two: one formal and one less formal. Since Kieślowski and Piesiewicz use the less formal 'Anka' throughout *Decalogue Four* we have decided to stick with it. This occurs again in *Decalogue Nine*, where Roman's wife is called 'Hanka' throughout except for the one time when she introduces herself formally as 'Hanna Nycz' when phoning the hospital from the ski resort.

7

At first the typewritten inscription on the faded yellow envelope is out of focus, but ANKA *can see it more and more clearly as she brings it closer to her face. She is standing next to the dresser we saw before in Michal's room. She takes the letter into her own room and examines it closely, perhaps not for the first time. It is quite thick, which suggests it contains several folded pages.* ANKA *holds it up to the light – she has taken the shade off the lamp specifically for this purpose – but is still unable to make out what is inside. She tries to peel back the flap of the envelope, but it is firmly stuck down and she has little success. She sniffs it, but no associations are aroused by the smell. Nevertheless she holds it up to her nostrils again and this time (if the actress is able to suggest this) the aroma reminds her of something. The doorbell rings.* ANKA *peers through the peep-hole.* JAREK *is standing on the other side with a massive head and unnaturally long legs, his whole body distorted by the convex lens. He is looking straight at her and senses that she is watching him from the other side of the door. He bends forward to the peep-hole, cups an imaginary face in his hands and looks at her submissively.* ANKA *smiles – the simple theatrical exercise has been executed skilfully and comically.* JAREK *places his finger against his lips and then moves it to a point just below the peep-hole itself, the finger growing to astronomical proportions due to the distortion of the lens.*

JAREK: Is this where your mouth is?

ANKA: Yes.

JAREK: Give it a kiss. Have you kissed it?

ANKA: No.

JAREK: You weren't at class today. They had to skip your scenes.

ANKA: I wasn't feeling well.

JAREK: What about tomorrow?

ANKA: Tomorrow I'll be there. Are you going to stand there for long?

JAREK: I'm frozen. I wouldn't mind a hot drink.

ANKA: There's no gas.

JAREK: I'll just look at you then.

ANKA: I'm not in.

JAREK: Oh yes you are.

>(JAREK *has stopped fooling around. He smiles sadly, the odd distortion of his face as viewed through the peep-hole making the smile seem even sadder.* ANKA *slides back the bolt and lets him in.* JAREK *tenderly puts his arms around her,* ANKA *succumbing to his embrace with a feeling of compassion rather than desire.*) Have I done something wrong?

ANKA: No, but not everything revolves around you, you know.

JAREK: Why don't we stay here, together?

ANKA: I prefer being with you when he's here. Then I do it to spite him. When he's away and I'm free to do what I like, I feel something's wrong.

>(*She is really talking to herself. In any case* JAREK *is not listening, more preoccupied with kissing her neck and earlobes, and then feeling her breasts.*)

JAREK: If you're feeling depressed or anxious, I could always stay.

>(*He slides down to her hips and presses his face against her stomach. She looks down calmly towards him from above, unmoved by his caresses.*)

8

ANKA *is walking through a small wood, the same wood we encountered in the first story about the lake, which extends as far as the banks of the River Vistula.* ANKA *jumps up on to the small wall which divides the wood from the shore and sits herself down on it before taking the yellow envelope and a large pair of scissors. She reads the inscription one more time – 'Not to be opened before my death' – and holds up the scissors as if to cut it open. She does not notice a young man paddling across the river in a small white dinghy, and is concentrating so hard on the letter that she does not see him reach the bank, get out the boat and lift it on to his shoulders either.* ANKA *slides the end of the scissors under the envelope flap and slowly, meticulously, starts to cut across it. She is surprised to find another white envelope inside. Since it is difficult as a rule to fit one envelope inside another,* ANKA *has difficulty extracting the second from the first. It too is firmly stuck down and also has an inscription: 'For my daughter, Anna'. The handwriting is completely different from that on the yellow envelope, the letters being round, soft and feminine. The white envelope is equally old. To be precise, once it was probably completely white, but the borders have now faded to a light yellow colour. The young man, as if oblivious to the weight of the boat on his shoulders, walks towards her. She holds the scissors up to the yellow-white envelope but then becomes aware that someone is watching her. She looks up: the young man with the boat on his shoulders is staring at her intently. He stands completely still, his expression fixed and unchanging, and then walks off.* ANKA *lowers the envelope, hesitates for a moment, and then scuffs up a little hole in the sand with her foot. She throws the scissors into the hole, puts the white envelope back into the opened yellow envelope, and then scuffs the sand back into place over the scissors.*

9

A rehearsal is in progress at the Theatre School. Young boys and young girls, and a PROFESSOR *are in attendance.* ANKA *and* JAREK *are acting out a love scene,* ANKA *perhaps in the role of Laura and* JAREK *as Jim from Tennessee Williams's* The Glass Menagerie. *Laura is naïve, while Jim is more experienced and sure of himself. We watch them enact the scene. Finally the* PROFESSOR *walks over and demonstrates how it should be played. It would appear that the acting could be considerably improved.*

PROFESSOR: It's very straightforward, but you, Anka, have to remember one thing. You are in love with him. If you forget that even for a second, then the whole tension of the scene is lost.

ANKA: Actually – why am I?

PROFESSOR: Why are you what?

ANKA: Why am I in love with him?

(*The* PROFESSOR *grimaces: they have been over this time and time again.*)

PROFESSOR: He's young and good-looking. He's good at rugby. All the girls are crazy about him. You're crazy about him,

[93]

even with that leg of yours. But when you finally get him here all on his own – don't you understand? Don't you find Jarek attractive?

(*Giggles. Everybody knows what is going on between* ANKA *and* JAREK.)

ANKA: So so.

PROFESSOR: You're on stage remember. You're in love with Jim. Is that really so difficult?

ANKA: Not if I have to . . .

PROFESSOR: Let's take a break.

(*Everybody slopes off. Cigarettes and chit-chat.*)

JAREK: Anka, what's up?

ANKA: Nothing. Why?

10

ANKA *tries to eat a sandwich in the kitchen but her mind is on something else. She is looking at the white envelope with the light-yellow borders standing propped up against a bottle of milk and at the inscription on its side: 'For my daughter, Anna'.*

11

ANKA *is searching for something in one of Michal's files and finds a stack of letters. None of them have the same character handwriting as the white envelope. Perhaps she herself does not really know what she is looking for. This is what we are led to conclude after she slumps down to the floor, which is now a mass of letters, throws back her head and sits completely still.*

12

It is dark in the basement corridor, since only a meagre light penetrates the little windows. ANKA *is a little afraid and moves nervously. She opens the door to their cellar – evidently she only rarely comes down*

[94]

here – and sees an old child's bicycle, a pair of old wooden skis, a
cardboard box, some dilapidated suitcases, an old rocking horse, and
what looks like an overall of some description. She drags out a black
suitcase, which must have looked quite smart in its day. She has
difficulty forcing open the rusty lock. The case is full of old books,
binders and an old vanity-bag which looks as if it has not been used for
years. This is what ANKA *has been searching for. She takes out a*
comb, some lipstick, a little compact mirror, and a worn handkerchief
with colourfully embroidered borders. They are all about twenty years
old, a fact evident not only from their condition, but also from their
dated style. She finds a photograph and a stationery set with notepaper
and envelopes in the side-pocket of the bag. ANKA *initially takes out*
the picture: it shows two young men and two young women standing
against a wall next to a tree. A banal holiday snapshot? Taken at a
sanatorium? While on some excursion or other? The people in the
photograph are dressed in the Polish fashion of the sixties. ANKA *looks*
at the picture for a long time. She has probably seen it on more than
one occasion before, but for no apparent reason seems keen now to
establish who is in it. There is no inscription on the back. ANKA *opens*
the stationery set to find several envelopes similar to the white one
which she found so intriguing and yet so disturbing. There are also
sheets of paper. ANKA *takes out one of the envelopes and one of the*
sheets of paper.

13

ANKA *has tidied up her table and placed both white envelopes on the*
top. From rummaging around in one of the cupboards in the flat, she
has discovered an old fountain pen and a bottle of ink. She cranes over
the paper and, carefully imitating the handwriting on the closed
envelope, writes out an inscription on the side of the envelope brought
up from the cellar: 'For my daughter Anna'. She places them side by
side – indeed they look very similar. She reflects for a while and then
writes: 'My darling daughter'. A ring at the doorbell interrupts this
striking achievement. ANKA *opens the door to find a stout, sympathetic*
man of forty-five wearing a checked shirt-cum-jacket.
ADAM: Hello. Sorry I didn't ring. Michal asked me to pick up

some drawings. Do you know what he's talking about?
(ANKA *brings the roll of drawings from her father's room.* ADAM *looks as if he wants to leave.*)

ANKA: Adam . . .

ADAM: Yes?

ANKA: You've been friends with my dad for quite a long time, haven't you?

ADAM: We studied together.

ANKA: Adam, what was my mother like?

ADAM: Very like you.

ANKA: Facially?

ADAM: Facially too. I meant in general.

ANKA: Do you think she could have had some kind of . . . some kind of secret?
(ANKA *notices that* ADAM *is blushing.*)

ADAM: How should I know?

ANKA: Something she didn't want me to know.

ADAM: She was just like you. If she had something she wanted to say, she would have said it.

ANKA: I was only five days old when she died.

ADAM: Then she would have written a letter. Why do you ask?

ANKA: I've been dreaming about her. She's always trying to tell me something but I'm never able to make out what it is.
(ADAM *nods understandingly.*)

ADAM: Look, I'm sorry . . . I really must . . . I'll drop by when Michal gets back.
(ANKA *goes back to the table with the envelopes and now with complete confidence writes a letter from her mother to herself. The writing is round, slightly inclined, feminine and fills one side of paper.*)

14

ANKA *is waiting at the airport bus-stop in her new glasses and scans all the new arrivals. A plane has just flown in from the south-east, where the black-market dollar rate is particularly favourable. The elderly man who makes a habit of courting women he has only just met walks down the steps from the terrace.* MICHAL *emerges from the arrivals lounge a short while after. Bent under the weight of his luggage and surprised not to see* ANKA, *he staggers over to the bus-stop, looking around every now and then. He finally spots his daughter and grins broadly.*

MICHAL: You're here . . .

(*He is surprised to see her in glasses.*)

Nice – pale frames as well.

(ANKA *looks at him without smiling.*)

Something the matter?

ANKA: No.

MICHAL: You're looking at me very oddly.

ANKA: 'My darling daughter . . .'

MICHAL: I'm sorry?

ANKA: 'My darling daughter, I do not know what you will look like or how old you will be when you come to read this letter. For sure you will already be grown up and Michal no longer in this world. You are tiny as I write here now. I only saw you once and then they stopped bringing you to me because they knew I am going to die soon . . .'

(ANKA *looks at* MICHAL, *her gaze fixed somewhere just below the level of his eyes.* MICHAL *lifts her chin with his finger and forces her to look him squarely in the eyes. She falls silent for a moment, then closes her eyes. Tears trickle down from beneath her eyelids. She continues, trying unsuccessfully but without much real determination to free herself from her father's hand.*)

'. . . There is something I have to tell you. Michal is not your father. It is not important who your real father is: it was an unthinking moment, an act of stupidity which caused much suffering. I know that Michal will love you as his own. I know him and am confident that you will be happy with him. I imagine you reading this letter in a place of your own. You have fair hair, don't you? You have thin fingers and a delicate neck, just as I would have wished. Your Mother.'

(MICHAL *releases her head. She buries her head deep into her neck and is trembling slightly.*)

MICHAL: You weren't supposed to read it. You weren't supposed to . . . until I was . . .

[97]

ANKA: I know.

MICHAL: So why did you?

> (*Again he forces her head upwards with his hand, this time sharply, almost brutally.* ANKA *winces.*)

Why?

> (*He is losing his self-control. He raises his hand and slaps her across the face. Only after the second slap does* ANKA *try to protect herself. Bystanders are staring at them both.* MICHAL *regains his composure. He lifts up the rucksack and strides off at a determined pace.*)

15

MICHAL *is looking out through the window, straining his eyes in search of his daughter. He looks down at the hand he had used earlier to hit her. He is angry with the both of them, but most of all with himself.*

16

ANKA *gets out of the taxi outside Jarek's house. It is a typical example of the old pre-war-style, low-built houses.*

17

JAREK'S MOTHER, *a fifty-year-old-woman who has come to terms with her age and appearance, opens the door. The flat is modest and the furniture spartan.*

ANKA: Is Jarek in?

> (JAREK'S MOTHER *is the kind of woman who switches quickly to informal terms with all her son's friends.*)

JAREK'S MOTHER: He popped out. Why don't you come in?

ANKA: Can I?

> (JAREK'S MOTHER *opens the door wider. She clears away various objects lying scattered over the dinner-table: a magnifying*

glass and some leaves arranged in a container divided into squares. She has either been labelling them or looking them up in a book.)

JAREK'S MOTHER: Take your coat off. It might be a while before he's back.

ANKA: I'm cold.

(JAREK'S MOTHER *looks at her in a way which suggests she is experienced in the trials and tribulations of life.*)

JAREK'S MOTHER: I could make you a hot drink . . . or perhaps you'd like a drop of vodka.

(*This had not occurred to* ANKA *but since it is on offer, why not?* JAREK'S MOTHER *takes out a carafe and fills Anka's glass to the brim while only pouring a drop for herself.* ANKA *holds the glass uncertainly.*)

ANKA: Did Jarek tell you he wanted to marry me?

JAREK'S MOTHER: Drink up.

(*They raise their glasses.* ANKA *knocks it back in one go without any difficulty.*)

He mentioned something about it –

ANKA: I'm ready to marry him now. Straight away if he wants.

JAREK'S MOTHER: What about your father?

ANKA: That's irrelevant. He isn't my real father anyway.

(JAREK'S MOTHER *looks at her intently, perhaps even shrewdly. She gets up and puts the carafe back in the cupboard.*)

JAREK'S MOTHER: This is all rather sudden. Once you go through with this, you can't change your mind or go back on your word.

ANKA: I know.

JAREK'S MOTHER: You shouldn't go ahead until you've sorted out the unfinished business of the past.

ANKA: I have.

JAREK'S MOTHER: I wouldn't be quite so hasty.

(ANKA *does not reply. Perhaps she realizes that* JAREK'S MOTHER *is right.*)

JAREK'S MOTHER: Perhaps you ought to move out for a while – you could always stay at my sister's. I could run you over there if you like, or you could go by yourself. Jarek keeps running off with the keys, so I guess you probably know

[99]

where it is already. But don't say anything to Jarek for the time being. He loves you. See how you feel after a few days. Do you want me to run you over?

18

ANKA *presses the front doorbell to her flat and holds the button down for some time. No one answers. She takes the lift down to the ground floor. It comes to rest and* MICHAL *opens the door. He gets into the lift and waits.* ANKA *presses the button and they move off upwards.*
MICHAL: I've been looking for you everywhere.
ANKA: I forgot my keys.
(*The lift stops at their floor but neither makes any move to open the doors.*)
This is our floor . . .
(*Still neither makes a move and after a while the lift moves off upwards. It halts again – this time the hospital* CONSULTANT *from the second story climbs in. He is surprised to see them there.*)
CONSULTANT: Ground floor?
(MICHAL *nods and the lift descends to the ground floor. The* CONSULTANT *climbs out but again they remain inside. After another moment of inertia,* ANKA *again presses one of the buttons.*)
MICHAL: I'm sorry. I'm sorry, Anka.
ANKA: You knew?
(*The lift has stopped in the basement.*)

19

This is where we were not so long ago and it is even darker this time. ANKA *hesitates, frightened.* MICHAL *switches on the light and leads her down the long corridor, bordered on both sides by the open-work wooden doors to the various cellars. The light in their cellar is not working.* MICHAL *strikes a match and lights two candles which are standing on the window-sill. Everything is repeated as before:* MICHAL *clears out the same objects which* ANKA *had to pull aside – the bicycle, the skis, etc. He opens the black suitcase, takes out the vanity-bag and gives*

ANKA *the holiday snap of the two men and women.*

MICHAL: Recognize your mother?

ANKA: Yes.

MICHAL: One of these two . . . I suspect . . . could be your real
father.

(ANKA *examines the picture for the second time.*)

Keep it. I don't know, maybe you'll want to find him, one day.

ANKA: What for?

MICHAL: I don't know. In films children are always trying to find
their real fathers.

(ANKA *returns the photograph.* MICHAL *shoves it back into the
vanity-bag.*)

ANKA: And that?

MICHAL: Your mother's. They gave it to me at the hospital.

(*He throws the bag back into the suitcase, unwilling, or so it would
appear, to discuss the subject further.*)

ANKA: How long have you known?

MICHAL: From the very beginning.

ANKA: You deceived me.

MICHAL: Yes. No. It was irrelevant. You were my daughter.

ANKA: You should have told me.

MICHAL: I planned to give you the letter when you were ten but
you were too little then. So I decided to give it to you when you
were fifteen but by then you were too grown-up. That was
when I decided to put it in the yellow envelope.

ANKA: So simple, wasn't it?

MICHAL: I thought it wouldn't change anything between us anyway.

(*The candles on the window-sill are slowly burning down.*)

ANKA: I think you're lying. You're lying, aren't you?

(ANKA *notices that the candle flames are beginning to flicker.*)

Look. Yours is the candle on the left. Mine's the one on the
right. Whoever's burns down first has the right to ask a
question. Agreed?

MICHAL: Agre—

(*The candle on the left is the first to burn out.*)

ANKA: Go ahead, ask me.

(*Now her candle burns out. They are now illuminated by a light
from further down the corridor.*)

[101]

Give me your hand.

MICHAL: Your hands are cold.

ANKA: Warm them up for me.

(MICHAL *breathes into the palm of her hand in exactly the same way adults warm the hands of small children, and doubtless in much the same way he used to warm her hands when she was a little girl.*)

20

ANKA, *wearing calf-length boots, flops into an armchair.*

ANKA: You won. You can ask me any question you like.

MICHAL: I already asked you it at the bus-stop.

ANKA: What was it?

MICHAL: Why you read the letter.

ANKA: The first time . . . the first time I saw it was when we were moving flat. It fell out of a file. That was when I was sixteen.

MICHAL: Fifteen and a half.

ANKA: I put it back but knew all the time it was there. At first I found it exciting. I thought it was an official document or something, perhaps even a will. I was reading adventure stories at the time and thought it might be some kind of 'words of wisdom'. You know, on how to live life decently and so on. Then I noticed you took it away with you every time you went away, so it couldn't have been a will or anything like that. The last time you went away, you left it behind.

MICHAL: Yes.

ANKA: On purpose? It was lying with all the other papers you were taking with you, but you left it behind all the same.

(ANKA *gets up, goes to her own room and brings back both envelopes and the letter she has written to herself. She lays them down in front of* MICHAL.)

Have you ever read it?

MICHAL: No.

ANKA: I read it because you wanted me to.

MICHAL: That's a pretty straight reply.

[102]

ANKA: At theatre school we're told: think why you're saying
something. What is the intention behind it.

(ANKA *gets up again and brings in an already opened bottle of
vodka and two glasses from the kitchen. She pours it out, raises her
glass and waits for* MICHAL.)

Don't you want to know the real intention behind what I've
just said?

(MICHAL *raises his glass.*)

MICHAL: No.

ANKA: So be it.

(ANKA *clinks her glass against Michal's.*)

How should I address you from now on?

MICHAL: Call me Daddy.

(ANKA *hooks her arm around his in the typical Polish drinking
tradition. This brings her closer to him.*)

ANKA: My name's Anka.

(MICHAL *plays along with her little game. Actually, he has little
alternative.*)

MICHAL: Pleased to meet you . . . Michal.

(*They drink from the glasses, arm in arm.* MICHAL *extracts his
arm and kisses* ANKA *on the cheek. Their heads are now close
together. She looks at him and brings her lips slowly towards his.*
MICHAL *does not move a muscle.* ANKA'S *eyes are closed but at the
very last moment her lips veer away and plant a kiss somewhere on
his chin.*)

ANKA: What I really intended to say was that for a long time I knew
. . . When I first lost my virginity, I felt, or rather, had the
feeling, I was being unfaithful to someone. At the time I didn't
realize that person was you. It's been like that ever since, on
many occasions –

(*The doorbell rings.* ANKA *pauses, but only for as long as it takes
for the bell to stop ringing.*)

I was always on the look-out for boys who were completely
different from you but whenever someone touched me, I
could only think about your hands. I just couldn't stop
myself. Whenever I'm close to someone, I'm not really with
them at all . . .

(*The bell rings again, this time insistently.* MICHAL *opens the door.*)

[103]

ADAM: You're back. How was it?

MICHAL: Come in. It was fine.

(ADAM *is carrying the rolled-up designs. He unbuttons his jacket but does not take it off.*)

ADAM: I copied them and sent them off. Arrival was confirmed by telex. (*He glances towards the table.*) Having a little vodka, are we?

MICHAL: Take a seat.

(*He steers* ADAM *towards the settee, brings over a third glass and pours out more drink, trying to give* ANKA *as little as possible.*)

ADAM: When do you get your diploma?

ANKA: May.

(*She leaves the room, throws herself on to her bed and buries her head in the pillow.* ADAM *drinks half the glass and prepares to leave.* MICHAL *remains seated in the armchair.* ANKA *looks out towards him from the bedroom.* MICHAL *looks towards her bedroom door, then gets up and quietly walks over to it. He watches her from the doorway, then moves closer, unfolds the blanket which is lying on the back of the armchair and covers her with it.*)

ANKA: Go to him.

MICHAL: He left.

ANKA: Well, go after him then. Or go and see someone else. You obviously don't want to talk to me!

(MICHAL *tries to answer, but* ANKA *covers her ears. She is wearing a wide-sleeved blouse and as she lifts up her arms* MICHAL *catches a glimpse of a small dark patch of armpit hair.* ANKA *is unaware of the erotic 'intention' of this gesture, but we are and so too is* MICHAL. *He lifts his hand and slides it towards her. We cannot be sure of his 'intention', but the motion ends only with the covering of this intimate–non-intimate place with the blanket. If* MICHAL *could be said to have been in a disturbed state of mind a moment ago, he has now regained his composure.* ANKA *looks as if she is asleep. Silence. Very softly, almost inaudibly,* MICHAL *sings the lullaby with which he used to send her to sleep so many years ago. Or perhaps he is whispering a verse from* Winnie the Pooh. *Unquestionably he is seeking a return to a time when everything was so much simpler and safer.*)

[104]

Who are you afraid of? Me, or yourself? There's nothing to
fear – I'm getting married.
(*The telephone rings.*)
MICHAL: You take it.
ANKA: It's probably Marta.
(MICHAL *doubts it with a shake of his head.*)
Or Krysia. (ANKA *goes over to the telephone.*) Hello. Yes. No,
I've just woken up. Tomorrow? Ring me first. (*She puts down
the receiver.*)
MICHAL: Your fiancé?
ANKA: My fiancé.
MICHAL: Does he know he's engaged to you?
ANKA: No. But I've told his mother.
(*Seeing that she is serious,* MICHAL *alters his tone.*)
MICHAL: And what about you? Who are you afraid of? You can
leave Warsaw, run away, get married, but it won't change
anything.
ANKA: Jarek's mother said the same thing. (*She sits down in the
armchair and stretches out her legs in their calf-length boots.*)
Help me take them off.
(MICHAL *bends down and pulls off first one boot, then the other.*
ANKA *leans forward and straightens her toes.* MICHAL
*instinctively touches the tips of her feet and then her legs, which
are resting on his knees.*)
MICHAL: They're wet. You'll catch a cold.
ANKA: We're not here to talk about blocked noses.
MICHAL: Take them off.
(ANKA *unfastens her stockings and pulls them off.* MICHAL
*returns with some woolly slippers. He bends down again and slips
them on to* ANKA's *feet.*)
Better?
ANKA: Warmer. It was like a sense of guilt, or betrayal. I always
felt I was betraying you when I was in bed with someone
else.
(MICHAL *lowers his eyes. Maybe it is a question of the different
generations, but he finds it harder to talk frankly about such
matters.*)
MICHAL: I never had that feeling.

ANKA: Liar.

MICHAL: OK. I – I felt distant whenever I was with anyone else. Almost as if I was moving away from you.

ANKA: I could never stand you always giving me so much freedom, as if you didn't care what I did. That's why I said I was going to get married. For ages I – I wanted you to say: no, enough is enough.

MICHAL: I couldn't. I didn't have the right. But that's not the only reason. I was afraid if I stopped you it would be because I was jealous. And not in the way a father is jealous of his daughter. I was afraid of what else it might be.

ANKA: But it was something else.

MICHAL: Yes. Well, no. I'm still not sure what it was – what it is.

ANKA: The time you caught me in bed with Marcin . . . Is that the reason you went away on a trip?

MICHAL: Yes. But no father likes it when his daughter starts sleeping around with other men. So I didn't feel guilty about that.

ANKA: But you knew I wasn't your daughter.

MICHAL: But you were. All those years . . . I often used to think your mother could have made a mistake. Women are supposed to know these things, but maybe she did make a mistake.

(ANKA *smiles: she knows what only women know.*)

ANKA: I don't think so. Women really do know these things.

MICHAL: How do you know?

ANKA: I just do.

(MICHAL *rises to his feet. There are the remains of some vodka in Adam's glass. He walks with the glass across to the window and now stands with his back to* ANKA.)

MICHAL: Have you ever had –

ANKA: Yes. Once.

(MICHAL *drinks the rest of the vodka from Adam's glass.*)

MICHAL: When?

ANKA: Last year.

(MICHAL's *eyes darken as they did when he slapped* ANKA *at the bus-stop. He moves away from the window and starts to pace around the room.*)

[106]

MICHAL: Listen, the reason why I used to go away on trips, the reason why I used to go out for long walks during the night was that I wanted something to happen which would change everything. Make it impossible to go back to the way things were. At first I thought it might be when you'd gone to bed with someone for the first time, but I was wrong. Then I hoped you'd have a child.
(*He is now standing over her.*)
I wanted you to have a child, do you understand?

ANKA: Which is why I got rid of it. So you couldn't give me that forgiving smile of yours and tell me everything was fine. That's why! That's why I didn't tell you when I went to the clinic. So you couldn't say: fine, little girl, go right ahead and scrape your insides out, see if I care!

MICHAL: That's not what I would have said.

ANKA: I'm not so sure!

MICHAL: Yes you are!

ANKA: What did you want me to have a child for? The happy home? Someone else to dote on and change nappies for? Someone else to keep you awake at night and make you feel all noble again? You wanted everything to resolve itself without actually having to take a decision of your own! Just like with the letter: 'Not to be opened before my death'! So there'd be no cracks in that precious moral armour of yours!
(MICHAL *looks at* ANKA *with the expression of a person who has been deeply wronged but stands little chance of being understood, whatever he might say in his defence.*)
And it's not even a question of what other people might think, but only your own opinion of yourself.
(MICHAL *walks over to the fridge, pours some milk into a small saucer and puts it down by a cupboard. He looks across and sees with relief that* ANKA *is no longer in the room. He walks across the big room and stands by the dresser in the doorway to his own room.* ANKA *is looking at some photographs of* MICHAL *when he was younger and of herself as a tiny girl: both are smiling at the camera. She is holding all the envelopes in her hand – the white one, the yellow one, the fake one and the real one . . .*)

[107]

MICHAL: You didn't put any milk out for the hedgehog.

ANKA: I'm putting them all back. See? (*She indeed puts the envelopes back into the drawer.*)

MICHAL: It's your letter.

ANKA: I don't want it!

(MICHAL *shrugs his shoulders.*)

I don't want it!

(*She runs over to* MICHAL, *puts her arms around him and buries her head in his chest.*)

I don't want it, I don't want–

(MICHAL *has no choice but to put his arms around her.*)

When I was little, you used to stroke my back whenever I cried. Sometimes I'd cry especially, so that you'd slide your hand under my pyjamas and stroke me. I loved it.

(MICHAL *draws back his hand which, again instinctively, had started to stroke the back of his trembling daughter.*)

You never wanted me to grow up, did you? You wanted me to stay a child, to keep me as I used to be. You never used to let me swim in a bikini top, even after my breasts started getting bigger. Every time my period was due you took me away to the mountains as if you thought you could hide me somewhere. But it didn't work. I grew up. You didn't get married, not even to Marta. I was afraid you would, but I needn't have worried because you wouldn't have got married anyway. You were waiting for me, weren't you?

(ANKA *draws back a little from* MICHAL, *although she still has her arms around his shoulders.*)

You were waiting . . .

MICHAL: I wasn't thinking that – I don't know.

ANKA: Well, I do. I know what you were thinking.

MICHAL: I don't know.

ANKA: Well, I do. I'm not your daughter . . . And I'm a big girl now.

(MICHAL *does not reply. His face is tired and sad.*)

Do you want to touch me?

(ANKA *takes his hand and places it on her neck.*)

Do you want to?

[108]

(*She slides his initially passive hand slowly downwards along
her neck, then along the buttons down the middle of her blouse,
and then tries to steer it towards her breasts.* MICHAL *tries to pull
his hand away but* ANKA *grips it even more determinedly.*
MICHAL *is now resisting strongly and finally succeeds in
wrenching it free.*)

MICHAL: Go to bed.

(*He moves aside to let her pass.* ANKA *walks past him slowly.
She goes over to the television set and turns to face him.*)

ANKA: You wanted to watch the downhill skiing.

MICHAL: Not any more.

(ANKA *switches on the television. Zurbriggen is speeding down a
huge mountain slope, the crowds roaring vociferously at every
bend. The volume has been turned up high.* ANKA *starts to walk
out of the room.*)

Anka! Turn it off.

(*He speaks in his usual, matter-of-fact tone of voice.* ANKA
switches the set off. Silence.)

ANKA: OK. Just one more question.

MICHAL: Just one.

ANKA: Why did you want me to read the letter?

MICHAL: Because I wanted something which was impossible.
Now go to bed.

21

Morning. MICHAL *has not undressed since the previous evening and
his night-light is still burning – he had evidently not switched it off. He
picks up the telephone receiver as quietly as possible and looks for a
number in his address book. He dials several digits and tries to keep his
voice as low as possible.*

MICHAL: 46417? Zielona Gora? Andrzej? I didn't recognize you
. . . Yes, it has been quite a long time . . . No, nothing. It's a
little . . . let's say a little business matter . . . I wouldn't be
ringing if it wasn't important . . . That's just the way things
are, you're right . . . Well, exactly. I've got a surprise for
you: I want to come over and stay . . . No, for a while . . .

longer than that. I want to move over there permanently . . .
exactly, work of some kind . . . perhaps rent a room or a flat
. . . Of course I could work as a teacher . . . Out of town if
there's the accommodation . . . No, on my own.
(ANKA *wakes up suddenly feeling agitated and is surprised to find
herself feeling so. A second later she realizes why. She creeps
softly into the kitchen. The milk, a butter dish, and some cheese
and rolls are lying on the table. A toy panda is standing propped
up against the bottle of milk.* ANKA *picks it up and tests the
fluffiness of the fur, then suddenly freezes in mid-motion. She
pokes her head into her father's room: it is empty – there is no
rucksack and no* MICHAL. *She runs over to the window. Again,
the spring weather is sunny and beautiful outside.* MICHAL *is
walking off in the direction of the bus-stop, bent under the weight
of his rucksack.*)
ANKA: Dad!
(MICHAL *does not stop.*)
Daddy!
(MICHAL *stops and turns round.*)

22

ANKA *runs down the stairs without waiting for the lift and takes the
steps two, three at a time.*

23

MICHAL *is standing there with his rucksack.* ANKA *is out of breath
and stops a couple of paces away from him.*
ANKA: Dad . . .
(MICHAL *says nothing.*)
I lied.
(MICHAL *is silent.*)
I never read the letter. I didn't even open it. It's lying in the
dresser.
(*The young man carrying the dinghy on his back is walking along*

the pathway which runs between the various blocks of flats.)
I wrote what you read myself. What I told you at the airport.
I saw my mother's handwriting on the envelope and copied
it, to myself.
(MICHAL *slips the rucksack off his shoulders. Out of the corner of
his eye he can see the young man with his dinghy. It is a rather
unusual sight in such surroundings and* MICHAL *instinctively
turns to look at him. It is the same man who sat around the fire in
the first story, who stood in the hospital corridor in the second
story, and who will continue to appear, for ever.)*
Dad – what's really in Mum's letter?
MICHAL: I don't know.
(*He glances again towards the man with the dinghy.* ANKA
follows his gaze.)
ANKA: Isn't there something written on the side? Of the boat?
MICHAL: Yes.
ANKA: What does it say? I haven't got my glasses on.
MICHAL: Gon— . . . gondola.
ANKA: I know what we'll do.

24

Still in her nightdress and overcoat, ANKA *opens the drawer in the
dresser and takes out the yellow envelope, the letter which she had
written herself, and finally the real letter in the firmly stuck-down
envelope.*
ANKA: Can you give me a hand?
(MICHAL *nods. They go into the bathroom –* ANKA *lifts up the
toilet seat and takes out a box of matches from her coat pocket.
The first fails to catch alight, so too does the second. She gives the
box to* MICHAL, *who strikes one and waits.)*
Here . . .
(MICHAL *moves the flame to the corner of the envelope. The letter
burns well and the flames slowly devour the several sheets of
paper. Tiny, black, charred flecks of paper flutter above the
toilet. The flame reaches the corner which* ANKA *is holding with
her fingers. She withstands the heat for as long as possible, then*

[111]

grimaces with pain, and MICHAL *extinguishes the dying flame. Only a small piece of paper remains in* ANKA's *fingers. She unfolds it. Several words written in a round, feminine handwriting have survived: 'My darling daughter . . .' – the rest of the line is charred. Only three words are visible from the first sentence of the first paragraph: 'I must tell . . .' – and that is all.*

They are seated around the table for breakfast. ANKA *is already in her blouse (but without a bra, naturally) and the furry panda is sitting by her glass of milk.* MICHAL *is trying on her glasses, but quickly takes them off.)*

ANKA: Everything looks completely different now.

MICHAL: There was a bloke called Krzysztof who used to work for us once. Have I ever told you this one? . . . He used to come to work on a bike from Michalina, about forty kilometres away. Every day, he would try to break his previous day's record. How long did it take you today, we'd ask? Twenty-six minutes and forty seconds, he'd say, or twenty-five minutes and three seconds, and so on. He must have been doing a ton or more. One day he doesn't turn up at work. Half an hour, an hour goes by, and we're all wondering what on earth's happened to him. He finally comes in looking as white as a sheet and wearing glasses. God in Heaven, Jesus Christ, he says. What's up? we ask. Gentlemen, he says, I had no idea how many people there were on the roads, how many cars, how narrow the road was, all those bikes and carts, God forgive me. It turned out he was shortsighted with minus four and a half diopters and never even knew it. He sold the bike, bought a suit, and never went near another bike again, right to this very day.

DECALOGUE FIVE
A Short Film about Killing

The cast and crew of *Decalogue Five* included:

JACEK	Miroslaw Baka
PIOTR	Krzysztof Globisz
TAXI-DRIVER	Jan Tesarz
Director of Photography and Cameraman	Slawomir Idziak
Producer	Ryszard Chutkowski
Composer	Zbigniew Preisner
Artistic Director	Halina Dobrowolska
Sound	Malgorzata Jaworska
Lighting	Jerzy Tomczuk
Film Editor	Ewa Smal
Production Managers	Pawel Mantorski
	Wlodzimierz Bendych
Costume Designers	Malgorzata Obloza
	Hanna Cwiklo
Director	Krzysztof Kieślowski

Stills: Miroslaw Baka as Jacek
Jan Tesarz as the taxi driver
Krzysztof Globisz as Piotr

*A powerfully built man emerges from the stairwell entrance to the
apartment block we know from all the previous stories and steps out
into the light of day. It is muddy and dismal outside. The man, who is
wearing a sleeveless padded waistcoat with a working overall on top,
is carrying something heavy and is whistling. His eyes are small, his
sideburns are those of a second-hand car salesman, and his Turkish
jeans are the sort smuggled in from abroad and sold on the black
market. A small shape suddenly flashes past virtually right in front of
his nose and hits the asphalt with a splat. He picks up the old, wet rag
off the ground and looks upwards.*

JACEK *is walking along Nowe Miasto Square. He is a short-haired
twenty-year-old, with a roundish face dotted with pimples, more
visible now due to the cold weather than they would be normally. He
has pale eyes and an unfriendly expression. He turns around on
hearing a voice shouting behind him.*

VOICE: (*Out of shot*) Hey, mate!

>(JACEK *does not know whether this shout is intended for him or
not. It appears, however, that it is. He waits for the* BLOKE *who
called over to him with the expression of a person who expects
nothing good to come out of it.*
>
>*A young man is reading a letter in the hall of the Council of
Defence Lawyers. He looks a sympathetic, sensitive and perhaps
even slightly too delicate sort of person. He lights a cigarette
instinctively, initially failing to find the tip of his cigarette with
the burning match.*)

VOICE: (*Out of shot*) Mr Piotr Balicki! Please go in.

>(PIOTR – *the very same sympathetic young man – turns away and
stubs out the cigarette. A hand appears on his shoulder, evidently
to wish him good luck.* PIOTR *swallows hard and moves off
towards the door.*
>
>*It should be clear from these three brief scenes that, although
these three characters are different and photographed in places
distant from one another, they are connected in some way. Or
rather, they* will *be connected in some way in the future.*)

2

The powerfully built man scans the block of flats with the rag in his hand. They look enormous from where he is standing. All the windows are closed and it is not obvious from which one the rag could have fallen. With a look of disgust, he carries it with his thumb and forefinger over to an area just next to the stairwell entrance. The doors are open and the CARETAKER *is sweeping the floor inside. He greets the* CARETAKER *and throws the rag into a dustbin. Our man is a* TAXI-DRIVER, *which is what he will be called from now on.*

CARETAKER: Throwing rags out? They can come in handy, you know.

TAXI-DRIVER: Someone threw it at me.

CARETAKER: Hit you, did he?

TAXI-DRIVER: No. Seen anyone with a rag like his?

(The CARETAKER *shakes his head: no, he hasn't.)*

CARETAKER: Maybe it just fell out.

TAXI-DRIVER: Maybe. Look.

(A cat is sitting on one of the dustbins.)

Pssst, pssst!

(The cat runs off like greased lightning. The TAXI-DRIVER *stamps his feet, grinning as the cat vanishes through the cellar window.)*

I hate cats. You can't trust 'em, just like people.

CARETAKER: They keep the mice down though.

TAXI-DRIVER: Let 'em, the bloody pests.

(He goes back to his two buckets of water and then walks over to his car, which is parked in one of the parking lots. He unties the pieces of cord which hold down the tarpaulin, pulls it off, and carefully folds it up in his own pedantic fashion. A blue Polonez with a taxi-driver's corona on the roof is revealed underneath. It does not look especially dirty, but the owner runs his finger along the polished surface nevertheless: not good enough. He opens the door and switches on the radio. The car is kitted out with a large number of tasteless accessories: additional lights at the front and rear, several stickers ('My Toyota is Fantastic', 'My Oil is . . .' etc.), a red aerial by the wing-mirror and an ET mascot. The TAXI-DRIVER *sets to work cleaning the vehicle.)*

[116]

3

The bloke who earlier called over to JACEK *on the square now walks up to him. He is large and square-shouldered, and would make anyone feel nervous if he were to approach them.* JACEK *is no exception. He moves the old airline bag a little closer to his feet. For the first time we notice what he is wearing: a Polish-made denim jacket with tacky studs pressed into the material and jeans which are a little too baggy for him. His hands are large, red and frozen. The other* BLOKE *casts a critical eye over him – he himself is wearing a badly worn fur jacket.*

BLOKE: Lend us a hundred zlotys.

JACEK: Sorry.

BLOKE: Fifty then.

(JACEK *looks at him with his pale eyes and their unfriendly expression.*)

JACEK: Sorry.

BLOKE: Look, I've got to get out of here somehow.

JACEK: I'm skint.

(*The* BLOKE *smiles, disbelievingly.*)

BLOKE: Well, fuck off then.

(JACEK *does not move. The* BLOKE *moves suddenly as if to head-butt him, but stops just short of his face.* JACEK *has not even flinched. The* BLOKE *is surprised.*)

OK then.

(*Maintaining his dignity, he walks off.* JACEK *starts walking in the opposite direction. He looks at a film poster in the display cabinet outside the Wars Cinema and disappears inside.*)

4

The CASHIER *is a woman of about thirty. Using the window which separates her from the customers as a mirror, she is combing her fingers through her hair.*

JACEK: Is the film any good?

CASHIER: No, it's boring.

JACEK: Boring? What's it about?

CASHIER: It's a love story – but it's boring. There's no
  performance at the moment anyway. They're all in a
  meeting.
JACEK: What are you doing?
CASHIER: I'm pulling out . . . grey hairs.
JACEK: Is there a taxi-stop near here?
CASHIER: On Castle Square.

  (*She has located another grey hair and plucks it out, wincing
  slightly. It is cold outside, perhaps one reason why* JACEK *had
  tried to prolong the conversation. He hunches himself up against
  the force of the wind and walks off towards the taxi-rank.*)

5

*Six middle-aged men, all dressed smartly and looking formal, are
seated behind a huge table in the grandly decorated office of the
Council of Defence Lawyers.* PIOTR *is sitting opposite them on the
other side of the table. He is deep in thought – presumably a question
has already been asked. One of the examiners smiles in an attempt to
give him some encouragement, another pushes forward a glass of tea –
a right evidently enjoyed by all those who appear before this august
body.*

PIOTR: I am not taking my time over this question because I don't
  know the answer. This question has been put to me on two
  occasions. When I was taking my entrance exams, the
  answer seemed straightforward. Four years on, I am not so
  sure. The question is a good one: why do I want to be a
  barrister? Would you like me to be completely honest with
  you, or would you prefer me to say what is expected?
  (*The man sitting in the middle smiles – he is perhaps the most
  important member of the examining board and is smoking a
  cigarette from a long holder.*)
CHAIRMAN: Our purpose here is to try to get to know you.
PIOTR: To answer truthfully, I would have to say: I don't know.
  Naturally I have some views on the subject, even though
  they may be a little vague. I have witnessed a great deal over
  the last four years. I suppose one reason for entering this

[118]

profession might be to correct the mistakes carried out by a huge machine which goes under the name of the administration of justice. Or at least to try. One might say this was – a social calling.

MAN 1: By all means, but –

PIOTR: Forgive me. I am afraid the passage of time makes this question a more and more difficult one to answer. Every person asks himself at one time or another whether what he does has any rationale. One's doubts seem to multiply. But you were going to say something . . .

MAN 1: No. That is precisely what I wanted to ask you.

CHAIRMAN: Fine. Any other questions?

> (PIOTR *wipes the corners of his mouth with a handkerchief. His hands are trembling. This exam is clearly very important for him.*)

6

The TAXI-DRIVER *is scrubbing the car roof with a brush. He bends back the windscreen-wipers just as a young teenage girl in a pale coat emerges from the stairwell entrance. She is neither ugly nor attractive and we would not have paid her any further attention if it were not for a shout from the balcony above which causes her to stop.*

WOMAN: Beata! Beata!

> (BEATA *turns, immediately exasperated.*)

BEATA: What?!

WOMAN: Get some pasta. Two packets!

> (BEATA *wants to be on her way, but the* WOMAN *yells even louder.*)

Money!

> (BEATA *has to go back and catch the little parcel wrapped in newspaper. Our* TAXI-DRIVER *watches all this with a grin. He follows her with appraising eyes: not bad, not bad at all. Sensing that someone else's eyes are on her,* BEATA *swings her hips and seductively – or at least that is how it seems – waddles off. This used to be known in our day as 'wiggling one's arse', but it is not clear whether it has the same connotations nowadays.*)

[119]

7

JACEK *walks along unhurriedly. He stops in front of the paintings hanging up on the wall outside the Fukier wine bar. The artists are cold and have draped plastic canvases over the paintings to prevent the rain from damaging them. Customers are few and far between. A Japanese tourist in an off-white trench coat is taking photographs with an instamatic camera. It is not clear exactly what he is taking pictures of, probably everything, since he snaps quickly and in all directions.* JACEK *likes the paintings of the Old Town, which are as faithful to the original buildings as a photographic print.*

PAINTER: Fancy one, my friend?

JACEK: How much is that one?

PAINTER: Seven grand.

(JACEK *thinks for a moment.*)

JACEK: How long does it take to paint?

PAINTER: What's your problem, mate?

(*He points to the picture with his finger. Each brick on the wall of the Old Town has been meticulously reproduced and looks like the real thing.*)

You don't get paid by the hour here. Look.

(*He spreads out his fingers. They are dirty from paint and from dealings. The fingernails are long and it is obvious that he washes them only rarely.*)

You get paid for talent here. I painted every single brick with these hands. Do you have a talent?

JACEK: Not really.

PAINTER: Maybe you know how to make shoes? Or grow a tree?

JACEK: A tree? Yes, a tree, yes.

PAINTER: Well, you'll be all right then.

(*He turns back to the other artists and has already cheered up a little, because a girl with long hair is telling them all an amusing story.* JACEK *touches his shoulder with his hand – the* PAINTER *turns round.*)

JACEK: Is Castle Square that way?

(*He points in the direction he thinks it is.*)

PAINTER: Straight as the crow flies.

[120]

8

CHAIRMAN: I think we can safely say we have found out your views as far as your knowledge of the history and theory of law and the various interpretations of the role of the Supreme Court are concerned. I would just like to ask one more question – what do you understand by the term 'deterrent sentencing'?

PIOTR: This is the delivering of a sentence not necessarily in relation to the crime committed, but as a warning to others. As a deterrent. It is called 'punishment by example' in Article 50 of the Penal Code.

CHAIRMAN: Am I correct in detecting a slight note of irony, let's say, a certain hostility to the concept of deterrent sentencing?

PIOTR: You are.

CHAIRMAN: May we know why?

PIOTR: It is one of the more dubious justifications for the harshness of a particular sentence. In my opinion, not only dubious but unjust.

CHAIRMAN: Do you not believe in the deterrent effect of punishment? After all, it is one of the cornerstones of our legal doctrine . . .

PIOTR: I believe that the inevitable application of the law is more important.

CHAIRMAN: I see you know your classics.
(*Smiles all round.* PIOTR *also smiles.*)

PIOTR: A little. I know it is written somewhere that 'since the time of Cain to the present day, no punishment in the world has ever prevented or deterred crime'.

CHAIRMAN: Well, gentlemen. What do you think? Shall we call it a day here?
(*The men look around at each other: time, perhaps, to call it a day.*)

9

The TAXI-DRIVER *scrupulously scrubs down the car doors and is liberal with his use of water.* DOROTA *and* ANDRZEJ *(whom we hopefully remember from the second story in our cycle) walk towards him from the apartment block.* DOROTA *is now in an advanced state of pregnancy. They stand and try to estimate how long it will be until he finishes.*

ANDRZEJ: Will you be free soon?

TAXI-DRIVER: Can't you see I'm cleaning it?

>*(He does not look up, engaged even more intensely in his work.*
>ANDRZEJ *seems to have recovered substantially after his illness.)*

DOROTA: We'll wait. It's cold.

>*(The* TAXI-DRIVER *does not respond, but instead throws some water demonstratively over the newly cleaned wing and moves around to the other side of the car. He does not even look up.*
>DOROTA *and* ANDRZEJ *walk off towards the nearest building and perhaps take refuge in the stairwell. The* TAXI-DRIVER *continues his scrubbing with an extinguished cigarette dangling from his mouth.)*

10

JACEK *has taken refuge behind a column to protect himself from the wind and it is now his turn to light a cigarette. He brings the Sports brand in his mouth to a burning match held in cupped hands. There are several people standing at the taxi-stop and* JACEK *is watching them all closely. Two girls in sheepskin coats are giggling to each other. A* MAN *with a briefcase shouts across the street on seeing two mini-cabs approaching.*

MAN: Marysia!

>*(The woman, who is clutching a bundle under her arm and has evidently been on the look-out from the other side of the road, scuttles over. Several new people take their places at the end of the queue. An old* WOMAN, *who is feeding pigeons as she walks along the square, advances towards* JACEK.*)*

[122]

WOMAN: Move away. You'll frighten them.

(JACEK *is nonplussed: the pigeons are eating perfectly calmly.*)
Move away.

(JACEK *stamps his feet on the ground and the frightened pigeons fly off. Another cab has pulled up at the taxi-rank. In the background, a* TOUR-GUIDE *is talking through a small, yellow megaphone to a group of tourists hunched up against the cold.*)

TOUR-GUIDE: These walls have witnessed some of the great glories of our nation in the past. One of the most modern constitutions of eighteenth-century Europe was proclaimed on this very spot: the 3 May Constitution. And this castle looks towards us once again, expectantly, and we must rise to the challenge hurled down by its great walls . . .

II

The TAXI-DRIVER *has finally finished cleaning his cab. He rinses his hands in what is left of the water and takes out a bottle of wax polish and a chamois leather from the side-door pocket.* BEATA *reappears in his field of vision carrying her two packets of macaroni.*

TAXI-DRIVER: Does our little neighbour fancy a lift?

(BEATA *smiles with an air of superiority but does not relax her swinging and seductive stride. The* TAXI-DRIVER *puts the bucket, the brush and the other cleaning utensils into the boot of the car, climbs into the driver's seat and starts the engine. The little ET mascot, which is stuck to the windscreen next to the rear-view mirror, vibrates in time with the running engine.* DOROTA *and* ANDRZEJ *have heard him start the engine and emerge from the apartment block. The* TAXI-DRIVER, *on seeing* ANDRZEJ *and his pregnant wife hasten towards him, the two who had had the nerve to bother him while he was in the middle of washing his cab, shifts the car into gear and drives off. He can see their disappointed expressions in the rear-view mirror and chuckles to himself with satisfaction. He slows down once out of the estate and pulls up alongside a dog sitting by the edge of the road. He winds down the window. The dog is a flea-bitten, miserable-looking mongrel.*)
Waiting, eh?

[123]

(The dog does not react: it does not wag its tail and does not even look at him. The TAXI-DRIVER *takes a sandwich out of his glove-compartment. He unwraps the paper, divides it into two pieces, and stows one half back into the compartment.)*
The wife made them for us. Go on.
(He throws the half-sandwich to the dog. Without moving from its spot, the dog bends down its muzzle and starts to eat it.)
Tasty, eh? Go on, go on. Get a bellyful.

12

Several young people are waiting in the hall for the examination results. The SECRETARY *to the examining board appears in the doorway and cheerfully calls out.*
SECRETARY: Mr Piotr Balicki!
(PIOTR is surprised. He did not expect to be called quite so soon and is unsure whether this is a good sign or not. He follows the SECRETARY into the room. The CHAIRMAN rises from his seat.)
CHAIRMAN: I am pleased to be able to inform you that you have passed your examination. After four years of studies and four years' apprenticeship, you may from today consider yourself one of our esteemed colleagues.
(He walks around the table, goes up to PIOTR and offers his hand.)
Congratulations.
PIOTR: Thank you, thank you all very much . . .
CHAIRMAN: All that remains is for you to get married.
(PIOTR smiles, still grasping the CHAIRMAN's hand. He had clean forgotten about his impending marriage.)

13

JACEK *walks along the buildings near the escalators. He looks back once more towards the taxi-rank and the older* WOMAN *who has again started feeding the pigeons. He stops suddenly as if he has caught a brief glimpse of something, and walks back to a photographic shop. The*

display cabinets are filled with pictures of young girls in white dresses,
wearing garlands in their hair, holding little candles. JACEK *stares at*
the photographs, as if forgetting for a moment that he had been on his
way elsewhere. A young WOMAN *is sitting behind the counter inside,*
sorting through a stack of male passsport photographs.

WOMAN: Yes?

JACEK: I've got here . . .

> (*He takes out a long coil of rope, a metal pipe for making holes in*
> *concrete, and finally an old shabby wallet from his airline bag. The*
> WOMAN *watches each individual object as it is taken out of the*
> *bag.*)

WOMAN: Are you a picture-hanger?

JACEK: No.

> (*He rummages through the wallet and pulls out a wad of*
> *banknotes. He finally finds what he was looking for and pulls out a*
> *small, damaged photograph from inside his identity card.*)

WOMAN: Just a thought.

JACEK: I've got this picture . . .

> (*The girl in the photograph, which is over-exposed and*
> *amateurishly touched up, is from the country. She is standing*
> *against a luminous background of artificial light in a white dress,*
> *with a garland of artificial flowers around her head, and holds a*
> *small candle.*)

Can you make an enlargement from this?

> (*The* WOMAN *examines the picture. She points to the fold marks –*
> *once upon a time the picture must have been carried around in a*
> *smaller wallet.*)

WOMAN: You'll be able to see the creases.

JACEK: That's OK.

WOMAN: When for?

JACEK: Is it . . .

WOMAN: Yes?

JACEK: Is it true you can tell from a photograph whether someone
is still alive or not?

> (*The* WOMAN *looks at him with astonishment. Is he an idiot? Is he*
> *making a pass at her?*)

WOMAN: Someone's been having you on.

> (*She takes the picture behind the curtain.*)

[125]

JACEK: You won't lose it, will you?

WOMAN: No.

(JACEK *smiles: if before he could have been described as an unsympathetic character, then he comes across as less so now. But this moment does not last long.*)

14

The small street which runs along the entrance to the Foreign Trade Centre building, not far from the central railway station, is dubbed 'Les Pigalles' by Warsaw taxi-drivers. One can hazard a guess as to why. This is the stalking ground for the young, moderately good-looking girls who once upon a time you would have been able to pick up in the Polonia Hotel. But in such weather, and at this time of the day, they are few and far between. The blue Polonez slowly pulls up alongside one of these girls. Youngish and not at all unattractive, she smiles at the familiar sight of the taxi-cab. The TAXI-DRIVER – *the one we saw cleaning his car earlier – opens the door for her. She hops in. It is warm inside, the car radio is playing, and the* TAXI-DRIVER *is smiling. There is a kinder look about him when he smiles like this.*

TAXI-DRIVER: Business good?

GIRL: In this weather? I'm frozen . . .

TAXI-DRIVER: Sit in here and take a break for a while.

(*The* GIRL *relaxes.*)

GIRL: You won't make any money sitting here.

TAXI-DRIVER: Doesn't matter.

(*The* GIRL *puts her hand on his thigh.*)

GIRL: Fancy a handjob?

TAXI-DRIVER: No thanks.

(*The* GIRL *removes her hand.*)

I like you.

GIRL: Really?

TAXI-DRIVER: Really.

GIRL: That's nice.

TAXI-DRIVER: I've got a sandwich – fancy half?

(*The* GIRL *shakes her head.*)

GIRL: I never eat in the mornings. I like you as well, even though

you've got huge hands and you're probably a real bastard.
You're good to me.

TAXI-DRIVER: Fancy a lift home?

GIRL: I'll put in a couple more hours. But come over this evening
. . . if you want.

(*The* TAXI-DRIVER *kisses her hand, the* GIRL *climbs out, and the
car drives off.*)

15

PIOTR *is riding a Vespa along a main road and leaning excessively into
the corners. His earlier tension has evaporated and we can see what a
lively and cheerful person he really is. He notices a smart car drawing up
beside him at the traffic lights and shouts out ecstatically to the driver.*

PIOTR: I passed my exam! I'm a barrister!

(*The driver cannot hear him and so winds down the window.*
PIOTR *happily repeats what he has just said.*)

I'm a barrister!

(*Several people can hear his shout above the general hub-bub of the
street, including the* TAXI-DRIVER *sitting one car back in his blue
Polonez. He shakes his head disapprovingly: what's this little git
got to be so happy about? The driver of the smart car also looks
disapprovingly at* PIOTR. *He winds the window back up again
without saying a word.* PIOTR *roars off straight ahead, the blue
Polonez following shortly afterwards.*)

16

JACEK *is walking along Krakowskie Przedmiescie. A small group of
youths wearing football scarves marches towards him from the
Mickiewicz Monument. Cars brake as they stomp across the road
without bothering to check whether anything is coming.*

YOUTHS: Widzew! Widzew! Legia – death! Widzew! Widzew!
Legia – death!*

* W.Z. Lodz, the first two letters pronounced 'Widzew', and Legia Warszawa are
two teams in Poland's football league Division One.

(There are only a few of them, but the atmosphere on the street has already turned unpleasant. Only JACEK *ignores them, walking straight ahead as if they do not exist. They pass him, their chants fading into the distance.*

JACEK walks up to an art gallery and stands by the window. It is opening night at the exhibition of huge, colourful nudes; they are tastefully portrayed and free of any vulgarity. Someone is pouring wine or possibly champagne into drinking glasses and we can hear laughter and snatches of an impromptu speech. A MAN *at the entrance is letting the guests through on presentation of their invitations and looks over sympathetically towards* JACEK.)

MAN: Do you have an invitation?

JACEK: No – no, I haven't.

(The MAN *smiles apologetically and closes the door.* JACEK *walks further on and sees the taxi-rank around the back of the Europejski Hotel. He starts to watch the stop with the same degree of intense interest as he did the rank on Castle Square and is about to walk across when he spots a policeman. He abandons this idea and, without moving from the spot, blows into the frozen palms of his hands.)*

17

A girl is standing in deserted Victory Square. She watches, smiling, as PIOTR *rides his bike up on to the pavement and stands on the pedals, revving the engine as high as he can before biking straight towards her.*

ALA: Did you pass? Piotrek, did you pass?

*(*PIOTR, *laughing happily, finally comes to a standstill.)*

PIOTR: Did you bring any flowers?

ALA: No!

PIOTR: Any present?

ALA: No!

PIOTR: Well, I passed then!

*(*ALA *runs over and puts her arms around the frozen* PIOTR.)

ALA: Piotr, you're a barrister now, you can't fool around like this any more.

PIOTR: Why not? Of course I can!

ALA: I'm inviting you for a coffee.

PIOTR: On you get then.

ALA: And you won't . . .

PIOTR: I'm not promising anything.

> (ALA *gets on the small saddle and* PIOTR *revs up the engine again before leaning and zigzagging his way across the square. They halt outside the Europejski Hotel coffee bar.*)

18

The blue Polonez is sitting at the taxi-rank in front of the Warszawa Hotel. It looks as good as new and is empty, its engine ticking over quietly. The DRIVER *watches with amusement a man who is walking a poodle dressed in a check-jacket. The* TAXI-DRIVER *blares his horn as they pass, causing the poodle to cringe with terror and bark with a high-pitched yelp. That was a good joke all right. The* TAXI-DRIVER *turns down the volume on the radio and moves off.*

19

JACEK has warmed his hands by now. The policeman is still standing in the same position as before. JACEK *moves off towards the hotel coffee bar. Some gypsies are standing outside the entrance. One of the women looks at* JACEK *with interest.*

GYPSY: Want your fortune told?

JACEK: No.

> (*He does not slacken his pace, but the* GYPSY *does not give up.*)

GYPSY: I'll tell if you're going to be lucky or unlucky.

JACEK: No.

GYPSY: Spare us some change for my kid here and I'll tell you a good one.

> (JACEK *does not reply.*)
>
> I see a journey. I'll tell you all.

JACEK: No!

> (*The* GYPSY *moves even closer to* JACEK *and speaks quietly.*)

GYPSY: I hope you burn in hell.

[129]

20

In the coffee bar itself, ALA *is pointing out the* GYPSY *and* JACEK *to*
PIOTR.
AKA: I'll tell you your fortune – and it really will be the truth.
(PIOTR *gives her his hand.*)
PIOTR: Go on then, the truth and nothing but the truth.
(ALA *examines his hand.*)
ALA: I see a great many words, a great many wise words. And a
great many victories . . .
PIOTR: What about my private life?
ALA: You'll need a very long life for so many words and victories.
PIOTR: What about my love life, and the two of us?
ALA: Your love line is long and very strong – I see two children.
PIOTR: When?
(JACEK *enters the coffee bar in the background. He reaches his
turn in the queue and casts his eyes over the various cakes in the
glass cases.*)
JACEK: One tea . . .
ASSISTANT: We don't serve tea here.
JACEK: What have you got?
ASSISTANT: Coffee.
JACEK: I'll have a coffee then. And that cake there. The poppy-
seed one.
(*He points his finger at the one he wants and then protests as the*
ASSISTANT *tries to take out a different one: no,* JACEK *was
pointing straight at that one there, not at any others. He takes his
coffee and cake over to the window where he has a good view of
the policeman standing outside the Bristol Hotel. He warms his
hands around the rim of the glass and then slowly, but greedily,
eats his cake. A police van pulls up outside the hotel and the
policeman climbs inside.* JACEK *pushes his cup of coffee to one
side and looks around: nobody is paying him any attention,
including* ALA *and* PIOTR, *who are sitting in the other half of the
bar. Beneath the table, he takes out the coil of rope from the
airline bag we have seen before. The rope is not that thick, but is
doubtless strong, having been factory manufactured from several*

[130]

thinner ropes twisted together. JACEK *winds it around his hand, making several loops so that all the rope will fit around it. At a certain moment he becomes aware that he is being watched. Two little girls have laid out their school pencils on the window-ledge outside and are swapping them for pink rubbers. One of the girls looks at* JACEK *and smiles uncertainly.* JACEK *returns her smile. For the first time we see how he smiles: his teeth are pearly-white and the brittle, stony expression in his eyes softens. They look at one another for a little while, then the girls nod their heads politely and pleasantly goodbye.* JACEK *is about to raise his hand and wave back to them, but then remembers the rope and so contents himself with a nod of the head. He reapplies himself to the slow, arduous task of winding it around the palm of his hand.*

PIOTR *is talking to* ALA *in the other half of the bar.*)

PIOTR: I feel this is one of those moments in life when virtually everything seems possible, when all gates are wide open to me.

ALA: You know what I think? I think you will be loved by many people. Just as I love you now.

(PIOTR *swallows. He looks tenderly at his fiancée, unsure whether he really deserves this compliment. By this time* JACEK *has wound half the length of rope around his hand. He seems to have enough and starts looking around for a knife; he eventually finds one at the far end of the table by a pile of dirty plates. He takes the knife and cuts the rope in two under the table with his free hand. The rest he puts back into the airline bag and walks out of the coffee bar.*)

21

JACEK *walks along the front of the Europejski Hotel holding the hand tightly bound with rope in his pocket.*

The blue Polonez turns into Victory Square at the same time. A woman tries to flag him down, but the DRIVER *points his finger in a certain direction: the taxi-rank is over there.*

JACEK *turns into a small street around the back of the hotel. The taxi-rank is just around the corner.*

The blue Polonez moves along Victory Square.

JACEK *is now standing at the taxi-rank with only one woman ahead of him. A Fiat draws up almost immediately and the woman is whisked off. The blue Polonez approaches from Victory Square. Just as the taxi is about to pull up at the stop, a* MAN *and a sixteen-year-old boy suddenly dash around the corner. The boy has a strangely distant expression on his face.*

MAN: You're not going to Dolny Mokotow by any chance, are you?

JACEK: No, Wola.

> (JACEK *gets in and loudly tells the* TAXI-DRIVER *where he wants to go, so that he can be heard above the noise of the radio.*)
> Dolny Mokotow.

TAXI-DRIVER: Where was the other bloke trying to get to?

JACEK: Wola.

> (*The car moves off.*)

22

PIOTR: And the one thing I really would like to know –

> (*He pauses.* ALA *looks at him with some surprise.*)

ALA: What's the matter?

PIOTR: Nothing. It's just I was thinking that perhaps things might not turn out so simply after all.

23

TAXI-DRIVER: Where in Dolny Mokotow?

JACEK: Biedronka. Stegny area.

TAXI-DRIVER: Along the Embankment?

JACEK: If you like.

> (*A small Fiat has braked sharply behind them and is impatiently flashing its headlights.*)

TAXI-DRIVER: Take it easy. Keep your hair on.

> (*The Polonez travels downhill and stops at a street corner. A young man holding a long pole is standing motionless in the*

middle of their lane with his back turned. The Polonez stops just
behind him. The TAXI-DRIVER *gently pumps his horn and the*
young man turns around. He is the same person we saw sitting by
the fire in the first story and standing in the hospital corridor in the
second story, the man who appears from everywhere. He stares
straight into their eyes. JACEK *shrinks back in his seat under the*
ferocity of his gaze. The young man is slowly shaking his head as
if to say: no, he will not abandon his post in the middle of the
road. Or perhaps this movement of the head could be interpreted
completely differently. The TAXI-DRIVER *waits until the*
oncoming lane is less busy, and then pulls out past him.)
Renovating again – they're a bloody nuisance.
(The Polonez moves along the Embankment.)
JACEK: Could you wind up the window a little. It's cold in the
back.
(The TAXI-DRIVER *winds up the window.* JACEK *looks down at*
his hands, which he keeps low so that the DRIVER *is not able to*
see them in his rear-view mirror. The hand tightly bound up with
rope has gone slightly blue, the swollen skin visible between the
strands. The car slows down and stops on the empty carriageway.
JACEK *looks anxiously towards the* DRIVER *– has he noticed*
something? The DRIVER *motions with his hand for a line of*
warmly wrapped children to cross the road. Guided by a smiling
and grateful nursery-school teacher, they step off the pavement
and into the road.)
TAXI-DRIVER: Bit of good manners never did anyone any harm,
eh?
(The car moves off. JACEK *turns his attention back to the hand*
tightly bound with rope. He tries to loosen it but realizes he will
have to unwind the whole lot and therefore abandons the attempt.
He looks up.)
JACEK: Left, just here.
TAXI-DRIVER: Straight on's quicker.
JACEK: I prefer this way.
(The car turns left. As it approaches another side-road, JACEK
issues another command.)
Right at the next turning.
(The car turns right.)

[133]

24

*They are now driving slowly along a muddy, uneven lane. A house
stands all by itself a little way off in the distance.* JACEK *unwinds a
section of rope and transfers it immediately on to his other hand, finally
leaving a half-metre-long stretch between the two hands. Both ends of
the rope are tightly wound around the palms of his hands. He carries
out this operation without actually looking down and, after he is
ready, says:*

JACEK: Stop here. You can't go any further.

TAXI-DRIVER: I wasn't even going to try.

> (*The vehicle slows down.* JACEK *whips both hands over the front
> of the* TAXI-DRIVER's *head, brings them down slightly and pulls
> back hard. The car rolls on a few metres and comes to a halt.*
> JACEK *has not quite caught his target, since the rope is actually
> pulling against the victim's mouth rather than against his throat.
> The radio is playing loudly. Visible now are the* TAXI-DRIVER's
> *contorted face and his chipped teeth.* JACEK *realizes that the rope
> is not where he wants it and slightly relaxes his grip. His victim
> immediately tries to catch hold of the rope with his hand and pull
> it away from his face. He is strong but his position is awkward.
> With a tremendous effort – he now has his knees firmly wedged
> against the back of the driver's seat for support –* JACEK *brings
> the rope down to where he wants it and pulls it back against the*
> TAXI-DRIVER's *throat. The* TAXI-DRIVER *now has one hand
> caught up in the rope and is thrashing around with the other in an
> attempt to grab one of his assailant's hands from behind the
> headrest. But his efforts are in vain.*
>
> JACEK *has now pushed himself back against the rear seat. The*
> TAXI-DRIVER *pumps the car horn with his free hand.* JACEK
> *tries to tie the rope around the back of the headrest without
> lessening any of the pressure. His victim tugs his other hand free –
> the rope slackens slightly, but* JACEK *pulls it back powerfully
> again. The* TAXI-DRIVER *is wheezing from lack of breath and
> his eyes bulging out of their sockets. He is growing weak, but
> manages to keep his hand on the horn, realizing that this is his
> only hope of survival.* JACEK *finally manages to tie the rope*

around the headrest with a complicated series of knots and gets out of the blaring vehicle. He struggles with the lock on his bag, eventually ripping it open and wrenching out the metal rod used for making holes in concrete.

The car-horn has stopped blaring: with his last ounce of strength the TAXI-DRIVER *tries to free himself from the rope.* JACEK *opens the front passenger-seat door and tries to hit him with the metal rod. There is not enough space to get a good swing, but he manages to wound his victim on the chest and on the hand he puts up to protect himself. The* TAXI-DRIVER *finally manages to rip the headrest out of the seat with his bloodied hand. Now freed, he tries to get out of the car, but is on the verge of losing consciousness.* JACEK *runs around the side of the vehicle just as the* TAXI-DRIVER *opens the door. He leans forward to climb out but, as he does so,* JACEK *smashes him over the head as hard as he can, once, twice. On the third blow, the bloodied bar flies out of his hand and hits the car bonnet with a dull thud before dropping to the ground somewhere. The* TAXI-DRIVER *slumps forward in his seat.* JACEK *is breathing heavily.*

Everywhere is deserted. JACEK *takes the keys out of the ignition and runs his fingers along the buttons and switches until he finds a small lever under the dashboard. He pulls it, runs around to the back of the car, and opens the boot. There he finds what he was looking for: a blanket. He goes back to the front, wraps the* DRIVER'*s head up in the blanket, and shifts the heavy, lifeless body with great difficulty over to one side. He gets in the driver's seat and switches on the engine. The car moves off slowly towards a nearby embankment, slipping in the mud as it does so.*)

25

The River Vistula lies on the other side of the embankment. Although the thickets, bushes and weeds are green at this time of year, the water at the river's edge is still frozen. JACEK *stops the car. He evidently knows this place well and has selected it especially, confident that at this time of day he is unlikely to run into anyone. He drags the* TAXI-DRIVER'*s body along by the legs and then halts on the bank to regain his breath. He suddenly notices a hand protruding from beneath the blanket – it is moving. A weak, spluttering voice reaches his ears.*

TAXI-DRIVER: Money . . . hiding-place . . . the wife . . . hiding-place . . . cash.

(It is difficult to catch the words, let alone make them out. But the hand is clearly moving, a little spasmodically, and almost even a little purposefully. JACEK looks around. He finds a large, ice-cold stone and pulls it out of the mud with a sucking sound, before carrying it back with both hands and standing astride the TAXI-DRIVER's body. The spluttering and wheezing is growing stronger.)

The money's in a hiding-place . . . it's yours . . . the wife's at home . . . there's a fair amount . . .

(JACEK puts the stone down to one side and runs back to the car. He turns up the volume on the radio once more and comes back to the body. He lifts the stone, but it is unwieldy. He kneels down and now actually sitting astride the body smashes the stone several times against the profile defined clearly beneath the blanket. This profile visibly flattens under the impact and a reddish-brown, sticky substance oozes up through the check pattern of the material.

The music stops. Now there is no longer either the body or the blanket on the river-bank. JACEK finishes unscrewing the taxi-corona off the roof and throws it and the metal bar far out into the water. He takes the money out of the glove compartment, but doesn't bother to count it before stuffing it into his pocket. He discovers the taxi-driver's breakfast wrapped up in a paper parcel. There is still half a sandwich left; the other half, if we remember, had been given to the dog. JACEK unwraps the paper and eats the bread and sausage. He notices a sticker attached to the windscreen: 'Please try not to slam the doors'. JACEK smiles and obligingly shuts the door gently. He is now feeling warmer and more relaxed. He turns the radio on softly. The GIRL from 'Gaweda'* is singing in a bright, cheery voice.)

GIRL: Good afternoon, Hans Anderson,
You've flown up high into the skies.

---

* 'Gaweda': a song-and-dance group aimed mostly at children or young audiences.

[136]

Down here a new generation
Demands the wherefores and the whys.

What will become of us, your children,
Will we join you up in the spheres,
Will we grow into fair, white swans,
The ugly ducklings of former years . . . ?
(JACEK's *expression is one of pain. He has been reminded of something, something he finds hard to live with and would prefer to forget. He violently rips the radio out of its socket and throws it out of the car window. It lands with a splash in the river-bank mud.*)

26

It is now dark. JACEK *pulls up outside the block of flats, the same one the* TAXI-DRIVER *emerged from earlier in the day and which appears in all our stories.*
He rings the intercom bell. A male voice replies through the speaker.
MAN: (*Voice over*) Yes?
JACEK: Is Beata there?
MAN: (*Voice over*) Hold on.
(BEATA *comes to the receiver. She speaks in a seductive, expectant tone of voice.*)
BEATA: (*Voice over*) Hello?
JACEK: Can you come down?
BEATA: (*Voice over*) Not really.
JACEK: Just for a second. I've got something to show you.
BEATA: (*Voice over*) OK.
(JACEK *softly hoots the horn as* BEATA *appears in the stairwell entrance. She walks over to the vehicle and nervously peers inside.* JACEK *opens the passenger door for her.*)
JACEK: Didn't I tell you?
(BEATA *gets into the car. She slams the door shut, causing the little ET figure near the rear-view mirror to start quivering.* BEATA *stares at it without saying a word.*)
You always said you wanted to get away. Now we can go wherever you like.

(JACEK *does not notice, but* BEATA *has shrunk back into the seat and is staring with terror at the quivering mascot.*)
I can leave the hostel now – and you can leave your mum's. We can go anywhere – to the seaside if you like. I've never been. I can pull out the seat and sleep in the back. I've got a blanket.
(*The ET mascot has stopped quivering.* JACEK *turns towards her.*)
BEATA: Where did you get it from?

27

There are only a few people in the largish courtroom: an elderly, rustic-looking woman with two grown-up sons, BEATA *and, on the other side of the aisle, a woman of about forty-odd dressed in black. Apart from them, there are only a few random spectators. Although we have not actually witnessed the sentence being delivered, the impact hangs heavily over the courtroom. Five judges, the prosecuting attorneys and stenographers start to make their exit: they have said their piece and it has all been noted down. The few people in the courtroom start to take their seats.* JACEK, *who has been standing guarded between two policemen, also slowly sits down.* PIOTR *is wearing his barrister's gown; his seat is just in front of the dock.*
JACEK: Is it all over, sir?
PIOTR: Yes.
(*The policemen make no attempt to restrain* JACEK *in his conversation with his defence lawyer. They escort him out of the courtroom and pass the worried, rustic-looking woman and her two sons. The woman stretches out her hand and touches* JACEK *for a second – again, the officers make no move to restrain her. One of the brothers gives* JACEK *a packet of cigarettes.* PIOTR *watches everything without moving from his seat. Only after the courtroom clears does he gather together his papers and leave.*)

28

PIOTR *stands alone by a window. From his vantage point he can see the policemen lead* JACEK *away across the courtyard towards an awaiting police van.* PIOTR *opens the window quickly and shouts out.*

PIOTR: Hey! Jacek!

(JACEK *lifts his head and looks up towards him.* PIOTR *has nothing to say to him, and vice-versa, but it is a demonstration of the fact that he is still there.* JACEK *climbs into the van.* PIOTR *shuts the window, walks down a long corridor past a number of doors and then finally turns and opens one of them.*)

Excuse me – is the judge back?

OFFICIAL: Yes.

(PIOTR *opens another set of doors. The* JUDGE *is standing by himself at the window, still in his gown, his case-papers thrown on to his desk. He turns on hearing the doors open.*)

PIOTR: Excuse me, your honour, I know this isn't normal pract—

JUDGE: No, it isn't.

PIOTR: I wanted to ask you – now it's all over – whether it would have made any difference – if someone older and more experienced . . .

JUDGE: None whatsoever.

PIOTR: Perhaps if I had adopted a different –

JUDGE: Your speech was one of the finest indictments of the death penalty I have ever heard. But there was no alternative. Your arguments were faultless. Please believe me, there was no other way.

(*The* JUDGE *is a short, well-built, elderly man with bushy eyebrows and closely cropped, grey hair. He walks over to* PIOTR *and offers to shake his hand.*)

Difficult circumstances admittedly, but I am glad to have made your acquaintance.

PIOTR: Goodbye.

JUDGE: If anyone should have a guilty conscience, it should be me. Does that make you feel any better?

PIOTR: No. You see, I know this is not really relevant, but when that young lad – when he was winding that rope around his hands in the bar on Krakowskie Przedmiescie, I was there.

JUDGE: Where?

PIOTR: In the same bar, at exactly the same time. That was the day I passed my exams. Maybe I could have done something?

JUDGE: I get the impression perhaps you are a little too sensitive for this profession.

PIOTR: It's a bit late to change now.

JUDGE: Why? You're still young.

PIOTR: I've aged a bit of late.

JUDGE: You still have a few years ahead of you.

PIOTR: A few years – well, goodbye.

29

The prison gates open and the barrister walks through.

GUARD: The governor will see you in a moment.

(PIOTR *stands by a barred window. The prison yard is empty but after a while a man with a ladder suddenly appears. He looks like a decorator and, indeed, probably is one. The* GUARD *bows in greeting to a tall, thin* MAN *who responds with a curt nod of the head. He walks into the reception area and takes out a key from a cupboard. He gives it to the tall* MAN *and at the same time pushes a signing-out book towards him.*)

What's the weather like outside?

MAN: Warm.

(*He signs the book and stands in front of the barred prison-door. The* GUARD *taps on the bars, signalling to another guard who appears on the other side with a set of keys.*)

30

The room, not unlike the interior of a recording studio, is padded out in soft, soundproof tiling. The man hangs up his jacket on a peg, rolls up his white shirtsleeves, and draws back a curtain at the far end of the room to reveal a small recess. A noose attached to a metal contraption hangs from the ceiling. It is an unexpected sight in a room which otherwise, with its small table, ashtray and hanging pegs, has every semblance of normality. The man – the EXECUTIONER *– checks the functioning of the gallows. The mechanism is straightforward enough; nevertheless it has to perform its task faultlessly and every detail has to be meticulously checked beforehand. The whole system is very simple: there is a trapdoor in the floor which opens with a gentle click after a button has been pressed in the wall. That is all. The* EXECUTIONER *checks the tension of the rope, using soap or grease to ease the movement of the noose itself. He inspects the functioning of the trapdoor by squirting several drops of oil into the hinges. He grimaces: the door is still squeaking too loudly, but it will have to do. When everything is checked and oiled, and functions as it should, the* EXECUTIONER *takes out a square of linoleum from its special place in his cupboard and places it on the concrete floor about a metre below the trapdoor opening. He then draws back the curtain, rolls down his shirtsleeves, and puts his jacket back on again.*

31

The EXECUTIONER *enters the prison governor's office. The* GOVERNOR *is standing behind his desk.* PIOTR *is sitting by a small table at the back of the room.*

EXECUTIONER: Everything is ready, sir.

GOVERNOR: Thank you.

> (*The* EXECUTIONER *leaves. The* GOVERNOR *dials a number on his internal telephone.*)

Number 24? You are wanted in my office.

> (*He puts down the receiver. It would probably be polite to have a few words of conversation with* PIOTR, *but perhaps they have too few subjects in common.*)

Well. He should be here at any moment.

> (PIOTR *ties up his cardboard file, which gives the impression of being empty. He gives it to the* GOVERNOR.)

PIOTR: Thank you. I expected something like this.

GOVERNOR: So did I. I can give you (*He looks at his watch*) half an hour at the most.

PIOTR: Half an hour. Fine.
(*The* GUARD *is standing at the door.*)
GOVERNOR: Please take him to cell number 24.
(*The barrister gets up from his chair and the two men, along with the* GUARD, *start to leave the room. As they pass through the doorway, they bump into the* PROSECUTOR: *he is a solemn, elderly man with a pointed nose.*)
PROSECUTOR: Greetings.
PIOTR: Good afternoon. I'm off to see him now. He wants to have a word with me.
PROSECUTOR: Perhaps this isn't the best moment – but since we see each other so rarely, I wanted to give you my congratulations. I understand your wife has given birth to a baby boy.
(PIOTR *brightens for a second.*)
PIOTR: That's right, not so long ago. That's very kind of you.
(*They move off, each in their different directions. Somewhere in the near distance we can see the young man on his ladder. He is stepping down it with his back to the camera. Perhaps he has just been painting the wall, since white paint is dripping from a brush which he is holding in his hand. The guard opens the door to the cell and lets the barrister pass through inside.*)

32

The cell looks no different from an ordinary, poorly furnished hotel room. It has an ordinary sofa, a table, some chairs and a sink – the only difference is the peep-hole in the door. JACEK *is standing with his back to the door and does not turn around, as if he has not heard it opening.* PIOTR *is unsure how to announce his arrival – 'Good afternoon' does not really seem appropriate. Fortunately, however,* JACEK *turns around of his own accord, without any prompting. They greet each other in the middle of the cell with a shake of the hand.*
PIOTR: You wanted to see me.
JACEK: Yes, I –
(PIOTR *sits himself down on one of the chairs.*)
Yes, I –

[142]

(PIOTR *wants to help ease the situation.*)

PIOTR: Take a seat.

(JACEK *sits for a while with his head lowered. He speaks so softly* PIOTR *finds it hard to catch exactly what he is saying and so has to crane forward over the table.*)

JACEK: Have you seen my mother?

PIOTR: Yes, I have.

JACEK: Was she crying?

PIOTR: Yes, she was.

JACEK: Did she have any message for me?

PIOTR: No, she just cried.

JACEK: Could you – can you drop in and see her from time to time?

PIOTR: Yes, of course. Of course I can.

JACEK: That's what I thought. Because you – because you called out to me when they were taking me away. You called: Jacek.

PIOTR: I wanted – I'm not really sure what I wanted.

JACEK: I thought you called out because you weren't against me. Maybe my brother wasn't either because he gave me some cigarettes. Even though I'd shamed the whole family. But you – all the others were against me.

PIOTR: They were only against what you did.

JACEK: It's the same thing.

(JACEK *seems to have forgotten what he wanted to say.*)

PIOTR: You wanted me to drop by your mother's from time to time.

(JACEK *brightens – he had clearly lost his train of thought.*)

JACEK: Yes. I wanted to ask Mum, my mother, whether she would bury me in the same grave as my father. Where his is. It's possible, isn't it, to have a decent burial?

PIOTR: Of course.

JACEK: The priest came to see me. He said it was.

PIOTR: Of course.

JACEK: Well, there, where my father's grave is, there's one – there's one space left where my mother was going to be buried. It was meant for her, that was how it was agreed, but I want her to let me have it instead.

[143]

33

The EXECUTIONER *is sitting upright on the edge of a chair in the corridor outside his room. He is smoking a cigarette but flicks the ash rarely and only when the column of ash is very long and about to fall off, carefully stretching out his hand towards the ashtray.*

    The prison GOVERNOR *still has half a glass full of coffee. The* PROSECUTOR *drinks up the rest of his and looks at his watch. The* GOVERNOR *dials a number on his internal telephone.*

GOVERNOR: Cell number 24?

GUARD: Right you are, sir.

    (*The* GUARD *replaces the receiver which is located in a little recess outside the cell and opens the door.* JACEK *pauses in his monologue and looks up.*)

    The governor wants to know if you've finished.

PIOTR: Not yet.

    (*He waits for the* GUARD *to leave and then turns back to* JACEK.)

    You were saying.

JACEK: I've forgotten.

PIOTR: You were talking about these grave sites . . .

JACEK: Yes. There's three of them. Marysia's buried there as well. Marysia, my father, and the empty one. Marysia's been buried there for about five – five years – yes, she was run over by a tractor five years ago. In the countryside where we live. She was in the sixth grade, just started. She was only twelve, in the sixth grade. Me and the tractor driver, me and a friend, the tractor driver was a friend of mine, we'd been drinking. Wine and vodka. And that's when he drove off and ran her over. In the field, by the edge of a wood. There was this meadow just at the edge of the wood . . .

    (JACEK *leans towards* PIOTR *and is now speaking more coherently. Clearly he has given the matter some thought and is able to formulate his thoughts.*)

    While I've been in this cell, I've been thinking. I was thinking maybe if she was still alive, maybe, maybe I would never have left. Maybe I would have stayed on. She was my sister, you see. I had three brothers, she was the only sister I had. We bought the grave site after she was run over by the tractor. She was – she was – she was everyone's favourite. She was my favourite as well. Everything would have turned out differently if it hadn't been for the – after that, I had to leave. Had to leave home, I mean. I didn't weant to and if it hadn't been for the – well maybe everything would have turned out differently.

(*We can hear the rattle of the bolts being slid back and, as a moment ago, the* GUARD *appears in the doorway.*)

GUARD: The governor and the prosecutor are asking if you're ready now, sir.

(PIOTR *gets up from the table and goes over to the* GUARD.)

PIOTR: Tell the prosecutor I'll never be 'ready'.

GUARD: You'll never be 'ready'. Right you are, sir.

(*He closes the door.*)

JACEK: We bought the grave site there because Marysia really loved trees. She loved green things. But she really loved trees. That's why she was walking through the field that day along the path. So we bought the grave, everyone chipped in. There were only a few trees in the cemetery and the other sites were already taken. But one of them had a tree, and as it happened it was free. So we bought it. We buried Dad there as well after he died. He had nothing else to live for after the accident. And there's still one empty space left.

34

The PROSECUTOR *and* GOVERNOR *are rising from their seats.*

GOVERNOR: Have you got the sentence?

(*The* PROSECUTOR *unties the little piece of string on the cardboard file: two sheets of paper are lying inside. He casts an eye over them.*)

PROSECUTOR: It's all here.

(*They leave the office and walk along the corridor. The* GUARD *gets up from his chair.*)

GOVERNOR: Please bring them out.

35

The GUARD *enters the cell.* JACEK *interrupts his monologue.*

GUARD: The governor instructs you to finish your conversation.

JACEK: Please – among my things, they'll give them back, in my wallet there's a receipt from a photographic shop. I left a picture there to be enlarged and there wasn't time to pick it up. They're supposed to have enlarged it. Could you pick it up and give it to my mother?

PIOTR: What's it a picture of?

JACEK: Marysia – after communion. I took it from my mother when I left. It's a little creased.

36

JACEK: Please – I don't want to go.

(PIOTR *stands motionless. The* GUARD *has finished locking up the cell and has also stopped still. They all stand for a moment.*)

GUARD: Let's go.

(JACEK *moves as if he hasn't quite finished what he had wanted to say. Then he starts walking forward, completely normally, without looking around. The* EXECUTIONER *slides back several bolts on the door, breaks the seals, and moves aside to let them in.* JACEK *walks in, followed by* PIOTR, *the* PROSECUTOR, *the* GOVERNOR, *a priest and a doctor. The door is closed. At that moment the young man who had previously been carrying the ladder, but whose face we have not yet seen, appears outside the room. He stares at the closed door as if able to divine what is happening inside. Still gazing intently, he slowly walks right up to the door and stops just in front of it. He looks as if he might have done some painting here before. His jacket and small cap are splattered with white paint, and several dried drops can even be seen on his face. No sound reaches him through the door from the inside.*)

37

GOVERNOR: . . . and the condemned man has not taken advantage
of the right to appeal.
 (*The priest whispers something into* JACEK's *ear.* JACEK *also
 whispers several words and lowers his head. The priest makes the
 sign of the cross on his forehead.* JACEK *inclines his head towards
 his hand. As he lifts his head again, the* GOVERNOR *takes a step
 towards him and pulls out a packet of cigarettes.*)
GOVERNOR: Cigarette?
JACEK: I'd prefer one without a filter.
 (*The* EXECUTIONER *pushes a packet of Sporty towards him.*
 JACEK's *hands are slightly shaking.* PIOTR *pulls out some
 matches, but the* EXECUTIONER *already has a lighter ready and
 lights Jacek's cigarette for him. Everybody is waiting;* JACEK *is
 the only one smoking.* PIOTR *takes a match out of the box and
 snaps it in two. The crack echoes loudly in the general silence.
 The* EXECUTIONER *holds out an ashtray.*)
 I would – I would like to relieve myself.
 (*The* EXECUTIONER *points towards a small door in a wall on
 one side of the room.* JACEK *disappears behind it. Again,
 everybody is standing and waiting. The* EXECUTIONER *goes
 over to the door and knocks quietly. Silence.*)

38

*The decorator with traces of dried white paint on his face stands as
before in front of the room and stares at it. Although there is only a
closed door in front of him, he seems to sense something greater.*

39

The silence continues. The GOVERNOR *is slightly anxious and walks
over to the door, but in the same instant the door opens.* JACEK *stands
there, calmly.*

JACEK: I can't go.

(*The* EXECUTIONER *ties his hands and pushes him towards the curtain. With one swift movement the true meaning of the room is revealed.* JACEK *walks through into the little recess followed by the* EXECUTIONER, *who draws the curtain back behind him with the jangling sound of the metal railings. Now in the middle of the recess, he slowly and conscientiously puts the noose around* JACEK's *neck. He walks over to the button and presses it. With a clatter which is slightly too loud for the* EXECUTIONER's *liking, the trap door opens up under* JACEK's *feet. His body twitches for a few seconds and gradually becomes still. The stiff legs swing gently to and fro. After a while, a thick brown liquid trickles down from beneath the trouser legs and drips on to the sheet of linoleum.*)

40

The young man in the cap flecked with paint walks away from the cell door down into the heart of the corridor. The coridor is dark and it is not long before his form gradually dissolves and finally disappears into the gloom.

DECALOGUE SIX
A Short Film about Love

The cast and crew of *Decalogue Six* included:

TOMEK   Olaf Lubaszenko
MAGDA   Grazyna Szapolowska
TOMEK'S LANDLADY   Stefania Iwinska

Director of Photography and   Witold Adamek
  Cameraman
Producer   Ryszard Chutkowski
Composer   Zbigniew Preisner
Artistic Director   Halina Dobrowolska
Sound   Nikodem Wolk-Laniewski
Lighting   Jerzy Tomczuk
Film Editor   Ewa Smal
Production Managers   Pawel Mantorski
                                           Wlodzimierz Bendych
Costume Designers   Malgorzata Obloza
                                           Hanna Cwiklo
Director   Krzysztof Kieślowski

Still: Grazyna Szapolowska as Magda and Olaf Lubaszenko as Tomek

1

It has long been dusk, but not one light is burning in the tall apartment block, which stands like a gloomy colossus silhouetted against the dark blue sky. Only the little red lights of bicycles being ridden around the block by small boys and the burning cigarette ends of smokers sitting in small groups on benches are visible in the dark. It is a warm, spring evening. Suddenly, the entire block bursts into light and we can hear the collective sigh of relief from all the open windows as the power cut comes to an end. The noise of television sets gradually fills the air as they, too, are reconnected at the same time.

2

Tomek's table lamp also comes on along with all the other lights in the block. TOMEK *licks the tip of his finger and puts out his candle. His room is poorly or modestly furnished, with a table, a couple of chairs and a cupboard. It has no personal identity of its own and looks as if it might be rented.* TOMEK *is sitting in a chair by the table. He is a tall, thin lad with a smallish face, nineteen years old and barely looks it. His table stands near the bedroom window. On the table, apart from a small mug, a metal coil for boiling water, and jars of sugar, tea and salt, there is a small, amateur telescope, covered with a piece of flannel cloth. Having now put out the candle,* TOMEK *closes his eyes and repeats several incomprehensible phrases to himself, checking them afterwards in an exercise book laid out open in front of him. He is deep in concentration and has perhaps made a mistake, since he repeats the whole series of incomprehensible words all over again. As he opens his eyes to check them in the book again, he glances over to the alarm-clock standing next to the telescope. His homework is interrupted by a knocking at the opaque glass window of his bedroom door.* TOMEK *gets up. A fifty-year-old woman, the* LANDLADY *of the flat, is standing in the doorway. She looks a simple sort of soul, but there is an attractive quality about her face, a kind of gentleness and serenity.*
LANDLADY: Miss Polonia's on the television.

TOMEK: I'm studying.
(They both smile at each other. Tomek's LANDLADY *is perhaps a little excited about the programme and looks faintly amazed at this demonstration of will-power.)*

LANDLADY: Have a little look, just for a second.
(The screen is filled with young girls in bathing costumes who are walking down some steps. TOMEK *nods so as not to offend his* LANDLADY.*)*

TOMEK: Looks great. Thank you.
(He is keen to cut this conversation short, perhaps because his alarm-clock is set to go off any minute. It starts ringing and he runs into the room to switch it off. His LANDLADY *closes the door behind him.* TOMEK *hurriedly pulls the cloth off the telescope and brings his eye towards the eyepiece. The telescope is evidently trained on a fixed, particular object. It magnifies this object by, let's say, about twenty-fold. A light comes on in the window opposite which is the object of the telescope's attention.* TOMEK *turns off his table-lamp.*

The woman on whom the telescope is trained enters her flat. She is an attractive blonde of about twenty-five to twenty-eight years old. She looks the sort of person who is capable of looking after herself and who does more or less what she pleases, without too many qualms. She dresses in loose-fitting, but not provocative clothes. MAGDA – *for this is the woman's name* – *shuts the door behind her and slides back the bolt. The net curtains in her flat are semi-transparent and so everything she does (and will do in future) can be seen reasonably clearly, even if not too precisely; in other words, exactly how one would imagine through semi-transparent net curtains and the viewfinder of a telescope.* MAGDA *has joined two rooms together in her flat by knocking down one of the walls and used part of the space for a little art studio. Unfinished tapestries hang on frames towards the back of the room. The design appears to be of various suns – large, yellow, red, orange balls – against a chilly landscape background.*

TOMEK *studies her with his eye to the viewfinder.* MAGDA *examines the letters she has taken out of the letterbox, presumably nothing of great importance, since she throws them carelessly on to*

[152]

the table. Still in her overcoat, she walks over to one of the
tapestries and then, much as painters do (although it is never
entirely clear why), takes a couple of steps backwards, cocks her
head slightly to one side and masks part of the tapestry with her
outstretched hand. Suddenly, also for no apparent reason, she
spreads her arms out and stands for a moment like a bird ready for
take-off, even making several flapping movements with her
hands. Maybe she is just in a good mood and is happy with the
way the tapestry is coming along. She walks up to it again and
places her scarf for a moment against a piece of the tapestry which
has not yet been completed, checking to see whether the colour will
match. She takes off her overcoat, folds it over the back of a
chair, and stretches, holding the pose long enough for us to see the
sweaty patches under the armpits of her blouse. She unbuttons her
blouse and skirt, and disappears into the bathroom.

    TOMEK *moves his eye away from the viewfinder. The first part*
of the showing is undoubtedly over. He picks up the mug from the
table and trying not to disturb his LANDLADY, *who is still*
watching the Miss Polonia contest, goes to the bathroom. He
comes back with the mug full of water. On the television set, a
blonde with permed hair is speaking into a microphone and
saying how much she likes animals and nature. Other blondes
looking strikingly similar are standing behind her. Tomek's
LANDLADY *turns away from the screen.)*

LANDLADY: Blondes, every single one . . . Did I ever tell you
    about the time I bleached my hair?

TOMEK: Yes.

(His LANDLADY *giggles.* TOMEK *closes the door, puts the metal*
coil into the mug of water, and peers into the telescope. Nothing is
happening: MAGDA *has still not emerged from the bathroom. He*
points the telescope at an old grandfather clock hanging up on the
wall in her flat: judging from the immobile pendulum, it has
stopped. He hears bubbling sounds in his mug, tears his eyes
away from Magda's flat, and sprinkles some tea from the jar into
the mug. Back to the telescope: MAGDA *is shaking her wet hair*
and wandering around the flat in a loose, unbuttoned blouse. She
opens the kitchen fridge and, from her blouse pocket, takes out a
pendulum attached to a piece of string. She solemnly dangles it

*over the food, possibly a piece of meat or cheese, with an intense
look of concentration on her face. The pendulum starts to swing in
a circle and* MAGDA *makes herself a sandwich.* TOMEK *also
starts to feel hungry, the normal reaction when one sees someone
else eating, and unwraps some processed cheese from tin foil.*
MAGDA *goes back into the main room. She has probably turned
on the radio, since she is moving to a rhythm which* TOMEK,
*naturally, cannot hear. He dials a telephone number (from
memory) and watches as* MAGDA *lifts the receiver.* TOMEK *can
now hear the melody* MAGDA *has been moving to. He can also
hear her voice.)*

MAGDA: Hello?

(TOMEK *holds his breath.*)

Look, I've just about had enough of this! Who are you? Who
the hell are you? I can hear you breathing, you bastard.
(*She angrily puts the phone down.* TOMEK *feels sorry for her. He
instinctively puts some sugar in his tea and then a thought
suddenly occurs to him. He quickly dials the same number again
and says quietly.*)

TOMEK: I'm sorry.

(*He replaces the receiver and looks back into the eyepiece.*
MAGDA *is standing astonished with the receiver in her hand. She
smiles after a while and then calmly puts it down. Her movements
around the flat become more agitated – perhaps she has heard the
doorbell. She runs into the kitchen, quickly rinses out her mouth
with tap-water, buttons up her blouse and opens the door. A
young, fair-haired man in a suit greets her with a cheerful smile.*
MAGDA *shuts the door and presses herself against him. Being
taller than she is, his hands easily reach around behind her down
to the tail of her blouse, which he lifts slightly before caressing her
buttocks.* TOMEK *pushes the telescope away: he is in no mood to
watch this scene develop further. Besides, he has no choice – his*
LANDLADY *is calling to him from the other room.*)

LANDLADY: Tomek! The Middle East!

(*News footage from some conflict or other is being shown on the
television. Tomek's* LANDLADY *is sitting even closer to the screen
than usual.* TOMEK *stands behind her chair.*)

TOMEK: Have they shown anything?

LANDLADY: No. Doesn't it look terrible . . .
(*She is not interested in the rest of the news and clutches* TOMEK's *hand.* TOMEK *stands stiffly.*)
TOMEK: But nothing's actually happened.
LANDLADY: I'm afraid . . .
(TOMEK *is unsure how to extricate himself from this trap. His* LANDLADY *is too absorbed in her own anxious thoughts and is thus oblivious to the awkwardness of the situation.*)
Do you think he'll ever come back?
TOMEK: Of course he will, everyone does sooner or later. I bet he'll be back within six months.
(*The screen is now filled with a queue of people waiting to come on to a rostrum for a variety performance: a man has lifted up his sweater and is moving his stomach muscles in time to the music. Another man with huge biceps is standing behind him. Tomek's* LANDLADY *releases his hand.*)
LANDLADY: They can play on their teeth . . . and do shadow puppets . . . you should go along. Why don't you go along?
TOMEK: I'm embarrassed.
(*He smiles helplessly – he really is embarrassed. He is probably even embarrassed to admit he is embarrassed. He returns to his room and looks reluctantly through the telescope. He knows what he will see and does not want to see it, but places his eye against the viewfinder nevertheless. He searches for a moment and then focuses the equipment so that he can see exactly what it was he was afraid of. He sees a small area of* MAGDA's *naked back and her hands held clasped behind her head. She moves up and down with slow, circular movements. A man's fingers slide up from her breasts on to her shoulders and alter her rhythm. This rhythm becomes faster and faster, and then breaks off abruptly. She lowers her shoulders, leans forward and gets up, exhausted.* TOMEK *follows her with the viewfinder as she disappears into the bathroom but swings it back just in time to see the man reach for the telephone. He dials a number and talks to someone, covering the mouth of the receiver with the palm of his hand.*

TOMEK *is angry: he has been witness to some kind of deception. He peers again into the viewfinder, but* MAGDA *and the man have presumably disappeared under the covers of her*

[155]

bed, which is standing too low off the ground for TOMEK *to see them. He opens his cupboard. A target with several darts stuck into it is nailed to one of the doors.* TOMEK *wrenches out a dart from section '10', puts it in his pocket, and walks through his landlady's room.*)

I'm off to throw out the rubbish.

LANDLADY: But the chute's not working!

(TOMEK *walks out of the stairwell entrance with his bucket full of rubbish and disappears behind the wall where all the rubbish is dumped. He re-emerges without the bucket, runs over to the apartment block opposite, and turns into a side alley, his eye roving along the many cars parked there and looking for one in particular. He finds the white, Yugoslavian Fiat and stoops down to plunge the sharp tip of the dart with surprising ferocity first into one tyre, and then into a second.*)

3

Back to the telescope. MAGDA *is sitting in an armchair. She is watching her visitor dress with a slight smile on her face, perhaps because he is putting on his tie and buttoning up his waistcoat with such fussy attention to detail. She does not get up from the chair when he leaves.* TOMEK *swings the telescope panoramically downwards. The man runs over to his white Fiat and starts to drive off, but brakes almost immediately. He gets out, takes a look at the wheels, and angrily kicks the flat tyres. He takes an overcoat and a briefcase out of the car and runs off towards the busy main road.* TOMEK *draws back from the telescope and smiles in sweet revenge.*

4

Tomek's large alarm-clock goes off at 4.30 a.m. He sits up in the bed, barely conscious. We see him a short while later pulling his little milk-cart through the estate.

5

TOMEK *listens for a while at Magda's front door: no sound emerges from the other side. He picks up the bottle which she has left outside and deposits it around the corner of the landing wall. He returns and presses the doorbell. Someone can be heard shuffling to the door.*

MAGDA: Who is it?

TOMEK: Milkman.

> (*The door opens:* MAGDA's *hair is dishevelled.*)

You forgot to put your bottle out.

> (MAGDA *disappears back into the flat and reappears a second later with a bottle.* TOMEK *gives her the milk, but then catches the sound of voices coming from the bathroom.* MAGDA *has probably turned on the radio – along with the gurgling of the bathwater, he can hear some bouncy, morning music.*)

6

TOMEK *is sitting in a navy-blue overall behind a post-office counter window. All his accessories – the stamps, the pens, a ruler, the paper chits – have been neatly arranged, each in its own particular place. He is having trouble making himself understood to an* OLD LADY *whom he is serving.*

OLD LADY: I'm a bit hard of hearing . . .

TOMEK: Your latest pension slip!

> (*The* OLD LADY *rummages around in her wallet as if she has understood.* MAGDA *is standing behind her. The* OLD LADY *looks up helplessly towards* TOMEK.)

OLD LADY: What was that you said?

> (TOMEK *leans forward from his seat and, although embarrassed in front of* MAGDA, *is forced to shout even louder.*)

TOMEK: Your pension slip.

> (*The* OLD LADY *looks towards* MAGDA.)

OLD LADY: Did you catch that?

MAGDA: Your pension slip.

> (*She takes out a felt-tip pen and writes the words 'pension slip' in*

large letters across the newspaper she is holding in her hand. The
OLD LADY *looks at the newspaper, her eyes watering.* MAGDA
*herself opens the woman's wallet and takes out the slip, which is
lying on the top. She gives it to* TOMEK. *He pays out the money,
the* OLD LADY *stuffs it back into her wallet along with Magda's
felt-tip, and walks off.*)

TOMEK: But your felt-tip.

(MAGDA *waves her hand: it is unimportant.*)

MAGDA: I have a money notice . . .

(*With Magda's notice in hand,* TOMEK *searches conscientiously
through the pile of postal orders. He cannot find it. He flicks
through the postal orders once more and then says apologetically.*)

TOMEK: It's not here.

MAGDA: But I received a notice.

TOMEK: Please have a look yourself.

(*He gives her the pile of postal orders.* MAGDA *flicks through them
and, naturally, finds nothing.* TOMEK *smiles.*)

You see . . .

(MAGDA *is in no mood for laughter.*)

MAGDA: (*Drily*) When should I come again?

TOMEK: Perhaps when the next notice arrives?

MAGDA: (*Mumbling under her breath*) Bloody mess.

(TOMEK *watches her walk out of the post office and along the
pavement outside the front glass window.*)

7

TOMEK *finds several letters beneath a pile of T-shirts and shirts, each
one with a multitude of stamps. He adds a similar letter with a more
recent post-mark to the pile. A glass paperweight with a little house
and a setting sun inside is also lying near the pile of clothes. When*
TOMEK *shakes it, snow rises up from the bottom of the glass ball and
slowly floats down again on the fairy-tale setting.*

Evening. Back to the telescope.

MAGDA *is showing someone her tapestries. A shortish, bearded man
is nodding his head appreciatively – he is probably a work colleague,
since he too takes a step backward and studies the tapestry with his*

head cocked to one side.

TOMEK *tries to adjust the telescope so that only* MAGDA *is in the field of vision, but the* MAN WITH THE BEARD *continually wanders into the picture. He appears to be giving her some advice on the composition, or so it would seem, since she steps towards him so as to study the tapestry from where he is standing. He puts his arms around her, almost as if by accident. Perhaps the view from where he is standing is indeed better, because* MAGDA *does nothing to break out of his embrace. Quite the opposite, in fact: she willingly nuzzles up to him. This friendly embrace quickly alters character. The* MAN WITH THE BEARD *slips his hands under her sweater, while* MAGDA *presses her whole body against him.*

TOMEK *reaches for the telephone directory with evident fury. He dials a telephone number.*

VOICE: (*Over*) Hello, emergency gas repairs.

TOMEK: I want to report a leak.

VOICE: (*Over*) How do you know it's a leak?

TOMEK: I can smell it and it's hissing.

VOICE: (*Over*) Where's it coming from?

TOMEK: The kitchen.

VOICE: (*Over*) Have you turned the mains off?

TOMEK: Yes.

VOICE: (*Over*) Address?

TOMEK: Flat 376, Number 4, Piratow Street.

VOICE: (*Over*) 376. We'll be round as soon as we can. Don't use any naked flames.

(TOMEK *grins into the receiver.*

TOMEK *'guides' the emergency gas vehicle with his telescope as it pulls up outside Magda's block opposite. Two men get out wearing caps and carrying little tool-kits.* MAGDA *is already stripped of her blouse and her skirt has been pushed up high over her thighs. Both of them are in the armchair. The doorbell rings – both freeze.* MAGDA *taps her temples to suggest they ignore it and seems keen to cuddle back up to her bearded friend again. But the gasmen are not going to give in that easily. They thump on the door (perhaps concerned that something inside may have exploded).* MAGDA *is finally forced to put the blouse back on which she had hastily thrown to the floor somewhere, smooth*

[159]

down her skirt, and run to the front door. The MAN WITH THE
BEARD *rearranges his clothes. The whole scene is really quite
comic and* TOMEK *watches with some satisfaction.* MAGDA *opens
the door and tries to explain something to the two men, they in
their turn try to explain something to her, after which she is forced
to let them into the flat. They walk around the stove with some
testing equipment. The mood in the flat has somewhat altered by
the time they leave.* MAGDA *puts the kettle on. The* MAN WITH
THE BEARD *studies her for a moment and then walks over to put
his arms around her again, but* MAGDA *this time slips out of his
grasp.*

This is exactly what TOMEK *had hoped for.)*

8

*Crowds of buyers and sellers at a second-hand market: stalls selling
suits, books, records and meats.* TOMEK *calls out to a* STALL-
HOLDER *wearing a small jacket.*

TOMEK: I'd like to have a look at that telescope . . .

STALL-HOLDER: Which one?

(*He studies* TOMEK, *who reminds him of someone. He hands
over the telescope, which is a great deal larger and bulkier than
the one* TOMEK *has at home.*)

Watch arse, do you?

(TOMEK *goes red.*)

So you do, do you. That's ten thou then.

TOMEK: It was nine before.

STALL-HOLDER: Arses come more expensive.

(TOMEK *places his eye to the viewfinder and searches for an
object on which to focus. He selects a distant corner of the market.
The telescope has a telephoto lens and so* TOMEK *zooms in closer
– it really is very good indeed. He trains the viewfinder on a stall
with old clocks standing displayed on pieces of newspaper. He
checks the time on the clocks and then focuses on the text of the
newspapers themselves. He draws his eye away from the lens to
check the real whereabouts of the objects.*)

9

LANDLADY: Look what's been delivered . . . it's got a military
postmark.
(*She hands* TOMEK *an opened letter. Inside, folded into quarters,
is the blue ensign with the United Nations emblem. The*
LANDLADY *reads what is written on the card again.*)
They've been in Damascus . . .
(TOMEK *looks at the ensign and then examines the Arabic letters
on the letter stamp.*)
Can you understand any of it?
(TOMEK *smiles. He has managed to slip the parcel with the
telescope into his room without his excited* LANDLADY *noticing.*)
TOMEK: No . . . this, no. What else does he say?
LANDLADY: Everything's fine . . . it's all going well. He writes:
'All the best to Tomek and tell him s.a.s.a. What's that?
TOMEK: It's a sort of code.
(*The woman sighs at these male secrets and looks through the
letter again.*)
LANDLADY: He's seeing so much of the world. It's a shame you
couldn't have gone with him . . .
TOMEK: I'm not that bothered.
(*The woman looks at him tenderly and then kisses him on the
cheek.*)
LANDLADY: That's from Marcin. I'm glad you're here.
(*She strokes his cheek in a motherly fashion and then suddenly
grows sad.*)
What will you do when Marcin comes back? It would be
good if you had somewhere permanent. I'm sure Marcin
won't stay here for very long. Maybe you'd like to stay here
with me . . . for ever?
(TOMEK *installs the new telescope: there is no one in Magda's
flat.* TOMEK *fills his mug up from the bathroom tap. His*
LANDLADY *is standing in the doorway.*)
Marcin mentioned something else . . . he's met a girl, an
Arabic girl. They've been to the cinema together. Tomek . . .
do you have anyone of your own?

TOMEK: No.

LANDLADY: You've probably never had anyone to tell you this
. . . but girls only pretend to be free and easy, flirting with all
the other boys. Gentle boys are what they like, boys who
they can rely on and be faithful to . . . Do you understand?

TOMEK: Yes.

LANDLADY: You shouldn't be embarrassed about ever bringing
someone home with you . . .

TOMEK: I won't be.

10

It is not clear what has woken TOMEK *up in the middle of the night.
Doubtless a premonition. He walks over to the bedroom window. The
white, Yugoslav Fiat is belching little puffs of smoke from its exhaust
pipe. Nobody gets out but* TOMEK *can see two dark figures inside. The
door on the passenger side finally opens but a man's hand leans across
and slams it shut again from the inside. It opens again and* MAGDA
*runs off towards her stairwell entrance. She stops, goes back, leans
down towards the open window on the driver's side and says
something. The Fiat roars off with a screech of the tyres.*

TOMEK *follows* MAGDA *along the lighted corridor and watches as
she opens the front door, breathes deeply, throws her overcoat angrily
to the floor and sits down at the kitchen table with her back to the
window and to* TOMEK. *He sees her shoulders begin to shake:* MAGDA
*is crying. She wraps a scarf oddly around her head, buries her face in
her hands, and sobs wretchedly for some time.* TOMEK *feels so sorry for
her that tears also well up in his eyes and he swallows noisily.
Suddenly he hears the soft voice of his* LANDLADY.

LANDLADY: Tomek?

> (*Tomek walks over to the door in his T-shirt and underpants and
sees that the small lamp by her bedside is switched on.*)
> Aren't you asleep? Come in and sit down.
> (TOMEK *walks over to her bed, with its feather-quilt and several
pillows in snow-white, starched pillow cases.*)
> Is anything wrong?

TOMEK: Why . . . why do people cry?

LANDLADY: Haven't you ever cried before?
TOMEK: Only once . . . a long time ago.
LANDLADY: When they abandoned you?
    (TOMEK *does not like this topic of conversation. He lowers his
    eyes as if feeling guilty about something.*)
TOMEK: Yes.
LANDLADY: People cry . . . when someone dies . . . when they've
    been abandoned . . . or when they can't cope any more . . .
TOMEK: With what?
LANDLADY: With life . . .
TOMEK: Even adults?
LANDLADY: Yes, even adults.
    (*She places her hand on his.*)
    Were you wanting to cry just then?
    (TOMEK *shakes his head: no, not him.*)

I I

TOMEK *is pulling his milk-cart along – the bottles clink softly. He
enters the block, takes a small piece of paper out of his pocket, and
carefully slips it into the letterbox marked flat number 376.*

12

MAGDA *walks up to Tomek's window counter.*
MAGDA: Was it you I dealt with last time?
TOMEK: Yes.
MAGDA: I have another money notice.
    (MAGDA *takes out the small piece of paper from her handbag: it is
    the same one* TOMEK *had slipped into her letterbox not long ago.
    As before,* TOMEK *flicks through the piles of postal orders and
    gestures helplessly.*)
TOMEK: There's nothing here.
MAGDA: This is the second time I've had to come here.
TOMEK: I know.
MAGDA: It's the second time a money notice has arrived and

there's no postal order.

TOMEK: I know.

MAGDA: It's a disgrace!

TOMEK: Yes.

MAGDA: I want to speak to your superior.

TOMEK: I'm sorry?

MAGDA: Your superior. The manager or someone.

(TOMEK *is not so sure now whether his idea with the money notices was really such a good one. A queue is slowly forming behind* MAGDA. TOMEK *comes back with the manager, who turns out to be a fat, old* SHREW *in gold-rimmed spectacles. She immediately launches herself into battle with a loud war-cry which makes itself heard throughout the post office.*)

SHREW: What's the problem?

(MAGDA *hands her the money notice.*)

MAGDA: This one arrived several days ago and this is the second. That's two notices when the money's not here, and no postal order either.

(*The* SHREW *examines the two bits of paper as if she has never seen anything like them in her life before.*)

SHREW: They're money notices . . .

MAGDA: Yes, but no money.

SHREW: Give them to me. Who's supposed to have sent you this money?

MAGDA: I don't know.

SHREW: So how do you know there's supposed to be any?

MAGDA: Because I keep getting these money notices.

(*The old* SHREW *is yelling the whole time. The entire post office is now staring at* MAGDA.)

SHREW: But the clerk told you the money's not here.

MAGDA: Well, how come I keep gett —

(*The* SHREW *throws the pile of postal orders on to the counter.*)

SHREW: You can see there's nothing here! Look for yourself if you don't believe me.

MAGDA: I've already looked. I didn't write them out myself you know . . .

SHREW: Well, I certainly didn't. Wacek!

(*The manager bellows out this summons with tremendous ferocity,*

although it would not have seemed possible earlier that her shouting could get any louder. A small, odd-looking postman appears behind the counter. The SHREW *waves the pieces of paper in his face.*)
What's this all about, Wacek? Did you write these out?
WACEK: No, I use a pencil.
MAGDA: But I found them in my letterbox.
SHREW: You heard him – they're not ours. The man couldn't have made himself clearer.
(MAGDA *is now enraged.*)
MAGDA: But they've got your stamp on them . . .
SHREW: This is a state post office! If you insist on writing slips out yourself, then go to the police and stop bothering us here with it!
(MAGDA *holds out her hand.*)
MAGDA: You're right. I'm going to the police.
SHREW: Well, you're not getting them back off me. They're fakes.
(*She rips them up right in front of* MAGDA*'s very eyes and throws them violently into the waste-paper basket.*)
What a nerve. And trying to swindle us out of money as well!
(TOMEK *has been watching the whole scene, for which he is entirely responsible and which has left* MAGDA *humiliated.*
MAGDA *marches out of the office while the old* SHREW, *evidently pleased with herself, disappears from behind the counter.* TOMEK *follows after her.*)
TOMEK: Excuse me . . .
(*The* SHREW *is now all sweetness and light, in stark contrast to a few minutes earlier.*)
SHREW: That's the way to deal with customers like that. Now you know.

13

MAGDA *is standing at the end of a small queue by a taxi-rank.* TOMEK *walks up to her but is unsure how to begin.*
MAGDA: Did you find it?

TOMEK: No . . . I . . .

(*A taxi draws up and the queue moves along.*)

MAGDA: Is there something you want?

TOMEK: About the money notices . . . It was me. I put them in your letterbox.

(MAGDA *does not understand. Another taxi draws up – they are now on their own.*)

I put them there.

MAGDA: And the postal orders?

TOMEK: There never were any postal orders.

MAGDA: What did you do that for?

(MAGDA, *who only a moment previously was looking around hurriedly for a taxi, is now intrigued.*)

I don't understand. Why put them there?

(TOMEK *is at a loss to know what to do with his large, red hands which are protruding from beneath the short sleeves of his post-office tunic.*)

TOMEK: I wanted to see you.

(*What was previously a matter of official business has now shifted on to the personal terrain.* MAGDA *thus takes a good look at* TOMEK *and notices how awkward he is, something she may find either moving or irritating.*)

MAGDA: You wanted to see me?

TOMEK: Yes. You were crying yesterday.

MAGDA: How do you know?

TOMEK: I . . .

(*He lifts his gaze and looks her squarely in the eye.*)

I watch you.

(MAGDA's *initial reaction is to laugh at this absurd confession, coming as it does at a taxi-rank of all places, but* TOMEK *does not lower his gaze and is clearly not joking. She starts to feel sorry for him.*)

MAGDA: You'll catch your death of cold in that tunic.

(*She speaks kindly, but starts to walk away.* TOMEK *wants to cling on to this moment, however embarrassing it may be for him: after all, he is actually standing next to her and she is talking to him! He runs awkwardly after her and calls out.*)

TOMEK: You said you wanted to go to the police . . . well, I'll

[166]

confess everything . . . you don't have to go to the station, there's a police kiosk right here.

MAGDA: Piss off.

TOMEK: I'll do whatever you want.

MAGDA: I said piss off. Back to work. Do you hear?

(*There is a hint of menace in these last words. To make her point, she motions with her head in the direction of the post office. TOMEK slowly retreats and MAGDA watches as he walks back, unhappy and awkward, with his long, gangly legs, his shoes which are too large for him and his sleeves which are too short for him.*)

14

Evening. TOMEK *is again practising his weird phrases. He shuts his eyes, repeats the words, checks to see whether they are correct in the exercise book, and then closes his eyes once more. His alarm-bell rings – TOMEK switches it off immediately. He is afraid of spying on Magda's flat this time and only uncovers the telescope after a while, almost as if in slow motion. The light goes on in Magda's flat and TOMEK peers through the telescope.* MAGDA *is standing at the window and staring straight at him. We remember of course that* TOMEK *has just acquired a new and more powerful telescope, and is thus able to see the way in which* MAGDA *scans the row of windows in the block opposite, her eyes roving up and down.* TOMEK *wants to switch off his table-lamp, but changes his mind at the last minute after realizing that if he switches it off now he is bound to give himself away.*

MAGDA *walks over to the grandfather clock on the wall and winds it up with a little key, glancing every now and then over towards Tomek's block. She returns to the window and slowly unbuttons her dress. There is something artificial in the way she does this, almost as if she were on stage, but she suddenly has an idea which would make her behaviour more natural. She turns the tapestries around with their back to the window so that* TOMEK *can no longer see them and with a malicious smile, or so it seems to him, pulls the sofa-bed away from the window. It is quite a struggle, the sofa-bed presumably being quite heavy. She positions it against the far wall so that it is in full view of the window, then picks up the telephone from the window-sill and sits*

down on the bed with it. TOMEK *dials the number and hears the
monotonous dialling tone.* MAGDA *waits. So, too, does* TOMEK.
Finally, after the phone has rung ten times, she picks up the receiver.
MAGDA: Hello.

> (TOMEK *does not answer.*)
> I'm going to count to three. One, two, three . . .

TOMEK: Hello.
MAGDA: Are you watching?
TOMEK: Yes.
MAGDA: Good. Make sure you get a good eyeful. I moved the bed
 over especially. Did you see?
TOMEK: Yes.
MAGDA: Have fun.

> (MAGDA *replaces the receiver and opens the front door. The* MAN
> WITH THE BEARD *has not even managed to close the door before
> she throws her arms around his neck. The full weight of their
> bodies actually closes the door.* MAGDA *takes off his jacket and
> pulls him towards the bed. The* MAN WITH THE BEARD *switches
> off the light but* MAGDA *immediately switches it back on again.
> As their naked bodies sink down on to the bed,* MAGDA *says
> something which makes him sit up suddenly and quickly cover
> himself with the sheets.* MAGDA *laughs delightedly as he walks
> over to the window. Still overcome with laughter,* MAGDA *points
> towards the apartment block opposite. The* MAN WITH THE
> BEARD *gets dressed, runs out of the room, and appears a few
> seconds later in the middle of the small square between the two
> blocks. He stands at the foot of Tomek's block and looks up.*)

MAN WITH THE BEARD: Hey you! Shithead!

> (*The huge block with its several hundred windows looks like an
> unassailable fortress from where he is standing.* TOMEK *tears
> himself away from the telescope and looks down at the* MAN
> WITH THE BEARD *through his window.*)

Hey you, shithead! Mr Postman! Come out of there!
(*People are beginning to lean out of their windows, but this does
not stop the* MAN *yelling even more loudly.*)
Come out of there, you feeble little bastard!
(TOMEK *moves. He walks through his landlady's room, ignoring
her look of astonishment at his sudden appearance, and runs*

down the stairs. The MAN WITH THE BEARD *is waiting for him outside the stairwell entrance.*)
So you're the lover boy, are you?
TOMEK: Yes.
MAN WITH THE BEARD: Raise your fists.
(TOMEK *obediently raises his fists in a boxer-like pose. The* MAN WITH THE BEARD *is short but stocky. He circles* TOMEK *for a while, nodding to himself all the while in astonishment. It is not really clear what he finds so surprising – perhaps Tomek's youth? Then he suddenly punches* TOMEK *in the jaw as hard as he can.* TOMEK *slumps to the ground. His opponent kneels down beside him and gently slaps his cheeks a couple of times.* TOMEK *opens his eyes. The* MAN WITH THE BEARD *helps him to his feet.*)
Don't do it again. It's unhealthy.

15

Tomek's LANDLADY *puts a cold compress against his jaw. He has a split lip and a swollen bruise under one eye.*
LANDLADY: Don't let it upset you. Really they don't like bullies at all. They like gentle boys.
TOMEK: Who?
LANDLADY: Girls.
(TOMEK *closes his eyes. Tomek's* LANDLADY *goes over to the table and, as* TOMEK *had done previously, carefully covers the telescope with the piece of cloth.*)

16

TOMEK, *his face partially swollen, takes his little milk-cart up in the lift to Magda's floor. He takes the bottle to her front door as quietly as possible, almost on tiptoe. Just as he is about to turn and walk away, the door opens and* MAGDA *appears, her hair all dishevelled.*
MAGDA: I thought it might be you. Want to come in? No one else is here . . . Was it you who hung a key on the door-handle for the grandfather clock?

(TOMEK *confirms with a nod of his head.*)
You look terrific . . . don't you know how to fight?
TOMEK: No.
MAGDA: Why do you spy on me?
TOMEK: Because . . . because I love you. Really I do.
(*They are both speaking in whispers.*)
MAGDA: And what . . . what do you want?
TOMEK: I don't know.
MAGDA: Do you want to kiss me?
TOMEK: No.
MAGDA: Do you want to go to . . . do you want to make love to me?
TOMEK: No.
MAGDA: Perhaps you'd like to go on a trip with me somewhere.
To the lakes, or to Budapest?
(TOMEK *shakes his head.*)
So, what then?
TOMEK: Nothing.
MAGDA: Nothing?
TOMEK: Nothing.
(*They stand for a while in silence.*)
You'll freeze standing there. It's cold in the mornings.
MAGDA: True.
TOMEK: I've got the round to finish.
(*He points towards the open doors of the lift and the little
milk-cart inside. He climbs in but a thought suddenly occurs to
him and he goes back to Magda's front door and knocks.* MAGDA
opens it straight away.)
Would you . . . would you come out for a coffee if I invited
you?

17

The television is already on and the LANDLADY, *holding a pen in her
hand, is sitting in front of the set with a newspaper spread out on her
knees.*
TOMEK: Could I . . . borrow Marcin's suit?
LANDLADY: Of course. I put it in a bag so the moths won't . . .

wait a second. (*She reads out from the newspaper.*) You take the initiative when it comes to livening up what is otherwise a boring gathering of friends. Yes or no?
(TOMEK *ponders for a while. He has never been out for the evening with a gathering of friends.*)

TOMEK: No.
(*He leaves the door ajar in the knowledge that more questions are likely to follow. He takes the navy-blue suit out of the plastic bag as his* LANDLADY *starts to ask him a further series of questions.*)

LANDLADY: 'You model yourself on someone you consider to be superior. Yes or no?'

TOMEK: No.

LANDLADY: 'You like making and spending money. Yes or no?'
(TOMEK *calmly puts on the suit.*)

TOMEK: No.

LANDLADY: 'You think sex and eroticism are binding for relationships. Yes or no?'

TOMEK: No.
(TOMEK *can see his ungainly figure reflected in the mirror: the suit is ill-fitting and too small. His* LANDLADY *has finished reading out the questions and is now counting up the points score. She appears in the doorway with the newspaper in her hand.*)

LANDLADY: You got zero points. From nought to twenty-five: 'You take decisions which are often not in your own best interests and pay a heavy price for this. Be more cautious in future – take life as it comes and make the most of it.'
(TOMEK *furtively takes the letters out of the cupboard which have been lying under the pile of clothing and slips them into his pocket. While his* LANDLADY *is preoccupied with reading out the results of the test, he also takes the glass paperweight.*)

18

The Telimen Coffee Bar. Several young people are lounging at the tables, their shirts unbuttoned at the top beneath their sweaters and bags slung casually over their shoulders. TOMEK *is wearing his absurd suit and clutches an equally idiotic bouquet of flowers. He is standing*

*by the cloakroom and getting in everyone's way, unaware that there is
a bar upstairs.*
MAGDA: (*Out of shot*) Hey!
  (MAGDA *calls down to him from over the balustrade.* TOMEK
  looks up, goes up the stairs and gives MAGDA *the huge bouquet.*)
  Thanks . . . What's your name by the way? I didn't know
  how to grab your attention . . .
TOMEK: Tomek.
MAGDA: Mine's Magda.
  (TOMEK *kisses her hand. He cannot stop staring at her and*
  MAGDA, *despite her age and experience, does not really know
  how to start the conversation and what to talk about. She wants
  to put the flowers down on a chair so they will not get in the way,
  but leaves them on the table instead.*)
  Cigarette?
  (TOMEK *does not smoke.* MAGDA *takes out a cigarette for herself
  – TOMEK, as is the done thing, rises from his chair with a
  lighter.*)
  How old are you?
TOMEK: Nineteen.
MAGDA: Tell me . . . about yourself.
  (TOMEK *smiles. His smile is engaging and alters the expression
  on his face. His teeth are even and pearly-white.*)
TOMEK: It said in the newspaper I should take life as it comes and
  make the most of it.
MAGDA: Quite right.
TOMEK: No, it's not. Life is what we make of it.
MAGDA: Don't you believe it. What else did it say?
TOMEK: That I make decisions which are bad for me.
MAGDA: That makes two of us then. I do exactly the same. The
  fact that we're sitting here together is a mutually bad
  decision.
TOMEK: Why were you crying the other day?
  (MAGDA *smiles sadly.*)
  What did he do to you?
MAGDA: Nothing.
TOMEK: Has someone you know died? Couldn't you cope any
  more?

MAGDA: No. Why?

TOMEK: People often cry when they can't cope with life any more.

MAGDA: More like when they can't cope with themselves any
more . . .

TOMEK: Why can't you cope with yourself?

(TOMEK *finds this impossible to grasp.*)

MAGDA: I always seem to be doing things to hurt other people and
only end up hurting myself . . . does that make any sense?

TOMEK: Sort of . . .

MAGDA: How long have you been spying on me?

TOMEK: A year.

MAGDA: That's a long time . . . You said something very
unfashionable this morning . . . You said . . .

TOMEK: I love you.

MAGDA: Listen, there's no such thing. Things can be nice,
relaxed, laid-back, out of this world even . . . but *that* doesn't
exist.

TOMEK: It does.

MAGDA: I'm ten years older than you and I say it doesn't. What
else do you do, apart from being in love with me. So you
work at the post office . . . what else?

TOMEK: I'm learning languages.

MAGDA: How many have you learnt so far?

TOMEK: Bulgarian . . .

MAGDA: Bulgarian?

TOMEK: There were two Bulgarians . . . in the orphanage . . .
where I was brought up. Then I learnt Italian and French.
Now I'm studying Portuguese.

(MAGDA *looks at him in amazement.*)

MAGDA: And you speak all these languages?

TOMEK: Not Portuguese as yet.

MAGDA: Say: 'I am sitting in a café with a strange boy.' In Italian.

(TOMEK *says the sentence in Italian.*)

And in Bulgarian?

(*He now says it in Bulgarian.*)

You're a strange one . . .

TOMEK: No . . . I've just got a good memory. I can remember
everything, from start to finish.

[173]

MAGDA: Do you remember the day you were born?

TOMEK: I sometimes think I can.

MAGDA: And your parents?

TOMEK: No. Them, no. I never wanted to. I wanted to forget my mother, and my father I never saw.

MAGDA: Do you remember the young man, the thin one, who used to come around last autumn . . .?

TOMEK: Yes. He used to bring you buns and rolls, and take away little parcels . . .

MAGDA: He left the country, and never came back.

TOMEK: He was . . . I liked him. Not at first though . . .

MAGDA: Yes. Well, he left for Austria and then moved on to Australia.

TOMEK: Australia?

(TOMEK *speaks in a way which suggests that all this is not totally news to him. He reaches into the depths of his jacket pocket and hesitates.*)

I had no idea it was him . . . you see . . . I used to intercept your letters.

(*He takes out the envelopes which he had been keeping under the pile of clothing at home. He gives them to* MAGDA.)

I work in the post office . . .

MAGDA: You seem to have me surrounded . . . sending me the gasmen, summoning me to the post office, pinching my letters, delivering the milk . . .

TOMEK: I'm sorry.

MAGDA: You waste a lot of time on my account.

TOMEK: I think about you a lot . . .

MAGDA: Who else do you think about?

TOMEK: My best friend. He's in Syria. In the Polish contingent of the United Nations. We were at technical school together. I'm lodging with his mother at the moment. He used to spy on you as well.

MAGDA: Did he tell you all about me?

TOMEK: No. He only showed me the telescope and pointed out your window when he left.

MAGDA: What did he say?

TOMEK: s.a.s.a. It's a special code.

MAGDA: What does it stand for? Tell me.

TOMEK: Sexy Arse . . . Screws . . . Screws Around . . .

WAITER: Good evening. Ready to order?

> (*Both break off from their conversation.* TOMEK *wants to order in style and appears to think this is the way it is done.*)

TOMEK: Two coffees, please. And two cakes.

MAGDA: I wouldn't mind a glass of wine. Red wine.

TOMEK: One wine, then. How much is it?

WAITER: Per 100 grammes? 240 zlotys.

TOMEK: Two wines then.

MAGDA: Give me your hand.

> (TOMEK *pulls his large hand out from under the table.* MAGDA *takes out her pendulum and positions it above his hand. It hangs still at first, but then slowly starts moving around in a circle, getting faster and faster.*)

You're a good person.

TOMEK: No. I've done some bad things in my life.

MAGDA: Well, you're good for me.

> (*She places her hand on top of his.*)

Stroke it.

> (TOMEK *squeezes the palm of her hand.*)

19

> TOMEK *is standing in Magda's room. Everything in the room looks different from his present perspective and he behaves as if this is the first time he has seen it. He takes out the glass paperweight and puts it on top of the tapestry frame.* MAGDA *emerges from the bathroom wearing a dressing-gown tied at the waist. Her hair is wet. She walks over to the tapestry and watches as the glass snow in the shaken ball descends slowly on to the fairy-tale house and the setting sun.*

TOMEK: Could you make an embroidery of a paperweight like this?

> (MAGDA *tosses her head, showering little droplets of water in* TOMEK's *face and causing him to screw up his eyes.* MAGDA *laughs. So, too, does* TOMEK.)

MAGDA: Do I always do this?

TOMEK: I can't say I've ever seen you.

MAGDA: Good. We wouldn't want everything to be a repeat.
(*She takes the glass ball into her hand.*)
Where did you get this from?

TOMEK: I've had it for ages. It was a present . . . a memento. It's
for you.
(MAGDA *pushes him towards the armchair, the glass ball in her
hand. If he had wanted to embrace her and felt capable of doing
so, no doubt they would have stopped there and then. But*
TOMEK *does not feel capable of doing so and so is forced
backwards, step by step.*)

MAGDA: I'm not a good girl. You shouldn't give presents to bad
girls like me.
(TOMEK *falls back into the armchair.* MAGDA *bends down over
him.*)
You know I'm a bad girl, don't you? I mean, really bad.

TOMEK: I love you and I don't care one way or the other.

MAGDA: What else do you know about me?

TOMEK: You drink a lot of milk.

MAGDA: And what else?

TOMEK: You walk around on tip-toes. Every day, for a minute.

MAGDA: But what do you see when one man after another turns
up here . . .

TOMEK: It's called . . . making love. I used to watch, but I don't
now. Not any more.

MAGDA: No. It's got nothing to do with love. Tell me what I do.

TOMEK: You get undressed. And then you . . . undress them as
well. Then you lie down on the bed, or on the carpet, and
close your eyes. Sometimes you lift your arms up and put
your hands behind your head.

20

*A female silhouette can be seen sitting next to Tomek's telescope. The
cloth has been put to one side. His* LANDLADY *is looking through the
eyepiece at the far window where it was trained before. Because she
finds it difficult to close one eye while keeping the other open, as is the*

[176]

*case with many women, she covers the other eye with the palm of her
hand. And watches . . .*

21

MAGDA *sinks down and crouches before* TOMEK. *She looks him
straight in the eyes.* TOMEK *wants to look away but finds himself
gripped by the intensity of her gaze.*

MAGDA: Have you ever had a girl before?

TOMEK: No.

MAGDA: And when you watch me . . . you do it on your own?

TOMEK: I used to . . . a long time ago.

MAGDA: You know it's a sin, don't you?

TOMEK: Yes.

> (TOMEK'*s voice is hoarse. He is trying to control his own feelings
> of lust.*)
> I don't any more. I only think about you . . .

MAGDA: Think about me now . . . you know I'm naked under this
dressing-gown, don't you?

TOMEK: Yes.

MAGDA: When a woman wants a man, she gets all wet inside . . .
do you want to see if I am now?

> (MAGDA *takes his hands and places them under her dressing-
> gown.* TOMEK *can feel her thighs. The gown parts in the middle
> above her waist.*)
> Don't close your eyes. You have gentle hands. Large, but
> gentle.
> (MAGDA *slides his hands further and further up her thighs.*
> TOMEK *begins to shudder, then breathes more and more quickly
> and shuts his eyes despite her command. He suddenly clutches her
> thighs and catches his breath, then violently releases his grip,
> takes another breath, and tries to restore his measured breathing.
> But it is too late. The expression of arousal on* MAGDA'*s face has
> vanished: she smiles.*)
> Already?
> (TOMEK *opens his eyes. He sees* MAGDA'*s normal, smiling face in
> front of him – without a trace of her previous excitement.*)

[177]

Well. Was it good?
(TOMEK *is still breathing unnaturally quickly but is fully
conscious of what she is saying. His face clouds over.*)
That's all it comes down to, Love. Now go to the bathroom
and clean yourself up.
(TOMEK *looks at her stubbornly as if he has seen everything in a
new light: her in front of him, then next to him, himself in front of
her, her in her parted dressing-gown . . . he suddenly springs to
his feet and dashes out of the flat.* MAGDA *watches him go,
reclined in the armchair, and then walks over to the window. She
sees him run awkwardly towards his own block. He passes a man
in a light overcoat carrying a large suitcase who follows him with
his eyes as he runs past.* MAGDA *grabs the window-handle but
TOMEK is already too far away. She shuts the window again
almost as soon as she has opened it, realizing the futility of the
gesture. She presses her face to the glass and with her other hand,
or rather fist, bangs the window-sill several times.*)

22

TOMEK *switches on the bathroom light. It is already quite late. He
quietly takes down the wash-bowl off the shelf and fills it up with
water from the shower grip so as not to make a noise. The water is hot
and steamy. He has taken off his jacket during this time and carefully
hangs it up on the back of a chair before rolling up his shirtsleeves. He
turns off the tap, replaces the shower grip on its hook, and unscrews the
razor-head. He takes out the blade, rescrews the head back down, and
puts it back on the shelf.*

23

MAGDA *is standing at the dark window looking through a small pair
of opera-glasses. She walks over to the tapestry frame, takes out a sheet
of card from underneath, and writes 'COME OVER' on it in large
letters with a felt-tip pen. Then in slightly smaller letters, she adds:
'FORGIVE ME'. She places the sheet against the window so that the*

message can be read from the outside. From her side of the widow, we can see the yellow sun through the dark-green glass, which recalls the scene in the paperweight.

24

TOMEK *kneels down by the bowl of hot water and then methodically, checking to see whether the blade is cutting effectively, slices through the veins of both wrists, first the left hand, then the right. He puts them into the wash-bowl: the water rapidly turns a shade of red.* TOMEK *props his head up against the white wall of the bathroom. The steam has condensed on his face to form what looks like a stream of tears.*

25

MAGDA *is in the process of fixing her encouraging–apologetic poster to the window when she notices* TOMEK *has left his overcoat behind. She reaches into the pocket but finds only a half-torn bus-ticket, nothing else. She suddenly hears the front doorbell and runs over with the coat in her hand, but decides to peer through the peep-hole first before opening it. She can see the bearded man's face, hugely distorted by the lens.*

MAGDA: I'm not in.
> (*He thumps on the door.*)
> I'm not in, do you hear? I'm not in!
> (MAGDA *goes back to the window. There is no light in Tomek's room but she notices some movement on the landing. Someone is climbing into the lift and someone else is running along the landing. An ambulance is waiting by the stairwell entrance and ambulance-men emerge carrying a stretcher. A body lies on it covered by a blanket. The vehicle drives off. An elderly woman with a shawl thrown over her nightdress watches as the ambulance drives off and then goes back indoors.*)

26

MAGDA *runs up to the fifth floor, Tomek's coat in hand. She searches for the right number but is unsure and so knocks gently. Tomek's* LANDLADY *opens the door, still in the shawl she has thrown on over the nightdress.*

MAGDA: I'm sorry, I must have woken you up . . .

LANDLADY: Not at all.

MAGDA: Does –

LANDLADY: Yes.

MAGDA: He left his . . .

(*She points to the coat.*)

LANDLADY: He's not at home . . . Please come in.

(MAGDA *enters the flat. The* LANDLADY *points to a chair.*)

Please leave it there.

(MAGDA *lays the coat down on the chair. The* LANDLADY *shows no sign of wanting to throw her out.*)

MAGDA: Has he . . . gone out?

LANDLADY: He's in hospital. It's nothing serious . . . he'll be out in a few days. It's nothing serious.

MAGDA: I want to see him. He's just been at my place . . .

LANDLADY: I know.

MAGDA: I think I hurt his feelings.

LANDLADY: There's no need for you to see him. He'll be out soon.

MAGDA: What's wrong with him?

LANDLADY: You'll probably find this rather amusing . . . he fell in love with you.

MAGDA: But why is he in hospital?

LANDLADY: As I said, it's nothing serious. Can I show you something?

(*The* LANDLADY *takes off the cloth covering the telescope.*)

This is a telescope. And this is his alarm-clock, set for half-past eight. That's when you get home, isn't it?

MAGDA: More or less.

LANDLADY: He made a bad choice, didn't he?

MAGDA: Yes.

LANDLADY: Well, I'm going to be looking after him from now on.

MAGDA: But you already have a son.

LANDLADY: He left the country. And when he gets back . . . he'll
    probably disappear again. He was always trying to run away
    . . . If I'm good to Tomek, he won't leave me. He won't run
    away . . .

    (MAGDA *leaves and is about to go down the stairs when she*
    decides to go back to the flat again.)

MAGDA: I'm sorry . . . what's his surname?

LANDLADY: Just Tomek.

    (*She closes the door, this time more loudly and demonstratively.*)

27

MAGDA *wakes up at dawn, frozen and lying fully dressed on the bed.*
Tomek's LANDLADY, *wrapped up tightly in her shawl, is pulling his*
little milk-cart across the square which separates the two apartment
blocks.

28

MAGDA *stands uncertainly in the post office. A sign is hanging up at*
the window where Tomek used to serve: 'Closed due to staff sickness'.
An elderly man brightens at the sight of MAGDA.

CLERK: Good morning. Are we registering in or registering out?

MAGDA: Neither, you don't happen to know . . . I wanted to
    know who lives in the block opposite. I have their address.

    (*She hands him the card. The* CLERK *runs his finger down the list*
    of names.)

CLERK: The main tenant there is Maria Karska, with her son
    Marcin.

MAGDA: There should be a Tomek there as well.

CLERK: He's not registered down here. Anything else?

    (MAGDA *shakes her head: no, nothing else.*)

29

MAGDA *is woken up in the middle of the night by the telephone. She leaps up and picks up the receiver.*
MAGDA: Hello . . . Hello!
    (*Silence on the other end of the line.*)
    Is that you, Tomek? Is that you?
    (*Silence.*)
    Say something.
    (*Nothing.*)
    Tomek, I've been trying to find you . . .
    (MAGDA *picks up the opera-glasses and puts them to her eyes. Tomek's window is dark. There is still no sound on the other end of the receiver.*)
    I've been looking for you everywhere . . . I've been to several hospitals. I wanted to tell you something . . . you were right.
    (*Silence.*)
    Do you hear? You were right . . .
    (*She holds the receiver to her ear for a second, then finally replaces it and is just about to walk away when it rings for the second time. She snatches it up again.*)
VOICE: (*Over*) Magda?
MAGDA: Yes.
VOICE: (*Over*) Hi, it's Wojtek. I can't seem to get . . .
MAGDA: Was that you a few seconds ago?
VOICE: (*Over*) Yes. But I didn't get through.
MAGDA: Could you hear what I was saying?
VOICE: (*Over*) No. We're at –
    (MAGDA *puts down the receiver, lies back down on the bed and does not react when it rings again, although it echoes loudly in the dark.*)

30

MAGDA *is waiting for the postman by her letterbox. When our odd little man turns up with his bulging sack, she immediately goes over to him.*

MAGDA: Excuse me . . .

POSTMAN: Number?

(MAGDA *replies automatically*.)

MAGDA: 376.

POSTMAN: No, nothing.

MAGDA: You wouldn't happen to know . . . what's happened to the young lad who used to work at your office? His name's Tomek . . .

(*The* POSTMAN *only now begins to take an interest in her. He smiles unpleasantly*.)

POSTMAN: He slit his wrists. They say it was unrequited love.

MAGDA: What's his surname?

POSTMAN: You'd have to ask the manager for that . . .

31

It is dawn and MAGDA *is standing in the hallway of her flat in her nightdress. She hears the clink of milk-bottles being brought nearer and nearer her front door. She opens the door. Tomek's* LANDLADY *is just about to deliver a bottle of milk.*

MAGDA: I'm sorry . . . is he back yet?

LANDLADY: Not yet.

(*She picks up the empty bottle and walks off.*)

32

The white Fiat is sitting outside the entrance to Magda's apartment block with its boot open. A MAN *in a suit and protective overall has put down the back seat and is making the most of what the car manual describes as 'the luxurious boot space'. He emerges with* MAGDA *from the stairwell entrance carrying two or three rolled-up tapestries. He loads them into the car and they drive off.* MAGDA *suddenly looks up as they they drive past Tomek's block.*

MAGDA: Stop!

(*The car halts.* MAGDA *looks back out of the rear window.* TOMEK *is walking home along the pavement with his*

[183]

LANDLADY. *He is obviously a little unsteady, because his* LANDLADY *is helping him along and holding an umbrella above his head – something which is slightly awkward since she is shorter than he is.* TOMEK *is in the same navy-blue suit he was wearing in Magda's flat.)*
Reverse.
(*The car reverses.* MAGDA *opens the door and wants to get out, but stays in her seat when she sees how carefully Tomek's* LANDLADY *is guiding him towards the block.)*
MAN: We'll miss the gallery. And you'll get wet.
  (MAGDA's *hair is indeed dripping wet with rain.)*
MAGDA: Drive on.

33

Evening. MAGDA *is standing at the window looking through the opera-glasses. The light is on in Tomek's room. She sees his* LANDLADY *walk over to the window and pull down the blind.* TOMEK's *silhouette can be seen seated at the table.*

DECALOGUE SEVEN

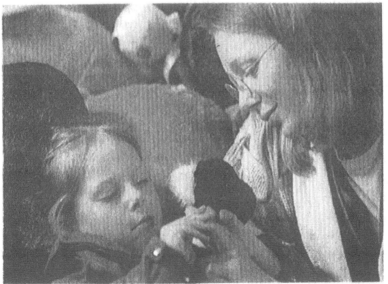

The cast and crew of *Decalogue Seven* included:

EWA	Anna Polony
MAJKA	Maja Barelkowska
STEFAN	Wladyslaw Kowalski
WOJTEK	Boguslaw Linda

Director of Photography and Cameraman	Dariusz Kuc
Producer	Ryszard Chutkowski
Composer	Zbigniew Preisner
Artistic Director	Halina Dobrowolska
Sound	Nikodem Wolk-Laniewski
Lighting	Jerzy Tomczuk
Film Editor	Ewa Smal
Production Managers	Pawel Mantorski
	Wlodzimierz Bendych
Costume Designers	Malgorzata Obloza
	Hanna Cwiklo
Director	Krzysztof Kieślowski

Stills: Boguslaw Linda as Wojtek
Maja Barelkowska as Majka, with Ania

1

Night. Our apartment block is asleep. Apart from the distant clattering of trams, the wind, and the windows rattling in the wind, all is quiet. This all-enveloping silence is pierced by the sharp-pitched, dramatic scream of a young child. A light immediately appears in one of the windows. The screaming continues.

2

MAJKA *bends over the bed of six-year-old* ANIA. *She tries to calm the child by taking her into her arms and hugging her gently:* ANIA *is crying less from pain than from fright and is not completely awake. She could be said to be screaming in her sleep and does not stop, despite* MAJKA'S *efforts. Majka's mother* EWA *hurries into the room wearing a shabby dressing-gown. She is a woman in her forties with stern, resolute features and purposeful movements. She goes over to the bed, roughly wakes the child up and takes her into her arms.* MAJKA, *who has been hanging around, is despatched from the room.*

EWA: Out of my way! If you can't quieten her down yourself, you
   might as well get out!
   (*The screaming gives way to the normal crying of a waking child.
   Still watching,* MAJKA *walks towards the door.* EWA *speaks to
   the young girl in a calm, matter-of-fact voice.*)
   There, there. There's nothing to be frightened of. The
   wolves have all gone. Did you have a bad dream? Well,
   they've all gone now . . .
   (*The crying grows fainter and we can now hear the lullaby* EWA
   is singing to the drowsy child.)
EWA: (*Out of shot*) We will rock you, rock you, rock you . . .
   (MAJKA, *a tall, slim, bespectacled girl in her twenties, goes into
   the room at the end of the corridor. It is a small room and every
   available space is taken up with organ pipes of various
   dimensions, thick ones and thin, all made of gleaming tin.
   Majka's father* STEFAN, *a cheerful, balding fifty-year-old, is*

[187]

sitting on the bed having been woken by the child's crying.
MAJKA *kneels down by his feet and her father clasps her to him as
if she were a small child.*)
STEFAN: Majka, my little Majka . . .
MAJKA: Today's her birthday . . . I can't take any more of this . . .
STEFAN: You used to scream like that when you were little.
MAJKA: But why does she . . . why does she . . .
(STEFAN *calms her just as* EWA *had earlier calmed down the
crying* ANIA.)
STEFAN: There, there . . .
(EWA *stands in the doorway.*)
EWA: I thought you had an early start tomorrow.
(STEFAN *motions for her to leave the room and picks up one of the
thinner little whistles.*)
STEFAN: Listen to this.
(*The sound produced by the whistle is pure and high-pitched.*
STEFAN *breathes more lightly, the whistling grows softer, and*
MAJKA *feels soothed.*)

3

*Several children are playing in a nursery-school garden, their top
buttons undone.* MAJKA *watches as* ANIA *is lifted on to the swings by a
bigger boy and giggles happily.* MAJKA *calls to her.* ANIA *runs over
and stands on tiptoes to give* MAJKA *a kiss through the garden railings,
although as likely as not, she would prefer to rejoin her playmate.*
MAJKA: It's your birthday today, isn't it?
(ANIA *solemnly nods her head.* MAJKA *gives her a little bunch of
flowers.*)
You're going to the theatre, aren't you?
ANIA: Mummy's taking me.
MAJKA: I've already seen the show – you'll enjoy it. Make sure
you try and understand everything.
(*A man on crutches is walking along by the nursery school.
Exhausted, or perhaps simply intrigued by the conversation, he
stops and studies* MAJKA *and* ANIA, *who by now is skipping back
to the swings.*)

[188]

4

MAJKA *takes her student index-card out of her handbag and smiles to the*
SECRETARY.
MAJKA: I'm handing it in.
SECRETARY: Aren't you going to appeal? It's your last year, you
    stand a good chance . . .
MAJKA: If they throw me out, they throw me out. I'm not going to
    appeal.
    (*The* SECRETARY *flicks through the index.*)
SECRETARY: Ten pages are missing . . .
MAJKA: The last two terms. I tore them out. I didn't want my
    parents to be disappointed.

5

*The puppet show is about to finish. The actors are disguised in animal
costumes – a good-natured hippopotamus is being completely
overwhelmed by mischievous monkeys and a crocodile.* ANIA *is rolling
about with laughter in the audience. A happy* EWA *glances over towards
her – both are clapping their hands enthusiastically.*
    Holding a bunch of flowers, MAJKA *pokes her head into the gym-hall
where several girls in their teens are dancing ballet. An energetic,
elderly-looking woman is shouting out commands in French –
everything looks very professional.*
MAJKA: Excuse me, Professor . . .
PROFESSOR: Majka?
MAJKA: I read how well you and the group were doing and I just . . .
    (*The* PROFESSOR *smiles happily.*)
PROFESSOR: How many years it must have been . . .
MAJKA: They weren't going to let me in until I mentioned your
    name . . .
PROFESSOR: Oh yes, they know me here. What are you up to these
    days? I had hoped you would keep on with your dancing.
    Girls? You're looking at one of the best students I ever taught!
    (MAJKA *is embarrassed by this praise.*)

[189]

MAJKA: I'm finishing my studies . . . I couldn't . . .

PROFESSOR: You were so talented, such a happy, smiling girl . . .
Do you remember how to do a tour chaîné?

(MAJKA *puts down the heavy canvas sack and executes a pirouette, faultlessly.*)

MAJKA: But I used to skip off during classes, do you remember?
There used to be some stairs at the end of the corridor, and
we'd run off in our leotards to watch the puppet show from
backstage. Are they still there?

(*The girls laugh.* MAJKA *kisses her* PROFESSOR.)

I just dropped in to say hello. They were good times . . .

(*She leaves, and her* PROFESSOR *drives the girls back to the bars.*
MAJKA's *expression becomes more crafty and businesslike as soon
as she is behind the door. She walks over to the backstage door: it is
open. The puppet-theatre is drawing to a close. The hippopotamus
invites the audience to come up for a dance, and the children jostle
their way up on to the stage, catching the monkeys by their tails and
stroking the hippopotamus's legs. Little* ANIA *is squealing with
excitement.*)

EWA: Do you want to go up there? You're not shy are you?

(*She nudges* ANIA *out of her seat. The little girl runs up to the stage,
captivated.*

MAJKA *is hiding in the little recess under the stairs. Judging by
the noise of the music and the screaming children, the stage is not
far away.* MAJKA *looks around cautiously and steals nearer.*

ANIA *disappears from* EWA's *view. Like other parents, she
leaves her seat and wanders over to the doors, then lights a cigarette
and observes the gaieties from the corridor. The music comes to a
close and the children applaud together with the actor-cum-
animals. The curtain drops and rises several times. Happy and
flushed with excitement, the children slowly make their way back
to their parents.* EWA *stubs out her cigarette and returns to her seat.
She sits on the back of the seat but immediately gets up again.* ANIA
*is nowhere to be seen. The last few children are decending from the
stage.* EWA *walks over, but the stage is empty by the time she
reaches it. She feels nervous in this unfamiliar surrounding, now
empty and quiet, and lit only with stage lights. She goes back to the
hall, but nobody is there either. She runs into the reception area –*

[190]

the last few are leaving the theatre. She runs back again into the hall – it is empty.)

6

EWA *runs out of the front entrance. Parents are walking down the steps with their children and chatting about the show.* ANIA *is still nowhere to be seen.* EWA *runs down several steps at a time and stumbles. She looks around, goes back, looks around again, and walks around the side of the curved building.*

MAJKA *pulls* ANIA *behind a large pillar at exactly the same moment. She crouches down next to her – neither can be seen by* EWA *as she searches for them near by.*

ANIA: Are we playing hide-and-seek?

(MAJKA *pulls out a little coat from her bulging bag.)*

MAJKA: Put this on.

(EWA *walks back up the steps and goes back into the theatre.)*

7

She pushes her way through the hall-doors. The cloakroom ATTENDANT *is holding two overcoats in her hand and bellowing throughout the whole theatre.*

ATTENDANT: I have two coats to be claimed!

(EWA *runs past her, pokes her head into the cafeteria, comes back, and runs over to the cashier who is counting up the petty cash. The first note of hysteria creeps into her voice.)*

EWA: I can't find my child. My daughter's gone missing! Do you hear me? I can't find my child!

8

An electric train pulls out of a Warsaw suburb. The carriage is packed with people. MAJKA *and* ANIA *are pressed against the window.*

MAJKA: Warm up your fingers and do a little drawing.
> (ANIA *tries to draw something on the pane of glass. This amuses her for a while.* MAJKA *breathes a sigh of relief and smiles for the first time today.*)

9

STEFAN *is making more organ whistles in his little room. This time they produce sounds which are lower down the register. They are already in their frames and* STEFAN, *forcing air into the container, listens carefully to the sounds they make. He is interrupted by the sound of the phone ringing.*

VOICE: (*Over*) Hello, is that you, Uncle?

STEFAN: Philip, hi.

VOICE: (*Over*) Listen, I wanted to ask you a favour. You know all that camping equipment you used to have, the tent, sleeping-bags, the gas-cooker, that sort of thing.

STEFAN: Yes.

VOICE: (*Over*) Would it be possible to borrow it? I'm off to the –

STEFAN: Listen, Majka's got the sleeping-bag and the cooker. She's gone off to the Bieszczady mountains with a group of friends from university . . .

VOICE: (*Over*) But I mean for the summer holidays . . .
> (STEFAN *hears the noice of a key turning in the lock and listens intently. The door bangs shut. Nothing more can be heard.*)

STEFAN: Look, ring me back in a week's time, OK? That's right, a week's time . . . Ania?
> (*There is no reply. He goes into the large room:* EWA *is lying on the sofa. She lifts her swollen, tear-stained eyes towards him.*)

EWA: Ania's gone missing.

10

The forest road leads to a small, brightly painted house. MAJKA *is standing with* ANIA *in front of the small, wicket gate, while a sympathetic-looking young man in his twenties is on his way out of the house. He lights a lamp and advances towards them, his step faltering as he gets nearer. He looks at the child as if hypnotized.* MAJKA *throws her sack on to the ground – perhaps it was beginning to hurt, or perhaps she wants to do something, anything, to break the tension.*

MAJKA: Ania, this is your daddy.

> *(The young man cannot tear his eyes away from the child. She studies him intently and then tugs at MAJKA's hand.)*

ANIA: Majka, wee-wee.

MAJKA: OK. I'll keep a look-out.

> *(The little girl is holding her legs together, but is still afraid to go into the thin forest.)*
>
> Don't be afraid. I'll be keeping an eye out.
>
> *(ANIA runs off to the edge of the wood and crouches.* WOJTEK *watches her as she runs off, completely ignoring* MAJKA.)

WOJTEK: Is that her?

MAJKA: Yes. She's nervous. She always has to have a pee when she's nervous.

WOJTEK: What do you want?

MAJKA: Aren't you going to let us in first?

> *(WOJTEK unlocks the gate with a key, but stands in her way.)*

WOJTEK: What do you want?

MAJKA: I've run away from home.

WOJTEK: So?

MAJKA: I want you to help us.

> *(ANIA returns, pulling up her knickers.* WOJTEK *crouches down next to her and examines her from close up.)*

WOJTEK: Hi.

ANIA: Hi.

II

In effect, the whole house consists of one large room with a small recess for a bed. The room is being used as a workshop: several hundred furry teddy-bears and cats are lying in a heap on the floor along with several large sacks full of cut-out materials, presumably intended for the bodies and paws.

WOJTEK: You can play with them if you like.

[193]

ANIA: Which ones?

WOJTEK: All of them.

(ANIA *moves shyly towards the toys.*)

MAJKA: Things have certainly changed around here.

WOJTEK: Yes. Dad died. Must have been around three . . . yes, three years ago . . .

(*A typewriter with a sheet of paper fed into it is standing on the table.* MAJKA *walks over to it.*)

MAJKA: So what are you up to these days?

(*She takes the paper out of the typewriter.* WOJTEK *has only managed to write three words in the middle of the page, where poets normally start their short verses: 'I make teddy-bears'.*)

WOJTEK: I make teddy-bears.

MAJKA: What about your studies? All your plans . . . ?

WOJTEK: Chucked them in.

MAJKA: And this?

(WOJTEK *makes a disdainful gesture with his hand.* ANIA *has found a comfortable little place for herself among the soft teddy-bears. She holds a tiny bear above her head and moves it around in the same way she remembers the actors doing from the puppet-show.*)

WOJTEK: Are you hungry?

MAJKA: Are you annoyed with me?

WOJTEK: Annoyed? No.

MAJKA: So tell me – why did you chuck everything in?

WOJTEK: Lack of talent.

MAJKA: But you used to talk beautifully about Rozewicz,* *Mr Cogito*,** Eliot . . .

(WOJTEK, *glancing over towards the young child, interrupts her.*)

WOJTEK: She's fallen asleep.

(*He gives* MAJKA *a blanket from his own bed. She covers the little girl with it.*)

---

* Tadeusz Rozewicz: a contemporary Polish poet who made his début in 1946 but who first attracted attention in 1947 with a volume titled *Anxiety*. Successive volumes established him as the most influential poet of the post-war period.
** *Mr Cogito*: the title of a volume of poetry by the contemporary Polish poet Zbigniew Herbert, first published in 1974.

Should we move her on to the bed?

MAJKA: No. She's perfectly happy where she is – look.

(*For the first time in their lives as parents they watch their own child sleeping.* WOJTEK *is evidently moved and looks as though he is about to lose control.* MAJKA *tries to cheer him up.*)

Do you still think about me?

WOJTEK: No. Not any more. Do they know?

MAJKA: I took her while they were at the theatre. Mum was running around like a blue-arsed fly . . . she even tripped on the steps and nearly cracked her skull on the bottom. I had everything planned . . .

WOJTEK: Why are you talking about her like that?

MAJKA: I've taken Ania from her and I'm not giving her back. I've been thinking about this moment for years . . . it was always meant to happen.

WOJTEK: I think you're wrong.

MAJKA: You don't understand. This is the first adult decision I've ever taken in my life. I finally stood up to her, and now I know I can do it. I never lied for the first fifteen years of my life. The first time was when I was pregnant and I realized it was easy – nothing could have been simpler. And now I realize I can take decisions. That's also very simple. I'm no longer the well-behaved little girl who was in love with her teacher because he used to tell her about *Mr Cogito.* All that's over.

WOJTEK: Well, if you think it's for the best . . . there's a lot to live for yet. You've never stolen anything, never killed anyone.

MAJKA: But can you steal something that belongs to you?

WOJTEK: I don't know.

MAJKA: I've taken back my own child, that's all. As for killing, I reckon I could kill my mother . . .

WOJTEK: You know nothing about her.

MAJKA: I've recently found out rather a lot . . .

(WOJTEK *goes over to the typewriter. He asks with his back to her:*)

WOJTEK: Like what, for example?

(MAJKA *does not notice his uneasiness. She is thinking what to say next.*)

[195]

MAJKA: Why she is how she is. She was unable to have children any more after I was born, but wanted to. And so when Ania arrived, she simply took her.

WOJTEK: But there was someone who agreed to all of this. Namely you.

MAJKA: I was only sixteen.

WOJTEK: Joan of Arc wasn't much older . . .

MAJKA: So you kept saying at the time. And they only wanted what was best, or so they said: I had a life to lead, studies, prospects and so on. But now I know it was the baby they were after. Why do you think I had to have the baby in the first place?

WOJTEK: But what about the scandal? Her, a headmistress; me, a young teacher; you, a pupil . . . but you always came first.

MAJKA: And what about you? I remember Mother telling you that if you wanted to carry on teaching and didn't want anyone to find out you'd seduced an under-age schoolgirl, then you'd better keep quiet about it. That's what she said, wasn't it?

WOJTEK: Is that what she told you?

MAJKA: I overheard her talking to Dad about it. Anyway, Dad –
(MAJKA *smiles*.)

WOJTEK: What?

MAJKA: Didn't want to know. He's shut himself off from the world. Do you know what he does now? Organs. His whole room's full of whistles.

WOJTEK: Organs?

MAJKA: He left the Party in December. Requested early retirement. Now he does nothing else – just makes organs. You'd probably get on with each other now.

WOJTEK: And what about your mum?

MAJKA: Mum? No, not with her. Even though she's changed. She was always dry and severe. I never knew she was capable of tenderness, I certainly had no experience of it. But she's so gentle with Ania. I watched her kiss her good-night once and then I understood she would never let her go. I remember coming back from summer camp once when Ania was only six months old – they were always sending me off to some summer camp or other – anyway, I came back early and saw

[196]

my mother feeding her, actually breast-feeding her. Ania
was sucking her breasts even though she didn't have any
milk. Or maybe she did. I once read somewhere that
bitches with phantom pregnancies can sometimes produce
milk . . .
(WOJTEK *rearranges the blanket covering* ANIA. *He is looking at
her little fingers.*)
They even wanted to buy me a car and find a flat. So I
couldn't be with her any more.
(WOJTEK *shushes her.* MAJKA *has been talking a little too
loudly.*)
WOJTEK: So what do you want to do now?
MAJKA: I want to be with her. Is that so strange?
WOJTEK: No. But how are you going to manage?
MAJKA: That I don't know. I used up all the strength I had when I
took her away. What happens now is anyone's guess.
WOJTEK: Do you think they'll call the police?
MAJKA: They're bound to.
WOJTEK: Will they figure out it's you?
MAJKA: No. I was due to leave today anyway to go on holiday. I
took my stuff and said my goodbyes.
(WOJTEK *rises to his feet – a thought has just occurred to him.*)
WOJTEK: I think perhaps you ought to give them a ring.
MAJKA: Why?
WOJTEK: Look, you can't just . . . There's no proof she's your
daughter. You won't be able to go or stay anywhere.
MAJKA: Well? So what?
WOJTEK: Ring them. Tell them you'll come back if they agree to
sort out the documents proving that Ania is rightfully yours.
MAJKA: And if they won't?
WOJTEK: Give them two hours to make up their minds.
MAJKA: Could be amusing.
WOJTEK: Do you want me to come with you? It's getting dark . . .
(MAJKA *puts on her coat. She turns around at the door and says
sharply:*)
MAJKA: Keep an eye on her.
(WOJTEK *is left alone with the child. He walks over to the table
with the typewriter and reaches towards a shelf. He takes down*

[197]

an old, grey file, unties the string, and eventually finds what he is looking for.)

WOJTEK: I'm going to read something to you, OK?

(ANIA *is asleep.*)

It's about your mummy, and your granny.

(WOJTEK *initially reads over to himself what he is intending to read to his daughter. He smiles and tries to strike the appropriate tone.*)

'An Italian film, a mother and daughter, several scenes I sense around me . . .'

(*A narrow streak of light appears through the window.* WOJTEK *lays down the grey file and sees a small van flashing its headlamps at the window. Glancing across to see if* ANIA *is still asleep, he goes outside. A small Nysa van is standing by the front gate.* WOJTEK *opens the gate and the van moves up the drive.*)

Good timing.

YOUNG MAN: Got any?

WOJTEK: A few.

(WOJTEK *opens the front door. Several packages doubtless full of teddy-bears and toy cats are lying in the hallway behind the door.* WOJTEK *points towards the sleeping child in the middle of the room.*)

Shhhh . . .

(*The* YOUNG MAN *looks over towards her.*)

YOUNG MAN: Who's that?

WOJTEK: My daughter.

(*They carry the packages over to the van.*)

Don't come over for a few days. I could have a problem here.

YOUNG MAN: With her?

(WOJTEK *nods. The van drives off.*)

12

WOJTEK *is standing on the front doorstep.* ANIA *is sitting on a pile of teddy-bears and gazes towards him, wide awake. She smiles a slight, hesitant smile.*

ANIA: Where's Majka?

WOJTEK: She's gone out. She'll be back soon.
ANIA: You're . . .
WOJTEK: My name's Wojtek. What woke you up?
ANIA: I often wake up. Majka told me today I haven't got a
    mummy.
WOJTEK: Hey, you can't have heard right. Of course you've got
    one.
ANIA: A mummy?
WOJTEK: Yes.
ANIA: And a daddy?
WOJTEK: A daddy too.
ANIA: Majka told me you were my –
WOJTEK: Aren't you sleepy?
    (ANIA *shakes her head: no, she isn't.*)
    Shall I show you how to make a teddy-bear?
    (ANIA *looks around: there are hundreds of the little bears.*)
ANIA: Like them?
WOJTEK: Yes, just like them.
    (ANIA *looks around and picks out one she has been sleeping
    next to.*)
ANIA: Show me how to make one of these.

13

A telephone ringing shatters the nocturnal silence. STEFAN, *in his room
full of pipes, tin and whistles, immediately picks up the receiver.*
STEFAN: Hello?
MAJKA: Dad?
STEFAN: Yes.
    (MAJKA *is standing in a kiosk on a station platform.*)
MAJKA: She's with me.
STEFAN: I thought as much. What do you plan to do?
MAJKA: Put Mum on the line.
STEFAN: Tell me.
MAJKA: You won't be able to help, Dad. I know you want to, but
    you can't.
    (STEFAN *tries talking as quietly as possible.*)

[199]

STEFAN: Your mother's been in tears all day. She's had to take
   some valium.
   (EWA, *tense and trembling, is standing in the doorway.*)
EWA: Who is it?
   (STEFAN *hands over the receiver without saying a word.* EWA
   *slowly and apprehensively takes the phone, fearing the worst. She
   speaks in a dead tone of voice, her lips completely dry.*)
   Hello . . .
MAJKA: She's with me.
EWA: Oh my God . . . you've got her . . . Oh my God . . .
MAJKA: Have you informed the police?
EWA: Yes, but it's not important. We did inform them. Where
   are you?
   (MAJKA *speaks clearly and deliberately. She has obviously been
   thinking all this out on the way.*)
MAJKA: Ring them back and tell them she's been found. That's
   number one.
   (EWA *has regained her usual vigour.*)
EWA: All right, I'll ring them. Where are you? We're coming to
   fetch you. Stefan!
   (*She has not heard a reply and so asks again.*)
   Where are you? We're coming to get you!
MAJKA: We're somewhere round abouts. I'm not telling you
   where. You have to change everything first.
   (STEFAN *enters carrying cigarettes, matches and an ashtray.* EWA
   motions to him to keep silent.)
EWA: Change what?
   (STEFAN *lights a cigarette and places it in* EWA's *mouth.*)
   What am I supposed to change? I don't understand!
MAJKA: Everything. Ania belongs to me. All the documents have
   to be changed. Every single one.
   (EWA *inhales.*)
EWA: That's impossible.
MAJKA: No it's not.
EWA: Nobody knows the truth.
MAJKA: I'll make sure they find out.
EWA: Ania's mine. Her birth certificate's in my name. Only
   Jadwiga knows she's your baby and she's not going to say

anything. Tell me where you are.

MAJKA: Listen to me carefully. You stole my child – it was straight theft. And I can't live with it any more. I'm giving you two hours to think of a way of giving her back to me. You'll find a way, somehow.

14

The little bear which WOJTEK *has just finished stuffing has no particular expression on its face. Only after* WOJTEK *has drawn the needle through the head and fastened a pair of eyes which he had taken out of a little box earlier does it come to life as a cuddly toy.* ANIA *is standing on his work-bench and is fascinated to see the bear acquire some form of identity.* WOJTEK *allows her to sew up the second eye and fasten it into position.* MAJKA *walks over to them.*

MAJKA: Why aren't you asleep?

WOJTEK: She woke up.

(ANIA *shows her the little bear.*)

ANIA: I put his eye in. Majka, look!

(*Since* MAJKA *displays little interest in it, the young girl stands up on the table so that she is the same height and pokes the bear under her nose.*)

Majka!

MAJKA: You're supposed to call me Mummy.

(ANIA, *holding the bear in her hand, thinks this is a game.*)

ANIA: Majka.

(MAJKA *lifts her off the table, holds her under the arms at eye-level, and speaks more loudly than before.*)

MAJKA: You're supposed to call me Mummy. Do you understand?

(*The little girl falls silent.* MAJKA *begins to shake her, shouting.*)

Say Mummy! Mummy, do you understand? Mummy!

(MAJKA *is shaking the child as hard as she can.* ANIA *is screaming hysterically.* WOJTEK *looks on in shock.*)

You must call me Mummy. You're mine. Say it, please say it. Well? Mummy . . .

(*The little girl says nothing.* MAJKA's *voice is now pleading tenderly.*)

Ania, say Mummy. Please.

(ANIA *is crying.* MAJKA *lays her down on the sofa, whispers entreatingly into her ear, strokes her dishevelled hair, and then says she is sorry. The little girl gradually begins to calm down. The telephone rings.* WOJTEK *darts over to pick up the receiver so as not to wake up the child, but waits for a second while motioning to* MAJKA *to keep an eye on her and only lifts it after the second ring. He pretends to have just woken up and feigns surprise.*)

WOJTEK: Hello, who is it? Ah yes, no, no problem. I've no idea. I haven't seen her for six years. By all means, fine. (*He yawns.*) Yes, fine.

15

STEFAN: He doesn't know anything. He was asleep. We've woken up enough people as it is.

(*He pens a line through the last name on a long list.*)

EWA: No harm's been done.

(*They are sitting in Ewa's large room.*)

STEFAN: We really ought to give the child back, you know.

(EWA *looks at him with an expression of anger.*)

EWA: I knew it: you don't love her.

STEFAN: I do, but we've made a mistake. We're in danger of losing them both.

EWA: But you agreed to it in the first place.

STEFAN: I didn't know it would turn out like this.

EWA: You said: I don't want that little brat –

STEFAN: I had my reasons.

EWA: So what's the problem?

STEFAN: There's no problem. It's just that things have changed . . .

EWA: You've changed, that's all. Martial law comes along and you just collapse under the pressure. And now you're completely useless – that's all that's changed.

STEFAN: I was only an engineer . . .

EWA: Rubbish! You were an engineer with a lot of pull!

STEFAN: Sit down! You're not in class now.
(EWA *stops pacing up and down the room.* STEFAN *repeats his request in an exhausted voice – presumably their arguments have always been like this, the moments of tension being acute but short-lived.*)
Sit down. Please.
(EWA *stands for a moment and then sits down beside her husband.* STEFAN *stretches out his hand and places it against her neck.*)
I'm sorry.

EWA: We know next to nothing about our child. Who she knows, where she might be. I never knew . . . I never thought she might . . .

STEFAN: You made too many demands on her, she just couldn't cope any more. She always had to dress the way you wanted her to dress and be interested in all the things you wanted her to be interested in. All those dance groups and orchestras, all the little discussion groups and committees you'd set up under that watchful eye of yours. She always knew she had to be best at everything so you wouldn't come home and say how much she'd let you down. She simply couldn't take it any longer. And the day you screamed at her when you saw her six months' pregnant in the bathroom with traces of bandages round her stomach, well, something snapped between you both.

EWA: You don't have to tell me the family history. I know it already.

STEFAN: But you don't seem to realize that she knows it as well.

EWA: Please, go and see if your friends can be of any help. You had so many at one time . . . I beg you.

16

MAJKA: Wojtek?
(*She has the grey file in her hand.*)
Can I?
(WOJTEK *pauses in pouring out the tea.*)

[203]

WOJTEK: It's all old stuff . . .

MAJKA: But you've taken it out.

WOJTEK: I wanted to read Ania something. Put it down.

MAJKA: Is the stuff about me here?

WOJTEK: Yes. But don't read it.

MAJKA: '. . . grey eyes breathing in every word, wiser than all the hundreds of blue–green–black others, alive and full of words still unspoken . . .' Is that how it went?

WOJTEK: More or less.

MAJKA: I don't remember the rest.

WOJTEK: Good thing too. It's not worth it.

(*He pours the boiling water into the mugs and puts them down on the table, slightly scalding his fingers.* ANIA's *piercing scream makes them jump to their feet. Similar to the scream which introduced the film, it is full of a terror which adults no longer experience. They both run over to the child. As at home,* MAJKA *is unable to calm her down. The still sleeping* ANIA *screams terrifyingly and loudly.*)

MAJKA: I'm no good at this. Mum usually does it at home. She wakes her up roughly.

(WOJTEK *hesitantly shakes* ANIA's *shoulder, then takes her into his arms and at first gently, and then more strongly, slaps her on the cheek.* ANIA *opens her eyes still screaming, but she gains consciousness and her screams give way to crying.* MAJKA *takes the child from him and says emphatically:*)

The wolves have all gone. There aren't any wolves now . . .

(ANIA *gradually calms down.* MAJKA *sits with her on the sofa.*)

ANIA: I had a dream about . . .

(*She does not finish her sentence.*)

MAJKA: Are you going to fall asleep again?

(*Quite unexpectedly,* ANIA *puts her arms around* MAJKA *and hugs her tightly.* MAJKA *happily puts her arms around her.* ANIA *tries to find her ear and then asks softly, so that* WOJTEK *cannot hear her:*)

ANIA: Is Mummy still not here?

(MAJKA *closes her eyes.*)

MAJKA: Everything will be fine, Anka. Go back to sleep.

(ANIA *slides away and moves towards the pillow.*)

Are you going to go back to sleep?

(ANIA *replies without turning around.*)

ANIA: Yes, I will.

(*After a while, her breathing becomes even: this is the third time she has fallen asleep in one day.*)

MAJKA: She screams like that virtually every single night. She has bad dreams, but never tells us what they're about. I don't know what she's frightened of.

WOJTEK: The future, probably. Once I –

MAJKA: Or the past. I read that children often scream when they're asleep because they are afraid of being born. They dream about still being in the womb.

WOJTEK: You read too much. About dogs and children.

MAJKA: You know something. I'm not that much older than her. There's only sixteen years' difference.

WOJTEK: Your mother wasn't that much older than you either.

MAJKA: I'm different from her. And I'm going to carry on being different.

WOJTEK: You talk about yourself the whole time. But what about her? Have you ever stopped to think about what she might want?

MAJKA: She's too little. She doesn't know what she wants.

WOJTEK: She won't survive this. All this running around, all this stress. She's a sensitive child. You should have tried to sort this whole thing out without having to put her under so much stress.

MAJKA: What are you afraid of? Mother can't touch you now.

WOJTEK: You can both stay here as long as you like, but it'll finish the child off. Sometimes you have to take decisions which aren't in your own best interest.

MAJKA: Like what?

WOJTEK: Go back. She needs a stable home, her own bed, her own cereal for breakfast.

MAJKA: I see.

WOJTEK: What do you see?

MAJKA: I see what you're trying to tell me. That she should have a stable home.

WOJTEK: I've got a friend here with a van. I'll go over and get it.

[205]

You'll be back home again before dawn.

MAJKA: Fine.

> (WOJTEK *is unsure whether* MAJKA *really has changed her mind,*
> *but gets up and puts on his coat.* MAJKA *is smiling at him.*)

WOJTEK: So, are you going to stay?

MAJKA: No. You're right. Go and fetch the van.

> (MAJKA'S *smile vanishes as soon as* WOJTEK *has closed the front*
> *door behind him.*)

17

WOJTEK *walks up to the front gate with an old, rusty bicycle. He puts*
the light over his shoulder and cycles off. The sky in the east is
beginning to turn a rosy pink as WOJTEK *cycles into the wood. He*
rides along a narrow path, comes out on to a tarmac road and comes to
a halt by the sort of wooden house which is quite common in the
district. He knocks at the door. His friend pokes his head out.

YOUNG MAN: Hi, Wojtek, what's up?

WOJTEK: Have you delivered them?

YOUNG MAN: Yes.

WOJTEK: Bring the van out. We've got to take my family home.

> (*The* YOUNG MAN *beams with relief.*)

YOUNG MAN: I thought maybe something was wrong.

WOJTEK: No, nothing's wrong.

18

STEFAN *is sitting in a large, impersonal room, one new to us, whose*
character is different from all the interiors we have seen up until now:
there is a large, circular table, cushions on the chairs and armchairs,
and a sofa-bed with sheets strewn all over it. A short man in glasses
enters the room wearing a dressing-gown over his pyjamas. He sits
down opposite STEFAN *without saying anything and spreads out his*
hands in an emphatic gesture. STEFAN *understands what he means.*

STEFAN: I woke you up. I'm sorry, it was stupid of me.

[206]

GRZEGORZ: It's not that simple, you see. I've rung around a few
people, but all they remember is that you abandoned us
when we needed you most. And that's all they've got to say
now that you've turned to us for help.

STEFAN: I wouldn't have come if it wasn't for Ewa. You've met
her, haven't you? She begged me. She's frightened of what
might happen to them.

GRZEGORZ: There's really very little I can do. I'll try to put out
an announcement on the TV news. That's all, I'm afraid.

19

The small van pulls up outside Wojtek's house. It is now dawn and
WOJTEK *walks quietly up the path to the front door. The flat is empty.*
Where ANIA *was sleeping earlier, there is only the check-blanket. He*
notices the grey file spread out on the table by the typewriter. On top is
a small sheet of paper with a verse on it, beginning with the words
'Mother and Daughter . . .'

WOJTEK: That's what I was afraid of. They've run away.
  (*He picks up the telephone receiver and dials. We can hear a brief*
  dialling tone: the number is engaged. He dials again. It is still
  engaged.)

20

MAJKA *is standing in the telephone kiosk on the station platform with*
the sleepy ANIA *in her arms.*

MAJKA: Your two hours are up.

EWA: Yes. Two and a half, actually.
  (EWA *is matter-of-fact and to the point – she has evidently*
  decided to take the matter in hand.)
  Now listen to me. Come home and bring Ania with you.
  Your father will sell the car and his organs. You'll be able to
  buy a flat and do whatever you like, we won't interfere. You
  can see Ania as often as you like and go wherever you want
  on holiday with her. You'll be able to have her on Sundays,

you can go with her to the cinema, you can take her wherever you want. Ania will belong to the both of us. While I'm still alive, that is. After that, she will be yours.

(MAJKA *listens calmly to this speech and says nothing.*)

Is there anything else you want?

MAJKA: Yes. Two million dollars.

(*Silence on the other end of the line.*)

Did you hear me?

EWA: Now you're just being stupid . . .

MAJKA: Did you understand what I said to you earlier?

(EWA *now speaks in a conciliatory, almost heartfelt tone of voice.*)

EWA: Majka, I can't. You know I can't live without her.

(ANIA *is falling asleep over* MAJKA'S *shoulder.*)

MAJKA: Then you'll never see us again. Ania is falling asleep on my shoulder and I don't give a damn any more. I'm going to count to five. If you don't agree before then, I'm putting down the receiver.

(MAJKA *counts quickly, not really giving her mother a chance.*)

One, two, three, four, five.

(*She immediately puts down the receiver.* EWA, *shocked, stands holding her end of the telephone.*)

EWA: Majka! I agree! Majka!

(*Only after a few seconds does she realize that her words are floundering unheard along several kilometres of telephone cable. Distraught, she replaces the receiver. The phone rings again almost at exactly the same moment.*)

Majka, come back! I agree, do you hear?

(WOJTEK *listens to her abrupt monologue with astonishment. As* EWA *pauses for breath, he quickly cuts in.*)

WOJTEK: I'm sorry, it's me, Wojtek.

(EWA *does not understand what is going on.*)

EWA: Who?

WOJTEK: Wojtek.

EWA: Wojtek? . . .

WOJTEK: Yes. It's me.

(EWA *begins to put two and two together.*)

EWA: You were lying to us, weren't you? You lied when we rang you before!

[208]

WOJTEK: Yes . . . I lied.

EWA: Is she there?

WOJTEK: She was. I told her she should take Ania home, and then I went off to fetch the van. I was afraid, you know what she's like. She ran off and took Ania with her while I was out picking it up.

EWA: Where's she gone? She said she didn't give a damn any more.

WOJTEK: I don't know. She can't have gone too far. I'll start looking for her in the car on the left-hand side of the railway track. You try the other side.

EWA: The one near your house?

WOJTEK: Yes.

21

It is now getting lighter. MAJKA *walks across a bridge with the sleeping* ANIA *in her arms. She stops, props the little girl up against a railing, and looks down at the rushing stream below. A car can be heard approaching. She takes* ANIA *and runs to the other end of the bridge and hides underneath it, slipping on the muddy embankment. She looks up towards the little Nysa van as it crosses the bridge.*

22

The small waiting room on the station platform is open. After stepping around a DRUNK *lying on the floor,* MAJKA *walks over to the ticket-desk. She has to knock several times on the cracked glass before a dishevelled* WOMAN *wrapped up in a blanket finally appears.*

MAJKA: What time's the train?

WOMAN: Where to?

MAJKA: It doesn't matter . . . to wherever.

(*Yawning, the* WOMAN *takes a good look at her.*)

WOMAN: Today's Sunday. Two hours' time.

(MAJKA *points towards the drunken man.*)

MAJKA: Is he all right?

[209]

WOMAN: His breath's so strong you could light a match with it.
He'll be all right.

(*The* WOMAN *adjusts the blanket more tightly around her
shoulders and* MAJKA *walks away from the window.* ANIA *is
heavy – she is sleeping.* MAJKA *nudges the* DRUNK *with her free
hand. He shifts sluggishly to one side and mumbles something.*)

DRUNK: The first's better, the second's worse . . .

MAJKA: Where's the main road from here?

(*The* DRUNK *opens his eyes, looks at her for a second, and then
drops off to sleep again.* MAJKA *can hear the whistle of an
approaching train. She runs out on to the platform. A steam-
powered locomotive is approaching the station, travelling slowly
and with dignity.* MAJKA *waves her hand as if she were trying to
hitch a lift. The locomotive slowly passes the frantically waving*
MAJKA *almost as if there was no driver in the front, and proceeds
majestically on its journey. The* WOMAN *runs out from the ticket
office. We can see now that she is actually quite young, but is
overweight and does not make a very good job of looking after
herself.*)

WOMAN: Man trouble, is it?

(MAJKA *does not understand.*)

On the run from your man?

MAJKA: No, just generally.

(*The* WOMAN *nods her head understandingly. She points to the
blanket.*)

WOMAN: Come and sleep in here. It's warmer.

(MAJKA *goes back with* ANIA *to the waiting room and from there
walks through the little doors leading to the small room behind the
ticket-desk. It is cramped. She positions* ANIA *with difficulty on
the narrow little bed. Through the window, she can see a Nysa
with its headlamps on driving up the station approach. She lies
back and cuddles up to her sleeping daughter.*)

23

*A large, dark Fiat is travelling along the main highway. A Nysa van
approaches from the opposite direction. They flash their lights at each*

other. The large Fiat brakes and they stop alongside one another on the
empty highway. EWA *gets out of the Fiat,* WOJTEK *out of the van.*
They meet in the middle of the road.
EWA:Nothing?
WOJTEK: Nothing.
EWA: I'm worried.
     (WOJTEK *says nothing and looks to the ground.*)
     Let's take a look around the stations.
WOJTEK: There won't have been a train yet. It's Sunday.
EWA: We never seem to bring you much luck, do we?
WOJTEK: We're going to try the forest. On the Otwock road.
EWA: What about me? Which way should I go?

24

It is light by now. A couple of people are waiting on the platform.
EWA *and* STEFAN *run up on to the platform from an underground*
passageway. Looking around, EWA *goes into the waiting room and*
knocks energetically at the cracked window. The WOMAN, *with a*
glass of tea in her hand, appears on the other side.
EWA: Have you seen a girl with a young child?
WOMAN: Are you from the police?
EWA: I'm looking for a girl and a small child. She's young and
     wears glasses, with a girl of about six. She's carrying a large
     sack.
     (ANIA *wakes and can hear* EWA's *voice. She leans out over*
     MAJKA.)
WOMAN: They were here about two hours ago, but then they left.
EWA: Which direction did they go?
WOMAN: She asked about the main road . . . I don't know.
     (ANIA *is now leaning out over the bed and can see* EWA's *face*
     through the ticket-desk window. She speaks softly, declaring a
     fact which is obvious to her.)
ANIA: Mum . . . Mummy.
     (MAJKA *opens her eyes and smiles. She hears the word 'Mummy'*
     repeated for the third time, this time more loudly. She sees ANIA
     gazing at a spot which is invisible to her, since her back is turned

to the window, and then watches as ANIA *slowly slips down off the bed and runs out of the small back-room, calling for her mother.* EWA *breaks off her conversation with the* WOMAN *and opens the door.* ANIA *throws herself at her.*)

EWA: Ania . . . Anka . . .

(MAJKA *gets up from the narrow bed. She lifts up her sack and throws it over her shoulder. The whistle of an approaching train can be heard in the distance.* MAJKA *contemplates her mother's happiness.*)

Majka . . .

(*Only one passenger gets off the train after it has stopped at the station platform: the man on crutches. He carefully lets himself down from the carriage and looks over towards the waiting room.* MAJKA *moves off towards the train, running past* EWA, *who has* ANIA *in her arms, and* STEFAN. EWA *shouts after her.*)

Majka! Majka!

(EWA *runs after her with* ANIA *in her arms, but* MAJKA *has managed at the last moment to leap on to the moving train. The man on crutches vanishes into the darkness of the underground passageway.*)

DECALOGUE EIGHT

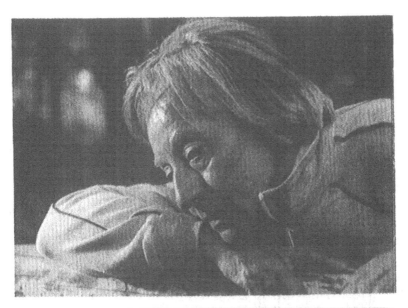

The cast and crew of *Decalogue Eight* included:

ZOFIA	Maria Koscialkowska
ELZBIETA	Teresa Marczewska
Director of Photography and Cameraman	Andrzej Jaroszewicz
Producer	Ryszard Chutkowski
Composer	Zbigniew Preisner
Artistic Director	Halina Dobrowolska
Sound	Malgorzata Jaworska
Lighting	Wieslawa Dembinska
Film Editor	Ewa Smal
Production Managers	Pawel Mantorski
	Wlodzimierz Bendych
Costume Designers	Malgorzata Obloza
	Hanna Cwiklo
Director	Krzysztof Kieślowski

Stills: Maria Koscialkowska as Zofia
Teresa Marczewska as Elzbieta

I

An early spring morning. A woman steps out of the stairwell entrance. She is about sixty years old, has short, grey hair, and moves briskly: a real lady who does not cause those around her to feel inferior on account of her class. An unshaven MAN *carrying a small suitcase is advancing towards her in the opposite direction.*

ZOFIA: Good morning! Are you off on one of your trips? Or on your way home?

MAN: On my way home. Night train from Szczecin. I'm telling you . . .

ZOFIA: Was it worthwhile? . . .

(ZOFIA *is fond of the* MAN *and knows all about his hobby.*)

MAN: Series commemorating the German flight over the North Pole. Nineteen thirty-one . . . Polarfahrt.

ZOFIA: By Zeppelin perhaps?

MAN: By three Zeppelins. I'm telling you . . .

ZOFIA: You'll have to drop by and show me them some day.

(ZOFIA *smiles and briskly walks off towards the little wood which we saw in the first and fourth stories of our series.*)

2

ZOFIA *reaches the Indian wigwam in the children's play area. She has taken off her coat and is now in a tracksuit. She begins her daily, morning jog, the route taking her in circles around the estate, during which she does simple gymnastic exercises. A* YOUNG MAN *is running towards her in the opposite direction. He steps to the side of the pathway to let her run past, but at the same time pulls something out from under his tracksuit: a book with a blue cover.*

YOUNG MAN: A friend brought it over from Paris. I was wondering whether you might be able to write a couple of words . . .

(ZOFIA *is intrigued and takes the book from him.*)

ZOFIA: This is the first copy I've seen . . . a weak translation,

[215]

though. Do you have something to write with?
(*The* YOUNG MAN *pulls out a pen.* ZOFIA *inscribes a couple of sentences, returns the book and the pen, and continues on her way.*)

3

Now back in her coat, ZOFIA *opens her letterbox. She takes out a pile of domestic and foreign letters and sorts through them while waiting for the lift to arrive. She tears several open straightaway and throws them into a waste-paper bin, but takes the rest with her and climbs into the lift.*

Zofia's apartment is fairly modestly furnished. It is full of books, papers and newspapers, but is clean, despite the mess. The most unfussy furniture belongs to a room at the back of the flat which ZOFIA *keeps locked. A picture of the Virgin Mary of Czestochowa can be seen hanging up on the wall, but apart from some flowers standing in a vase on the table, there is little sign of it being inhabited.* ZOFIA *throws out the flowers, changes the water in the earthenware pot, and replaces them with a bunch of asters. She puts one of the letters which she had opened earlier on the bedside table, alongside a pile of other envelopes already lying there. She then closes the door and locks it.*

A small piece of paper is attached by a magnet to the refrigerator door. She examines what is written on it and then repeats to herself quietly:
ZOFIA: One slice of cheese. One lettuce leaf. Coffee, no sugar . . .
(*She takes the products out of the fridge. She tries to light the gas-ring by pressing the ignition button several times in quick succession, but has again forgotten that there are problems with gas on the estate and so plugs in the metal heating-coil and places it in the kettle.*)

4

ZOFIA *is collecting her Trabant-Combi from the car-repair workshop, where it is standing in the forecourt. The* OWNER *accompanies her over to the car.*
ZOFIA: What was wrong with it?
OWNER: Nothing serious, just a blocked carburettor. But there

have been a couple of dents and a cracked headlamp since I
last saw it. You really must be more careful on the roads in
future.

ZOFIA: It was on a roundabout – I never saw the tractor coming, I
swear it. How much do I owe you?

OWNER: It's my pleasure. Regular customers and all that . . .
(ZOFIA *climbs into the car. The* OWNER *comes over to her once
more.*)
My daughter is trying to get a place at the university . . .

ZOFIA: Really? Good for her.

OWNER: You wouldn't by any chance know an assistant lecturer
or someone who might be prepared to give her a few extra
lessons before the exam?

ZOFIA: Naturally assistants do give private lessons – they have to
make a living somehow. But I am afraid I don't think such
methods make any difference. Good day.
(*She moves off, but then stops and reverses.*)
Perhaps I do owe you something after all?

OWNER: You're one of our regular customers, Professor. Please
don't mention it.

5

ZOFIA *parks in the university courtyard. Young and old alike bow
their heads politely in greeting.* ZOFIA, *wearing a two-piece suit and
training shoes, and with a large briefcase tucked under her arm, greets
them back with a smile.*

6

*A similar scene along one of the Department corridors. Students sitting
on the window-ledges leap off in order to greet her respectfully.*

7

The Department secretary's office. A middle-aged lady abruptly interrupts her typing.

WOMAN: The Dean wondered if he could have a brief word with you.

(ZOFIA *walks into the Dean's office. He is sitting at a small table and entertaining a dark-haired woman of some forty odd years with a cup of coffee. They both rise to their feet,* ZOFIA *greets them both, and the* DEAN *introduces her to the woman with dark hair.*)

DEAN: (*In English*) Mrs Elizabeth Loranz from New York.

ZOFIA: But we have already met, if my memory serves me correctly. Aren't you my translator in the States?

ELZBIETA: That's right, Professor.

(*Her Polish is quite good – the* DEAN *is surprised.*)

DEAN: And here I was getting my tongue in a twist, all for nothing . . .

ELZBIETA: You were doing marvellously.

DEAN: Mrs Loranz is here as part of a cultural-exchange programme. She finds your work very interesting and wants if possible to participate in a couple of your classes.

ZOFIA: It will be a great pleasure. Are we starting from today?

8

The amphitheatre with its tiers of seats is not large but the auditorium is packed. ZOFIA *quietens the chattering students with a friendly glance.*

ZOFIA: We have several guests here again today. Mr Muabwe has come over from Nigeria and does not speak Polish, so perhaps one of you would like to volunteer as a translator.

(*A* STUDENT IN SPECTACLES *puts up his hand and goes to sit down next to the grinning Mr Muabwe.*)

Messrs Toreczik, Nemelaszi and Gardos from the University of Budapest you already know – they have been taking part

[218]

in our classes for several months now. Mrs Elzbieta Loranz is from New York – she speaks Polish and works for an institute which researches the fate of Jewish war survivors. We shall continue where we left off before: ethical hell. Who would like to volunteer first?

(*It is late afternoon and the auditorium is bathed in the red, angular rays of the sun.* ZOFIA *is sitting in the shade. Her eyes come to rest for a moment on* ELZBIETA, *who is fiddling unconsciously with a gold chain hanging around her neck.*)

Let me remind you that we are here to consider two examples taken from the sphere of politics, and one which for simplicity's sake we shall call the sphere of social convention.

FEMALE STUDENT I: Let us imagine the following situation. A man is dying of cancer . . .

(*The auditorium explodes with laughter.*)

ZOFIA: This is the third story involving cancer this term.

FEMALE STUDENT I: It's not important what he is actually dying of and in any case he is not the hero of this particular story – he is only dying. This man is being treated by a first-rate doctor who, and this is important, believes in God. This doctor lives in the same apartment block as his patient, and the wife of the dying man starts to pester him to try and find out what his chances of survival are. The doctor is unable and unwilling to tell her. He has seen too many people live even though medical science had given them up for dead. The wife of the dying man gets more and more persistent. As it turns out, she has a very special reason for wanting to know what will happen to him. She is pregnant with another man's child. Her husband knows nothing of this. She was unable to have children previously – she loves the unborn child as much as she loves her husband. If he lives, she will feel morally obliged to have an abortion. If he dies, she can go ahead and give birth to the baby. The doctor is told all this and holds the fate of the child in his hands. If he tells her that her husband is going to live, then he signs the child's death warrant. If he tells her that her husband is going to die, then the child lives. That, in broad outline, is the story.

[219]

(The students have forgotten that they burst out laughing when she first began to tell the story and are now listening intently and busy making notes.)

ZOFIA: I know how this story ends, as it happens. In order to make your task more difficult, I can tell you that the child is alive and that this, perhaps, is the most important –

(ELZBIETA, interrupting ZOFIA, gets up from her seat and brings her tape-recorder a little closer. She explains why she has had to move.)

ELZBIETA: I'm afraid she's too far away . . . I can't record from there.

ZOFIA: *(Repeating)* I was saying that the child is alive and that I consider this to be the most important thing. I want you now to try to decide for yourselves the character traits of the main protagonists in the story and also the motives for their actions . . . Is there anybody else? Or can we make a start on analysing our previous stories?

(ELZBIETA puts her hand up. ZOFIA smiles.)

Yes.

ELZBIETA: If I may . . .

ZOFIA: By all means. Everyone has equal rights here.

ELZBIETA: I also have a certain story which I would like to tell everyone.

ZOFIA: I am sure it will be most interesting.

ELZBIETA: You may perhaps consider it to have one drawback in that it took place in the past. But it does also have one virtue: it is a true story.

ZOFIA: Not all the dilemmas we are here to consider have to be from contemporary life.

ELZBIETA: This happened during the wartime occupation.

ZOFIA: Excellent. The events of war often appear in a much sharper focus than those of the present day.

(The students are intrigued by their overseas guest. She has dark eyes and dark, curly hair, and tells her story sitting down, perhaps because she considers this to be a privilege of seniority, or perhaps because this is what she is accustomed to.)

ELZBIETA: It is the winter of 1943. The hero of this story is a six-year-old Jewish girl. She has been sheltered up to now in

[220]

a Polish family's cellar, but suddenly finds she has to move –
the villa in Zoliborz where she is staying is about to be
commandeered by the Gestapo. Friends of the girl's father,
who has stayed behind in the ghetto, try to find a new
hiding-place for her. They have one possibility, but the
future guardians have laid down one condition: the little girl
must have formal documentation proving she has been
baptized.

(ZOFIA, *who until now has been making brief notes on the story,*
looks up. She discovers that ELZBIETA *is looking directly at her*
and is in fact telling her the story rather than her students. She
lowers her eyes and continues making notes.)

The girl's protectors thus start searching for a couple who
will agree to become her fictional godparents. It is a pure
formality, but the godparents must be genuine, living
people. They also start looking for a priest who would be
willing to give the girl a fictitious baptism.

STUDENT IN SPECTACLES: Was this a problem?

(*He asks the question on behalf of Mr Muabwe, for whom he is*
translating.)

ELZBIETA: No, there were plenty of priests who were willing to
assist. The problem was to track them down, arrange a time,
and agree all the necessary details.

(ELZBIETA *waits for the bespectacled interlocutor to translate her*
reply. Mr Muabwe raises his hand as a gesture of thanks and
smiles contentedly: he has understood.)

In the end, everything is arranged. It is a cold, winter
evening. The girl and her guardian arrive at the place where
her fictional godparents live. They are a young couple. The
girl is frozen, having spent the entire afternoon threading her
way through the city in order to reach their house. Her
guardian, a man, is nervous. Their hosts offer them a cup of
tea. The girl is desperate for a hot drink, but time is running
short, the priest is waiting, and curfew is not long off. But
despite this, their hosts, instead of putting on their coats, ask
them to sit down.

(ZOFIA *is behaving a little strangely. She is sitting rigidly still*
and stares at ELZBIETA *with a stony expression.*

ELZBIETA *is now addressing her directly*.)
So they both sit down at the table. The host is pacing nervously around the table. The hostess sits down in the chair opposite the girl's guardian and tells them what they have found so difficult to explain. They have to withdraw their promise of help. After a great deal of thought and consideration, they have decided that they cannot go against their religion which, while admittedly commanding acts of charity, also forbids the bearing of false witness. To bear false witness, even in a matter of such importance, cannot be reconciled with their religious principles. That is all they have to say. The girl and her guardian get to their feet. 'Stay and drink a little of your tea,' says the young lady. The girl takes a sip but puts the glass back down again after glancing towards her guardian. Later, at the bottom of the stairs, the young girl looks impatiently across at her guardian, who is standing by the entrance gate and staring out into the night and the empty street. 'Come on,' she says, but her companion does not move. 'Come on, it'll soon be the curfew.'

(ELZBIETA *has concluded her story. There is silence in the auditorium for a few moments*.)

ZOFIA: Was there anyone else in the flat at the time?

ELZBIETA: Yes. An elderly man. He sat with his back to us – I think he may have been in a wheelchair.

ZOFIA: Are there any other specific details you remember?

ELZBIETA: The tea-cups were made of good-quality porcelain, each one unique. There was a green oil lamp on the table, but it had not been lit – they had switched on the light bulb overhead instead. The windows were blacked out with newspaper. The man held his hands in his pockets for the entire two or three minutes of the conversation. That's all I remember.

ZOFIA: This was in Warsaw?

ELZBIETA: In Outer Mokotow, Odyniec.

(ZOFIA *leans back in her chair. Her hands are shaking slightly. She picks up her pen and her hands regain some of their steadiness*.)

[222]

ZOFIA: Does anybody have any questions? No one? Any doubts?
(*A small, slender girl puts up her hand.*)
FEMALE STUDENT II: The Decalogue only mentions the bearing
of false witness against your neighbour. But this wasn't a
case involving a neighbour. If the couple really were devout
Catholics, then the reason they gave couldn't have been the
real one.
ELZBIETA: This was the only reason they gave me. At the time it
seemed genuine.
(ZOFIA *now turns to* ELZBIETA.)
ZOFIA: What other reasons do you think there could have been,
Mrs Loranz . . .?
ELZBIETA: I really don't know. As far as I am concerned, there is
no justification for such a decision.
(*The young* LAD IN SPECTACLES *puts his hand up on his own
initiative.*)
LAD IN SPECTACLES: Maybe the reason was fear. For instance, if
a Jewish family had been discovered in the same block only
an hour earlier and had been executed along with the Polish
family who were protecting them, then they could have been
afraid.
ELZBIETA: Yes. Fear, yes. But is that any justification as far as
you are concerned? Fear?
LAD IN SPECTACLES: I'm only suggesting a possible motive. I'm
not debating whether –
ZOFIA: I'm sorry, but I think we have gone as far as we can on this
one. I want each of you to decide for yourselves the
characters of the protagonists, and the motives for their
actions. Thank you, and we'll meet again to discuss it in two
weeks' time.
(*She rises to her feet and is the first to leave the auditorium. Only
after she has left do the students get up from their seats.*)

9

The secretary's office is now dark and deserted. ZOFIA *switches on the
light, but then switches it off again almost immediately. A faint orange*

glow from the setting sun filters gently through the window. ZOFIA *sits in the low-slung armchair and grips the sides. This lasts for some time. She gets up, picks up the briefcase with her usual sense of purpose, and walks out of the room.*

10

ZOFIA *walks along the corridor, which is deserted and badly lit at this time of day. She can dimly make out a figure seated on one of the window-ledges ahead of her smoking a cigarette. She approaches nearer – it is* ELZBIETA. ZOFIA *stops a couple of paces away from her. They look at each other for a few moments.*

ZOFIA: It wasn't in Mokotow, was it?

ELZBIETA: No, it was in Srodmiescie.

ZOFIA: On Nowogrodska Street.

ELZBIETA: Yes.

    (ZOFIA *is searching for words.*)

ZOFIA: So it is you.

    (ELZBIETA *replies completely calmly.*)

ELZBIETA: Yes. It is me.

ZOFIA: And you are still alive . . . My whole life I thought . . . how many times I must have seen someone playing with a gold chain and thought: Holy God . . .

ELZBIETA: I stopped doing that years ago.

    (ZOFIA *suddenly smiles.*)

ZOFIA: You're alive.

ELZBIETA: I hid with people in Praga who were relations of the man who brought me to see you that time. They used to make moonshine vodka – I spent two years living with the stink of fermented potatoes. They're with me now in the States, but he's no longer alive . . .

ZOFIA: So you came to see how I would react, to your story.

ELZBIETA: I had wanted to tell you earlier, while you were in the States. I was going to write, or fly over. If you hadn't said what you did about the child, I would have never . . .

ZOFIA: Yes. I see.

ELZBIETA: There is a theory that saviours have certain character traits in common, like the people they save. I wonder if one can isolate these traits to create a model of the person who is capable of saving others and the person who isn't. A sort of reverse victimology . . .

ZOFIA: I dare say you are right. Such traits undoubtedly exist.

ELZBIETA: You have them.

ZOFIA: I do?

ELZBIETA: Your conduct after the incident with me is well known. Quite a few of my people would not be alive today if it were not for you.

ZOFIA: You are exaggerating.

ELZBIETA: No. I have the figures. Interesting, isn't it, that the girl was so quick to see through the falsity of their explanation, which was only superficially Catholic.

ZOFIA: There is nothing odd about it at all. People here are interested in Catholicism.

ELZBIETA: It took me several years longer to work it out.
(ELZBIETA *has finished her cigarette and looks around, seeking to throw the stub out of the window.*)

ZOFIA: There is an ashtray over there.

ELZBIETA: But you don't smoke.

ZOFIA: But I have eyes in my head. Where are you staying? Perhaps I could drop you off? I remember you driving me all over New York.

ELZBIETA: The Victoria Hotel. It's only three hundred metres away – not a very fair exchange, I'm afraid.
(ZOFIA *moves closer.*)

ZOFIA: Perhaps you would come and have supper with me?

II

ZOFIA *opens the door to the Trabant and moves aside to let* ELZBIETA *climb in. She starts the engine.*

12

The Trabant stops in front of an arched entrance on Nowogrodzka Street. ZOFIA *switches off the engine.* ELZBIETA *looks around, intrigued.*

ELZBIETA: Is this where you live?

ZOFIA: No.

ELZBIETA: Then why . . . Ah, of course . . . Is this where it was?

ZOFIA: Yes. 'Come on, it'll soon be curfew' . . . this is where it was.

(ELZBIETA *climbs out of the car and walks through the archway. It is quiet and deserted, her heels echoing like rifle reports against the concrete paving stones. A small shrine of the Virgin Mary stands with a small, burning candle in the courtyard.* ELZBIETA *stands for a moment in the middle. From somewhere in the near distance she can hear a telephone ringing and a voice shouting, 'I'm not yelling, I just can't stand it any longer,' and then trailing off. From another window she can hear the beginning of the sports programme on the television.* ELZBIETA'S *face clouds over. She walks slowly out of the courtyard, past the gate, and stands to one side of the arched entrance, concealed among the shadows. She can see* ZOFIA *looking over anxiously – she has got out of the car and is now standing next to it.* ELZBIETA *does not move and* ZOFIA *is not sure whether she can see her or not. She cautiously walks over to the arch, convinces herself it is* ELZBIETA *and breathes a deep sigh of relief.*)

ELZBIETA: Let's go.

ZOFIA: There was something I wanted to tell you . . .

(*She draws closer and wants to touch her, but* ELZBIETA *draws back sharply.*)

Is anything the matter?

ELZBIETA: Come on, it'll soon be curfew.

13

The Trabant parks outside the block amid a cloud of exhaust fumes. ZOFIA *locks the little doors.*

ZOFIA: I only picked it up from the garage today . . . What on earth
could have gone wrong again?

ELZBIETA: I know nothing about (*She checks the make of the car.*)
Trabants . . .
(*She is willing to carry Zofia's large briefcase for her, but* ZOFIA
refuses her offer and moves off towards the stairwell entrance.)

14

ELZBIETA *puts a book back on the shelf, returns to the kitchen, and
watches as* ZOFIA *prepares a modest supper.*

ELZBIETA: I had no idea.

ZOFIA: Of what?

ELZBIETA: That you lived like this – the flat, the car, the
briefcase. . . .

ZOFIA: I have everything I need. You may not believe me, but
others have less.

ELZBIETA: I believe you.
(*She examines a sliced radish.*)

ZOFIA: I am on a diet . . . and I am afraid I wasn't expecting guests.
(*They sit down for supper.*)

ELZBIETA: You can't possibly be the same woman I remember
from the war. Your thoughts, your books, even you yourself
are so far removed from the sort of arguments she used
then . . .

ZOFIA: If you flew all this way expecting to discover some
mysterious explanation for what happened, then I am afraid
you will be cruelly disappointed. The reason I was forced to
abandon, well yes, abandon a Jewish child is really quite banal.
The man who was pacing around the room with his hands in
his pockets was my husband. He died in 1952, in prison.

ELZBIETA: I know.

ZOFIA: During the war he was in the KDW.* We had received

---

* KDW: Komisja Diwersji Wywiadowczej, the counter-espionage section of
Poland's Home Army, the clandestine military resistance to the Nazi occupation
during the Second World War.

information that the people who were due to hide the girl were agents of the Gestapo, and that through her, her guardian and the priest, they would eventually have been led to us. That is the whole secret for you.

(ELZBIETA *is surprised at the simplicity of the explanation.*)

ELZBIETA: It all sounds terribly simple . . .

ZOFIA: We could not really have told the girl's guardian because we did not know him. So we had to think of an excuse, any excuse, which as you saw earlier even students of today can see through. But you believed it and lived with the certainty for the last forty years. And I . . . never knew you were still alive . . . in fact I took you for dead and believed that for forty years. What is more, the information we received about these people turned out to be false, although they only narrowly escaped execution because of it.

ELZBIETA: None of this had occurred to me . . .

(ZOFIA *smiles bitterly to herself.*)

ZOFIA: If I was to say that evening has haunted me ever since . . . I sacrificed you, despatched you to almost certain death in full knowledge of the consequences, in the name of values which I believed in passionately at the time.

ELZBIETA: And now? What do you believe in now?

ZOFIA: I believe there is no idea or cause, nothing, more important than the life of a child. From life . . .

ELZBIETA: Yes, I've always thought the same myself. But what do you tell your students? How to live?

ZOFIA: I am not there to tell them anything. I am there to help them reach their own conclusions.

ELZBIETA: About what?

ZOFIA: About Good. I believe everyone has it in them. The world gives birth to either Good or Evil. That particular evening in 1943 did not bring out the Good in me.

ELZBIETA: And who is the judge of Good and Evil?

ZOFIA: He, who is in all of us.

ELZBIETA: I've never read anything in your work about God.

ZOFIA: I am reluctant to use the word 'God'. One can believe without having to use certain words. Man was created in order to choose . . . if so, perhaps we can leave God out of it.

228

ELZBIETA: And in his place?

ZOFIA: Here, on earth – solitude. And up there? If there really is no life after death, if there really is nothing, then . . .

(*There is a ring at the front doorbell.* ELZBIETA *looks over towards* ZOFIA, *who smiles apologetically and gets up to answer the door. An elderly* MAN *walks into the flat, the same one we met earlier on his way home from Szczecin.* ZOFIA *moves aside to let him through. He is already pulling out the three stamps wrapped in cellophane from his little address-book. He gives them to* ZOFIA *and only then notices that there is somebody else in the room.*)

MAN: Forgive me . . . I didn't realize you had guests. Good evening.

(*He greets* ELZBIETA *with a little bow.* ZOFIA *looks at the stamps.*)

ZOFIA: They're beautiful. Really . . .

MAN: I thought I'd drop in to show you . . . forgive me. If you happen to bump into my son by any chance, perhaps you would tell him.

ZOFIA: Of course, Polarfahrt, three Zeppelins, 1931. Elzbieta, would you like to have a look?

ELZBIETA: It's all right, thank you . . .

(ZOFIA *gives him back the stamps and the* MAN *leaves the flat.*) A neighbour?

ZOFIA: Yes . . . You know the doctor and his patient we were talking about today – they live in this block.

ELZBIETA: Interesting block.

ZOFIA: Like any other. Everyone has a story to tell, and so on.

ELZBIETA: The people . . . who I was supposed to go and hide with . . . do you still know them?

ZOFIA: Yes.

ELZBIETA: Do you think it might be possible to go and see them?

ZOFIA: I'll run you over tomorrow. He works in a small tailor's outfit. But I'll let you go in by yourself. The last time I saw him was after the war, and he still hadn't come to terms with the fact that his integrity had been questioned. I told them I was very sorry. What more could I say?

ELZBIETA: The girl mentioned the Decalogue . . .

ZOFIA: Yes, it had been transgressed – the same commandment about bearing false witness against your neighbour. Only that other people were affected in the end.
(ZOFIA *smiles. She adds some water from the kettle into the tea-cups, which are made of elegant porcelain, each one unique.*) It all seems so ridiculous, everything repeating itself in circles. The same commandments, the same transgressions, especially in our day and age . . .

ELZBIETA: People always say 'especially in our day and age'.

ZOFIA: True. But the mess is getting worse. Do you have the same problem in the States?

ELZBIETA: Yes. I suppose we are looking for a 'way' just like everyone else. What this 'way' is, I'm not so sure. (*She smiles.*) Thank you for supper. I must be going.
(ZOFIA *looks up at her from her armchair.*)

ZOFIA: It would give me great pleasure if you stayed the night here. I have a spare room . . . it's not often I have guests.
(ZOFIA *rises to her feet and shows her guest to the room which she keeps locked. She switches on the bedside lamp, making the crude furnishings and someone's physical absence even more apparent.* ELZBIETA *watches as* ZOFIA *takes the black quilt off the bed and arranges the sheets.* ZOFIA *then puts out the bathroom light and checks to see the front door is locked before walking back to Elzbieta's room and looking through the gap in the door:* ELZBIETA *is kneeling by the bed, her hands clasped in prayer.*)

15

ZOFIA *is running along the path in her tracksuit. She is running more quickly and energetically than usual. She runs to the bottom of a small embankment and leans on a tree to get her breath back. There is nothing extraordinary about this – she is simply taking a rest after more intensive exercise than usual. She looks around, not having run this far before. On the other side of the embankment, the wood yields to a kind of park with a small wooden platform. A strange little human figure can be seen on the podium.* ZOFIA *has to approach closer in order to identify what it is exactly, but the closer she approaches, the more*

*bizarre this human shape appears to be. She finally walks right up to
it. A* MAN, *who has bent over so far backwards that his head is
between his knees, is on the middle of the podium. Moreover, this head
is smiling at* ZOFIA, *if 'smile' is the right word, since the head is at
roughly the same height as his ankles.* ZOFIA *takes another step nearer.*

RUBBER MAN: What do you think?

> (ZOFIA *finds the idea of conversation with such a head completely
> unnerving, especially since the* MAN, *without straightening, hops
> several steps nearer.*)

What do you think?

ZOFIA: What are you doing?

RUBBER MAN: There's a guy on television . . . who everyone
reckons is the best. People compete against him and I want
to prove that I'm better.

ZOFIA: Could you . . . show me how you look normally?

> (*The* MAN *straightens in one unbroken movement. He is a tall,
> handsome young man. He looks at his watch.*)

RUBBER MAN: I've already done better by thirty-eight seconds.
I'm sorry.

ZOFIA: How did you learn to do it?

RUBBER MAN: It's a question of practice. Anyone can do it . . .
try bending backwards yourself.

> (ZOFIA *bends over backwards as far as she can, but it is not very
> far.*)

A little bit more, yes . . .

> (ZOFIA *tries her best while the* RUBBER MAN *watches her,
> standing expertly to one side.*)

Can't you manage any further?

ZOFIA: No.

RUBBER MAN: Well, I'm afraid you're past it then. Sorry.

> (*The* RUBBER MAN, *with one movement, rolls himself up into a
> little ball again.* ZOFIA *returns to her jogging. A dog is sitting on
> the spot where the road to the estate turns off the main road. We
> have seen it before – it is the same dog who was fed a sandwich by
> the taxi-driver in story number five.* ZOFIA *walks up to the dog,
> stops several metres away, and then inches her way towards it,
> step by step, while looking it straight in the eye. The dog makes no
> move towards her, but curls his lip after a couple of steps and*

warns her with a throaty growl. ZOFIA *stops. She makes a mark
in the earth with her foot and compares it with yesterday's. She
has clearly managed to get a little closer this time.*)

ZOFIA: See? Nearer already . . . and I'll be even nearer tomorrow,
just you see . . .

(*The dog curls its lips again.* ZOFIA *retreats as slowly as she had
approached and then, when at a safe distance, resumes her usual
brisk stride in the direction of the block.*)

16

ZOFIA *tries to enter the flat as quietly as possible but turns on hearing a
noise.* ELZBIETA *is standing smiling in the kitchen, already dressed. A
shopping bag lies on the kitchen table and we can see a bottle of milk
and fresh bread rolls inside.*

ELZBIETA: Are you allowed to have anything apart from (*She
reads from the card stuck to the fridge door*) 'five grammes of
cheese and coffee without sugar'?

ZOFIA: I'll make an exception.

ELZBIETA: How about a normal breakfast? Eggs, bread rolls and
butter?

ZOFIA: Fine.

(ELZBIETA *tries to light the gas, without success.*)
The gas isn't working.
(*She points to the metal heating coil.* ELZBIETA *pours water into
the saucepan and adds the eggs.*)

ELZBIETA: What about the milk?

ZOFIA: We'll have to have it unboiled.

(ELZBIETA *pours some milk into the mugs.* ZOFIA *notices how
naturally she copes in the kitchen.*)
How many children do you have?

ELZBIETA: Three. The eldest is a doctor. The next eldest is in
Canada – he writes about once a year. The youngest has just
given up his studies. I also have a grandson.

ZOFIA: You certainly know how to slice bread rolls . . . I have a
son.

ELZBIETA: Was his room . . . the one I was sleeping in . . .?

ZOFIA: Yes, it was.
  (ZOFIA *responds naturally, as if this was no longer a sensitive issue.*)
ELZBIETA: But he no longer lives here, I take it?
ZOFIA: He didn't want to be with me.
ELZBIETA: Where is he?
  (ZOFIA *smiles.*)
ZOFIA: To put it simply . . . a long way away.

17

The Trabant crosses the bridge, past the zebra crossing, then turns left, then right and pulls up outside several small workshops. ZOFIA *points one of them out to* ELZBIETA.

18

ELZBIETA *looks through the window into the small tailor's workshop. A young man is sewing something on a machine and an elderly* MAN *in a V-neck sweater is cutting some material on the top of a large bench.* ELZBIETA *walks in, causing the small bell to ring above the door. The* MAN *with the scissors looks up at the customer entering the shop and then returns to his work.* ELZBIETA *takes a look around: there is a Singer sewing machine, which the young lad is using in the back of the shop; a counter, which looks as if it has seen thousands of hands and been cleaned hundreds of times; old magazines; a moulting old chair; a newspaper cutting with a picture of the Pope. The* MAN *finishes cutting his material and walks over with the smile he usually reserves for customers.*
ELZBIETA: Could I have a word with you?
MAN: Oh God! What about?
ELZBIETA: My name's Elzbieta Loranz.
  (ELZBIETA *pronounces her name as if she expects everything to suddenly become clear.*)
MAN: Your name means nothing to me.
ELZBIETA: I know, we haven't actually met. But we were due to,

during the war. It was in the winter of . . . You offered to –
MAN: Stop.
(ELZBIETA *trails off in astonishment.*)
I refuse to talk about the war. I refuse to talk about what
happened after the war. We can talk about the present, if you
like. Or if you prefer I can make you a dress, a coat or a suit.
You can even choose the style.
(*The* MAN *gives* ELZBIETA *several second-hand magazines. She
flicks through them perfunctorily, perhaps only in order to collect
her thoughts.*)
ELZBIETA: You were prepared to save my life. I wanted to thank
you for it.
MAN: Have you chosen the material? It's difficult to get any
material worth covering your back with these days.
ELZBIETA: I was six years old. The winter of nineteen forty-
three . . .
MAN: And I was twenty-two. What's it going to be – a suit or a
coat?
ELZBIETA: These magazines are very old. Would you be offended
if I sent you some more up-to-date ones?
MAN: Not at all. They're all sent from abroad.
ELZBIETA: Are you really not prepared to talk to me?
MAN: No, I'm not. Really I'm not.

19

ELZBIETA *walks across to the parked Trabant.*
ZOFIA: I decided to stay, just in case.
ELZBIETA: He wanted to make me a coat.
ZOFIA: That is what I feared. He has suffered a lot – it's probably
all been too much for him. He was in the same cell as my
husband but was released in 1955. That was when I went to
see him, to say I was sorry.

20

The Trabant is travelling along a road somewhere a long way away from Warsaw. ZOFIA *enters a small town, passes through the main square, and turns into a side-road leading to a church.*

21

ZOFIA *enters the main part of the church without having knelt or dipped her hands in the holy water. She looks around, evidently searching for someone or something. She notices a silhouette in the confessional and moves towards it. The* PRIEST *is a middle-aged man and looks exactly like the sort of priest you would expect to find in a small-town, provincial church. He has dozed off to sleep with his hands holding the stole.* ZOFIA *smiles on seeing his face with its closed eyes behind the confessional box mesh. She taps on it gently. The* PRIEST *slowly lifts his eyes, trying to pretend he had not actually been asleep, and wakes up instantly.*

PRIEST: What are you doing here?

ZOFIA: I have something important to tell you. She is alive.

(*The* PRIEST *looks at her through the mesh.*)

You'll never guess, she's alive. The little girl.

DECALOGUE NINE

The cast and crew of *Decalogue Nine* included:

HANKA   Ewa Blaszczyk
ROMAN   Piotr Machalica

Director of Photography and   Piotr Sobocinski
   Cameraman
Producer   Ryszard Chutkowski
Composer   Zbigniew Preisner
Artistic Director   Halina Dobrowolska
Sound   Nikodem Wolk-Laniewski
Lighting   Jerzy Tomczuk
Film Editor   Ewa Smal
Production Managers   Pawel Mantorski
                                           Wlodzimierz Bendych
Costume Designers   Malgorzata Obloza
                                           Hanna Cwiklo
Director   Krzysztof Kieślowski

Stills: Ewa Blaszczyk as Hanka
          Piotr Machalica as Roman

I

Early afternoon. Little ANIA *(from story seven) is playing with a doll in front of the apartment block.* HANKA *steps out of the stairwell entrance, a vivacious, attractive woman of around thirty. She is in a hurry, but suddenly slows, as if having forgotten something. She turns back and hurries home at an equally speedy step.*

2

HANKA *enters the living room without taking off her overcoat. She sits down in an armchair and waits. She does not have to wait long before the telephone rings. This is precisely the reason she came back and she immediately picks up the receiver.*

ROMAN: *(Voice over)* Hanka! Hi.

HANKA: Hi. I had a feeling you'd ring.

ROMAN: *(Voice over)* What do you mean?

HANKA: I was already on my way out and had to come back. Where are you ringing from?

ROMAN: *(Voice over)* I'm still in Krakow. I'll be back in the evening.

HANKA: Drive carefully. Bye.

3

ROMAN *is sitting in a doctor's surgery. The doctor is not there.* ROMAN *is around forty and has the face of a man who understands a great deal about life. He is well built, perhaps just slightly overweight, and has powerful hands; as we shall discover later on, they are the hands of a surgeon.* MIKOLAJ *enters the room wearing a short, doctor's overcoat. He clears away the ashtray from the desk and sits down next to* ROMAN *before taking out a Marlboro and offering it to his friend. He takes some papers out of his pocket and spreads them out pedantically on the table. He casts his eye over them, although knowing perfectly well what they contain.*

MIKOLAJ: How do you want it?

ROMAN: Straight.

MIKOLAJ: Aha. Well, my friend, that's too bad. We could look on the bright side, but I'd have to ask you a question first. How many have you had in your time? You know – women, birds, call them what you want.

ROMAN: Eight, ten. Maybe even fifteen if I was counting properly.

MIKOLAJ: That's not bad.

ROMAN: I've been married for ten years.

MIKOLAJ: Not bad either. A good wife, is she?

ROMAN: Very good.

MIKOLAJ: Do you want my advice? As a friend, not as a doctor? Get a divorce.

(ROMAN *leans back in his chair – he is prepared for anything.*) Fancy a drink?

ROMAN: Are you sure? I'll never be able to – with any woman at all?

MIKOLAJ: Positive. It's a classic case – both the symptoms and the test results.

ROMAN: I didn't tell you that much about the symptoms.

MIKOLAJ: Doesn't matter, I can guess. Three and a half, maybe four years ago, you started noticing . . .

ROMAN: Four.

MIKOLAJ: There you are, you see. So, four years ago you started having trouble getting it up. You probably couldn't get it up at all. You put it down to fatigue, went skiing, and it got better. You were relieved. But it got worse again. That little, faithful friend of yours just refused to take orders. You remembered medical school and reached for the primers. You're a dynamic sort of bloke, so you arranged to get hold of some ginseng and paid through the nose for it. Then you took yohimbine and strychnine, but they didn't help either. You couldn't turn to anyone in Warsaw because they all knew you and it was a bit embarrassing. So you panicked and came to me. Am I right?

ROMAN: More or less.

MIKOLAJ: What's more, there's no cure.

ROMAN: None whatsoever?

MIKOLAJ: I shouldn't really be so blunt, of course. Other doctors in a case like this would tell you to try it with another bird. Or what they call another partner. Don't do it. You'll only raise your hopes and it'll be a disaster.

ROMAN: Thanks. You couldn't have been more honest.

MIKOLAJ: Well. I've been straight with you. But then again. I'm straight with everybody these days. As old Grotzber always used to say –

ROMAN: Look, I'm sorry, Mikolaj, but I really don't give a shit what old Grotzber used to say.

4

Roman's diesel-powered Mazda emerges from behind the crest of a slight incline, travelling at great speed. He can see the road ahead curving gently downwards into a wood below and straightens the wheel. The road is empty; nothing is travelling in the opposite direction. ROMAN *shuts his eyes. The car gathers momentum. Nothing happens initially because the road is straight, but as it begins to curve to the left and to the right, the car wheels begin to slip off the tarmac on to the gravel of the hard-shoulder. The car continues to gather momentum but* ROMAN *still does not open his eyes. The car hits a bollard on the hard-shoulder with a tremendous impact and rips it right out of the ground. Crash.* ROMAN *brakes sharply. The car dances, the sharp braking causing it to slew sideways until it finally comes to a halt.* ROMAN *presses his head back against the rest, a small stream of saliva dribbling out of the corner of his mouth.*

HANKA *looks up from the ticket desk at the Foreign Travel Agency and stares straight ahead, almost as if into space. Not a muscle moves on her face. The smartly dressed man for whom she was writing out the ticket looks at her in surprise.*

MAN: Hello there. Hey!

(HANKA *does not react.*)

5

The Mazda stands parked outside the block. It is now dark. The green light of the car-alarm signal is flashing and music is playing softly on the radio. ROMAN has forgotten to turn it off.

6

HANKA *is lying in bed reading a newspaper but listening at the same time to the murmur of water coming from the bathroom. She looks over towards the door on hearing it open.* ROMAN *walks into the room with a towel around his waist. He walks over to the cupboard without looking over towards* HANKA, *takes out his pyjamas, and returns to the bathroom. Later, now in his pyjamas, he switches off the lamp on his side of the bed. He folds his duvet into a smallish rectangle, places a pillow on top of it, and begins to fold the sheet.*

HANKA: Come and sleep with me.

> (*Her voice is tender and soft – she is trying to be nice to him.* ROMAN *unfolds the sheets without saying a word and puts the pillow and quilt back in their normal places. He settles down beside her. She reaches over to the light switch. Both of them lie in silence.* HANKA *usually sleeps naked. She pulls the quilt down slightly and places* ROMAN'*s hand against her breast. Music can be heard in the silence.* ROMAN *turns off the radio standing beside the bed.*)

ROMAN: I forgot to turn the car radio off.

HANKA: It doesn't matter. How was it in Krakow? Meet any girls?

> (*She slides her hand under the covers.*)

ROMAN: I loathe myself.

> (HANKA *snuggles up more closely to her husband and puts her arms around him, although careful not to suggest any erotic intent. She speaks softly and calmly.*)

HANKA: I feel good.

ROMAN: Liar.

HANKA: No. I love you, maybe that's why.

ROMAN: I went to see Mikolaj. I told you about him.

HANKA: I remember. The bastard.

ROMAN: He told me – he knows about these things. He gave me a check-up, did all the tests. Do you want to know the results?
(HANKA *indicates with a nod of her head that she does.*)
It's no use trying to get around it or pretending. He told me straight. There's not a hope in hell. Either now or in the future. Never.

HANKA: I don't believe it. I don't believe all those medical check-ups and tests. In any case, there are more important things in life – like feelings, love . . .

ROMAN: There are also facts. At least if we discuss it now seriously, we'll part without one of us feeling let down or betrayed. To put it bluntly, your feeling let down by me.
(ROMAN *speaks in the neutral tone of voice of someone who has decided to deal with the problem rationally.* HANKA's *face is buried in his pyjamas.*)

HANKA: Tell me you love me.
(HANKA *endures the silence for a moment, then turns away and takes two cigarettes from the bedside table. She lights one and hands the other over her back to* ROMAN.)
You're afraid to say you love me, even though you do. Love isn't just a five-minute screw every week, you know.

ROMAN: But it's part and parcel.

HANKA: That's just biology. Love isn't about what you've got between your legs. What's more important to me is what we already share with one another, not what we'll never share again in the future.

ROMAN: You're still young . . .

HANKA: I'll manage.

ROMAN: You'll want to take a lover sooner or later.
(HANKA *rolls over – they are now face to face with one another.*)
If you haven't already. After all, it's been like this for several years now.

HANKA: No. You don't have to say it. Certain things don't have to be completely spelt out.

ROMAN: Hanka, they do. We have to discuss these things if we want everything to work out and stay together in future.

[243]

HANKA: You say you'll never be able to make love to me again –
or at least that's what the doctor says. I'm telling you that I
still want to be with you in spite of all that. As for . . . well,
women can look after themselves and their men don't have to
be any the wiser. The things we don't talk about don't exist,
which is why not everything has to be discussed. Unless
there's something you haven't told me. Is there?

ROMAN: No.

HANKA: Something I ought to know?

ROMAN: No.

HANKA: You're sleeping with someone else and all this story
about some illness or other is just a pretext?

ROMAN: No.

HANKA: Or . . .

ROMAN: Or?

HANKA: You're jealous.

(ROMAN *is silent.*)

Are you?

ROMAN: Everyone gets a little jealous. It's all part of the way we
lead our lives, part of our agreement. We sorted all that out.
We've never interfered in each other's lives. Not everything
has to be completely spelt out.

HANKA: You're right. Stupid question.

(ROMAN *touches her back.* HANKA *snuggles back down into the
bed and lies with her back against his chest. Both take a drag on
their cigarettes simultaneously: two little lights in the darkness of
the room.*)

ROMAN: We never wanted children anyway.

HANKA: True.

ROMAN: Maybe things would be easier if we had.

HANKA: Maybe. But we didn't and we're not going to. Did
anything happen on the way back from Krakow?

ROMAN: Why do you ask? Have you seen the car?

HANKA: No.

ROMAN: Somebody smashed into the bumper while it was
parked.

HANKA: I mean on the road. I was writing out this ticket at work
and I suddenly had this terrible attack of anxiety – as if

[244]

something was going to happen. Something dreadful.
ROMAN: Nothing happened.

7

Morning. ROMAN *climbs into his car. He leans over the dashboard
and looks up towards the block.* HANKA *is waving to him from the
window.* ROMAN *waves back. He is about to drive off when he notices
a young man in a bright jacket who then deliberately seems to turn
away as their eyes meet.* ROMAN *watches him, and then drives off
slowly, keeping an eye on him in his rear-view mirror. He turns the
corner at the end of the next block and stops the car. He goes back – the
young man is no longer there.* ROMAN *walks quickly towards the
stairwell entrance.*

8

He opens the door and quickly walks into the flat. HANKA *is sipping
some coffee and reading the newspapers. She leans across on hearing
the door open.* ROMAN *sizes up the situation with one quick glance.*
ROMAN: I forgot the receipt for the cleaners.
    (HANKA *gets up and scatters some small objects out on to the
    table.* ROMAN *has meanwhile taken out a folded piece of paper
    from his jacket pocket and dropped it furtively on the floor. He
    picks it up.*)
It's all right. I've got it. It must have fallen out.

9

ROMAN *pulls up outside the hospital. His attention is caught by the
sight of a refined-looking man in a sheepskin jacket and silver-rimmed
spectacles, who is having trouble pouring petrol into his car with a
funnel and petrol canister.*
ROMAN: Good morning, doctor. Can I give you a hand?
CONSULTANT: If you could. I'll hold the funnel. I'm afraid the

[245]

canister's too heavy for me.
(ROMAN *lifts the canister while the hospital* CONSULTANT *inserts the funnel into the tank.*)
What is the world coming to – the best heart surgeon in the hospital and a consultant pouring black-market petrol bought illegally from a spiv into an old banger which probably won't start anyway. You're lucky you've got a diesel.

ROMAN: It's certainly something of a relief.

CONSULTANT: So I imagine.

ROMAN: You wanted me to have a word with Miss . . .

CONSULTANT: Ah yes. She's a young girl and I don't really understand what she's on about. The name's Jarek. Ola Jarek. Her mother has a very noble and respectable profession, you'd like her. She stands for a living.

ROMAN: What do you mean, 'stands'?

CONSULTANT: She stands. You want a washing-machine, she'll stand in the queue for it. You need some furniture, she'll stand for you. Twenty-five per cent on top, but guaranteed delivery.
(ROMAN *has poured in all the petrol and puts the canister down to one side, careful not to spill a drop. The* CONSULTANT *sniffs his hands.*)
They stink to high heaven.

10

ROMAN *is sitting with a young girl in that part of the corridor designated as a smoking area. She is an average, plainish-looking girl, and is wearing a hospital dressing-gown.* ROMAN *lights a cigarette.*

OLA: Can I have one?

ROMAN: It's not good for you.

OLA: It won't kill me.
(*She holds out her hand for a cigarette and* ROMAN *rather reluctantly gives her one.*)

ROMAN: You can still change your mind.
(OLA *smiles, a smile which breathes life and charm into her*

[246]

expression. ROMAN *also smiles: a sort of mutual accord has been struck.* ROMAN *thus decides to come straight to the point.*)
The consultant says he's having trouble understanding what it is you want.

OLA: Well, it's very simple really – I may not look it, but I have a good voice.
(*She smiles again, this time a little embarrassed.*)

ROMAN: A voice?

OLA: A voice. A singing voice. My mother works hard and, well, you know, she wants me to make something of myself. She wants me to sing. The music school won't take me because I have a weak heart. I'm not supposed to sing because my heart can't take it. But my mother wants me to give it a go.

ROMAN: What sort of things do you sing?

OLA: Bach, Mahler – do you know any Mahler?

ROMAN: Yes.

OLA: He's difficult, but I can sing him. My mother wants me to be a famous singer and for that I need an operation. My mother wants the consultant, or perhaps even better, yourself . . .

ROMAN: What do you want?

OLA: I'm quite happy to be alive, that's enough for me. The singing isn't that important. And I'm nervous about the operation – the consultant said you'd put my mind at rest. Tell me there's no risk involved and that I'll be able to do anything I like afterwards. So tell me.

ROMAN: I wish I could. An operation like that is only done as a last resort, to save . . . when there's no other choice.

OLA: And I do have a choice, right?

ROMAN: To tell you the truth, yes, you do. Not to sing.
(OLA *smiles again.*)

OLA: It's a problem of who wants what. My mother wants me to have everything. All I want is . . . well, about this much.
(OLA *moves her forefinger and thumb together to show how much she really expects from life: it would appear to be not very much.*)

11

ROMAN *puts on a record manufactured abroad. The stereo system reproduces the Mahler perfectly but the music is interrupted by the sound of the telephone.* ROMAN *turns down the volume and picks up the receiver.*

VOICE: (*Over*) Good afternoon. Is Hanka there?

(ROMAN *is standing by the window with the receiver and can see* HANKA *walking at her customary pace towards the block.*)

ROMAN: No, she's not back yet.

VOICE: (*Over*) Thank you.

(HANKA *disappears from* ROMAN'S *view into the stairwell entrance.*)

ROMAN: Any message?

(*But the other end of the line is already dead.* ROMAN *stands rigidly for a couple of seconds with the receiver still in his hand. He puts it down and turns the music volume back up again. He takes out a little calendar and places a bold little cross against today's date. Previous days also have the little crosses marked against them. The calendar has been hidden away by the time* HANKA *comes through the front door.* ROMAN *listens with his eyes shut as* HANKA, *still in her overcoat, kisses him on the forehead. Only now – or at least that is how it appears – does* ROMAN *seem to notice her.*)

HANKA: What's playing?

ROMAN: Mahler. It's beautiful, isn't it?

(HANKA *is leaning against the door and listens without taking her coat off.*)

HANKA: Beautiful.

ROMAN: You had a phone call.

HANKA: Who was it?

(ROMAN *shrugs his shoulders: he does not know.* HANKA *also shrugs her shoulders, clearly unconcerned. The Mahler comes to an end.* ROMAN *switches off the amplifier.*)

Beautiful.

(*Only now does she remember the large parcel she has tucked under her arm. She takes out a brand-new jacket.*)

[248]

Try it on.
(ROMAN *gets out of his chair and slips into the jacket – it fits perfectly. He steps back to show* HANKA *just how perfectly.*)
See?!

12

ROMAN *presents a popular television programme which explains the functioning of the heart. In front of the camera he demonstrates why the heart sometimes functions badly and the way in which doctors try to repair the defect. He also demonstrates, with the help of various film aids and visuals, what sort of heart operations are carried out. He is humorous and approachable, but also serious when the subject-matter requires it. He is wearing his new jacket and is at present precisely explaining the most dramatic part of the programme: the transplant – the insertion of a new heart to replace an old, sick one.*

13

The television programme continues, this time watched by ROMAN *and* HANKA *on their own set at home. On screen,* ROMAN *says a few words and then the credits start to roll.* HANKA *switches off the set with the remote-control –* ROMAN *looks at her questioningly. She nods her head.*
HANKA: It was fine, a big improvement.
ROMAN: Are you sure?
HANKA: I suppose people will be coming up to me again and saying what a wonderful husband I have. A couple of girls at work have already got a crush on you. It won't be long before you have your own fan-club.
ROMAN: I think it was worth a try.
HANKA: But didn't you want . . .
ROMAN: I thought maybe it should have been more serious, but it's simpler and better like this. Hopefully it'll give the public some food for thought – that is, if they watch that sort of thing at all.

[249]

(*The telephone rings,* ROMAN *tenses.*)

HANKA: Here comes the proof. (*She lifts the receiver.*) Yes, I'll give him to you now.

(*She hands the receiver over to* ROMAN.)

ROMAN: Hello? Good evening. Thank you. I'm very touched. Really? – that was my wife's idea. Fine, I'll pass it on. Goodbye.

(*He replaces the receiver. The phone rings again.*)

HANKA: I bet it'll be non-stop like this for the rest of the evening. You take it.

(ROMAN *picks up the receiver.*)

ROMAN: Hello. (*He listens briefly.*) It's for you.

(*Although* HANKA *has signalled to him not to, he hands over the receiver and leaves, making his way over to a small room at the back of their apartment which he has turned into something like a workshop. We can see a cluttered-up table, a soldering iron, a holder, a saw and a hammer.* ROMAN *reaches towards the telephone standing on the table and connects it up with a clip to an earpiece at the end of a long piece of wire. The plug fits snugly into his ear.* ROMAN *listens – the conversation is clearly audible.*)

HANKA: (*Voice over*) Yes, I can.

VOICE: (*Over*) At six, OK?

HANKA: (*Voice over*) Fine.

VOICE: (*Over*) On Dobra Street?

HANKA: (*Voice over*) Fine.

(*Her voice sounds the same as it did while* ROMAN *was still in the room: cold and impersonal.* ROMAN's *face is wracked with pain, but something forces him to carry on listening to the end of the conversation, despite the evident agony. He walks out on to the long balcony. It is windy outside.* ROMAN *leans against the balcony railing, his head buried in his hands. His body is shaking violently – perhaps simply because of the cold.* HANKA *pokes her head into the small room, then the bedroom and the kitchen, before knocking on the bathroom door and the toilet. Nothing but silence. Agitated (perhaps she is also feeling slightly guilty), she rips down her overcoat from the peg in the hallway and runs out of the flat.* ROMAN *recognizes her, her coat billowing in the wind.*)

[250]

ROMAN: Hanka!
(HANKA *recognizes his outline on the balcony of the sixth floor.*)
HANKA: I came out to look for you!
(*She wraps herself up more tightly in the coat and slowly returns home.* ROMAN *walks out of the flat and on to the landing.* HANKA *waits, having already pressed the lift button. No sooner have the lift doors opened than she is in* ROMAN's *arms.*)
Where have you been? I was frightened.
ROMAN: I was out on the balcony – it was a nice sunset.
HANKA: I was frightened.
ROMAN: What of?
HANKA: I don't know. I couldn't find you anywhere.

14

HANKA *is a good driver and* ROMAN *smiles as she riskily overtakes a heavy lorry, squeezing deftly between it and a Fiat coming the other way. The car pulls up outside a swimming-pool.*
HANKA: I'll be waiting here in two hours' time.
(ROMAN *disappears through the entrance.* HANKA *drives off.* ROMAN *does not go into the cloakroom, however, but greets the attendant with a nod and walks straight out through the back entrance. A taxi is waiting in the side-street.* ROMAN *opens the door.*)
ROMAN: Are you waiting for me?
DRIVER: Dobra Street?
ROMAN: That's right.
(*He climbs in. The taxi moves off.*)
It's on the corner of Dobra and Solec.
(*The taxi stops on the corner and* ROMAN *pays him.*)
I'll be back in a few minutes.
(*He walks through the gateway and passes a tiny garden – there in front of him is the house he wanted to see. The young man in the bright jacket is standing outside.* HANKA *pulls up in the Mazda a moment later and parks in a nearby space, almost right next to him. She climbs out of the car and slips her arm into his.*)

[251]

15

ROMAN *is standing in his swimming trunks on the highest platform of the diving board. He looks down, slowly leans forward so that his legs form a vertical axis, and then dives into the water. He swims underwater towards a pool ladder and, holding himself down with the last rung, tries to stay underwater as long as possible. He gasps convulsively for breath after coming to the surface, allowing oxygen to flow into his air-starved lungs.*

16

ROMAN *is making himself a cup of coffee in the doctors' rest-room. The door opens without anybody knocking.*

WARD-ATTENDANT: Coming for lunch, doctor?

ROMAN: What's on the menu?

WARD-ATTENDANT: Pig's brawn.

ROMAN: Thanks.

The WARD-ATTENDANT *disappears.* ROMAN *walks over to the door, which has not been shut properly. He notices* OLA.

Not going to lunch?

OLA: My mother brings me things.

ROMAN: Come in. I've been thinking about you.

(He clears some papers off a chair and invites OLA *to sit down. He himself settles back deep into the back of a settee with his cup of coffee.* OLA *looks enviously at it.)*

You're not supposed to drink coffee.

OLA: No, I know.

ROMAN: I went out and bought a record after our conversation the other day.

OLA: Mahler?

ROMAN: Yes. In German – it's superb.

(OLA visibly perks up.)

OLA: Do you remember any of it?

ROMAN: A little.

(ROMAN tries to hum a few half-remembered notes, but it all

[252]

sounds rather vague. OLA *laughs. She picks up the tune from the notes he has been singing and, still sitting down, manages easily to sing a couple of bars with a pure, vibrating, elegant voice. It is not a tutored voice, but its beautiful quality is already evident.* ROMAN *stares at her in amazement. He has not mentioned which concert he had been listening to, but* OLA *is singing the piece of the music they have been talking about. On seeing* ROMAN *staring at her,* OLA *trails off with embarrassment.*)
That was beautiful. It would be shame for such a voice . . .

OLA: That's exactly what my mum says.

ROMAN: She's right.

OLA: What were your ambitions when you were my age?

ROMAN: I wanted to be a surgeon.

OLA: Didn't you dream about having a home, a family?
(ROMAN *thinks for a while: he would rather not be reminded about such things.*)

ROMAN: I don't remember.

OLA: Maybe you didn't think it was important then. I've got a boyfriend, he works in a shop. I'd like to marry him and have a couple of children, maybe even three. And live away from the city centre in Brodnia or Ursynow. I'd settle for that.
(ROMAN *smiles.*)

ROMAN: Don't you want to be fêted and adored?

OLA: He adores me the way I am.

17

ROMAN *walks to his car, which is parked in front of the hospital. There has been a slight frost during the night and the windows are frosted over. He wipes them down and climbs into the car. As he opens the glove compartment to put away a hairbrush, he finds an exercise book which someone has evidently left behind by mistake.* ROMAN *tenses. The words 'Mariusz Zawiszki. Physics. VI Term' are written in felt-tip pen on the cover.* ROMAN *flicks through it: it is full of mysterious, unfamiliar equations. He drives off. He stops the car by one of the rubbish skips on the estate, gets out, and throws the book on to it. He drives on but decides to brake several hundred metres further on, then reverses, climbs out again and goes over to the skip. He cannot find the book. He looks around, finds a stick and pokes through the rubbish, eventually finding the book. He reaches for it with evident disgust, brings a rag from out of the car, and endeavours to restore it to an acceptable state of repair. He then drives off.*

18

ROMAN *cautiously opens the door of the apartment and hangs up his coat. His bed has been made.* HANKA *is sleeping in it, slightly uncovered.* ROMAN *delicately covers her back up again with the quilt. Her bag stands on the floor at the foot of the bed. He picks it up and walks out of the room with it on tiptoe. He flicks through her address-book and rummages through the scores of receipts, various photographs and make-up paraphernalia. A telephone number has been noted down on the cover of a creased little savings book. He repeats the number to himself in order to memorize it, but finds nothing else which warrants any interest. He replaces the lot and goes back into the bedroom.* HANKA *is sleeping as before.* ROMAN *puts the bag back down on the floor.*

19

FEMALE FRIEND: Didn't you have a number for the petrol station? I've run out of oil again.
   (HANKA *reaches for her handbag and searches for the address-book – it is not where it was lying before. She gives her friend the number and anxiously thinks about the handbag. She dials a number.*)
HANKA: It's me.
VOICE: (*Over*) Hi.
   (HANKA *takes a look around and drops her voice.*)
HANKA: Can you do me a favour? Don't ring me at home unless you really have to.
VOICE: (*Over*) Is something wrong?

HANKA: No, nothing. It's just better to ring me at work.
VOICE: (*Over*) From ten till six.
HANKA: That's right, ten till six. Until eight on Tuesdays and Thursdays.
VOICE: (*Over*) Your wish is my command.
HANKA: Thanks.
VOICE: (*Over*) Bye.

20

Evening, and they are both already in bed. ROMAN *is reading* The World According to Garp *and chuckling quietly to himself.* HANKA *is listening to a tape on Walkman earphones, the music she is listening to faintly audible.* ROMAN *touches her shoulders –* HANKA *speaks unnaturally loudly because of the earphones.*
HANKA: What?
(ROMAN *hands her the book and points to the passage which he has found so amusing.* HANKA *reads it and begins to chuckle to herself quietly at the same passage* ROMAN *had found so amusing a few seconds earlier.*)

21

ROMAN *gives* HANKA *a lift to her travel bureau. She climbs out and* ROMAN *notices with pleasure how naturally and beautifully she moves:* HANKA *remembers something and comes back to the car.*
HANKA: I've forgotten something.
(*She looks at her watch.*)
ROMAN: What?
HANKA: Mum rang – she asked me to send her umbrella and scarf over. The plane's flying to London today.
ROMAN: Can't she buy them over there?
HANKA: She's rather fond of her own.
(ROMAN *looks at his watch.*)
ROMAN: What time's the plane?
HANKA: Twelve.

ROMAN: My operation's not until the afternoon. I could go over
  myself.
HANKA: You're a darling.
  (*She gives him the keys.*)
  The umbrella's on the hat-stand and the scarf, you know, the
  woollen one with the navy-blue and black check pattern, is in
  the chest of drawers. The one in the bedroom.
  (ROMAN *takes the keys.*)
ROMAN: I'll find them.

22

ROMAN *is standing at the key-cutting stall in the Centrum department
store. He handed over the key a few minutes earlier and is watching
the man place it alongside the new and as yet shapeless key. The
machine precisely cuts little chinks out of the new one.*

23

ROMAN *pulls up outside the house on Dobra Street and opens the glove
compartment. It is empty – the exercise book has gone.* ROMAN *climbs
out of the car and walks towards the house.*

24

ROMAN *tries both keys: they both fit well. The flat is unused, tidy and
empty, and the furniture is covered in dust-sheets.* ROMAN *looks
around, full of depressing thoughts and forebodings. He stands for a
moment by the wide unfolded sofa bed and then suddenly rips off the
cover. The sheets underneath are clean and unsoiled. He goes over to
the bathroom and opens the automatic washing machine: some twisted
bed linen is lying inside.* ROMAN *untwists the sheets and examines
them to find a yellow stain in the middle of one of them. He puts them
back in and walks into the living room. He notices several newspapers
and picks them up, finding exactly what he expected. The exercise*

[256]

book is lying underneath, now drier than before, although slightly soiled after its brief, albeit eventful sojourn in the rubbish skip. ROMAN *dials the number he had learnt by heart. After several ringing tones, someone picks up the receiver.*

WOMAN: (*Voice over*) Hello.

ROMAN: Is Mariusz there, please?

WOMAN: (*Voice over*) Mariusz! Telephone!

(ROMAN *covers the mouthpiece with his hand. He hears a pleasant-sounding male voice on the other end of the line.*)

MARIUSZ: Hello.

(ROMAN *says nothing.*)

Who's there? Hello?

(*Without waiting for a reply from* ROMAN, *who is silent,* MARIUSZ *puts down the receiver. So too does* ROMAN. *He opens the chest of drawers and hears the phone ring. He thinks for a moment and then picks up the receiver.*)

HANKA: (*Voice over*) Is that you?

ROMAN: Yes.

HANKA: (*Voice over*) I've been getting an engaged signal all the time. Have you been on the line?

ROMAN: No, I only just got in. You must have got a wrong number.

HANKA: (*Voice over*) Have you found them?

ROMAN: Not yet. Hold on.

(*He opens the cupboard and takes out the scarf. It looks just as* HANKA *described it. He walks over with it to the telephone.*)

I've got the scarf. I saw the umbrella as I came in.

HANKA: (*Voice over*) Well, come back then.

ROMAN: OK.

HANKA: (*Voice over*) Roman, don't do any poking around. Mum likes to have everything in its proper place.

ROMAN: I know. I'm on my way.

25

There are quite a few customers in the travel bureau, but not enough to make it crowded. HANKA *goes straight over to* ROMAN *and takes the scarf and umbrella.*

HANKA: They still haven't gone yet. I'll be here until six.
(ROMAN *takes out the keys to the car.*)
ROMAN: I'll leave you the car.
HANKA: Will you make it in time?
ROMAN: Easily. I've left the registration card in the glove
compartment.
(*He watches for her reaction.* HANKA *smiles.*)
Fine.
(ROMAN *leaves.* HANKA *hurries across to a* YOUNG MAN *in
airline uniform.*)
Can you take this for me? The captain knows all about it. My
mum's picking them up at the other end.
YOUNG MAN: Is there anything else I can do for you?
(HANKA *replies without the trace of a smile.*)
HANKA: No, that's all, thanks.
(*She does not notice* ROMAN *standing outside the front window
and watching her through the glass.*)

26

HANKA'S *face is twisted in ecstasy. She turns her head to one side,
tears streaming down her face: from pleasure? disgust? humiliation?
The young man looks tenderly at her tears and wants to stroke her
cheeks with a sympathetic, caring gesture of his hand, but she pushes it
away. He strokes her hair and kisses the hand which has rejected him.*
    ROMAN *enters the room adjoining the operating theatre. The*
CONSULTANT *has a cigarette in his mouth and is washing his hands.
Doctors and nurses are bustling around the room and operating theatre.*
CONSULTANT: At last, you're here.
ROMAN: Look, I –
CONSULTANT: Get changed. We're starting in a minute.
ROMAN: I was wondering whether . . . I'm not feeling up to an
operation today.
CONSULTANT: What's wrong?
ROMAN: I don't feel well. I'd be grateful if you could –
CONSULTANT: We've got two operations as well.
ROMAN: I'm really sorry.

(*The* CONSULTANT *studies him intently.*)

CONSULTANT: Did you have a word with the young girl?

ROMAN: Yes, I did. She really isn't that desperate to go through with it.

CONSULTANT: Fine. Off you go then.

(*The young man is sitting, still undressed, in the flat on Dobra Street. He is examining his exercise book in astonishment.*)

MARIUSZ: What did you do to it? Drop it in a puddle or something?

HANKA: No, I didn't. You're sure you left it in the glove compartment?

MARIUSZ: I think so. It was as clean as a whistle. A whole term's physics down the drain . . . Where was it?

HANKA: In the glove compartment.

(*The young man nuzzles up to her.*)

MARIUSZ: I'm sorry.

HANKA: What for?

MARIUSZ: For forgetting it.

27

ROMAN's *taxi pulls up outside the house on the corner of Dobra and Solec Street.*

ROMAN: What time do you make it?

DRIVER: Half-seven.

(ROMAN *climbs out and walks through the gate we have seen before. The Mazda is in the parking lot, as he expected and feared. The automatic alarm-light is flashing. He feels the bonnet – it is still warm.*)

28

ROMAN *reaches the first floor, walks up to the front door and listens intently. No doubt he is debating whether to go inside (since he has a spare key) or wait outside alone with the desperate misery he feels inside but which he conceals from the outside world.*

[259]

He eventually decides to creep up a couple of steps and sit on the stairs, tightly hunching up his knees and burying his head in his hands. We cannot be sure whether he suspects what is going on inside or knows for sure. In any case, he sits motionlessly until he hears the rattle of the lock. He gets up and walks up to the mezzanine. From there he sees HANKA *lean out of the doorway and then step back inside as the young man in the bright jacket leaves the flat. He runs nimbly down the stairs, his light-hearted, jaunty whistling descending the steps to the same rhythm as his feet.*

ROMAN *waits for a while and then walks right up to the front door with sudden determination. He takes out the keys and is about to put them in the lock when he hears* HANKA *stepping towards it from the other side. He leaps to one side, totally instinctively, as if he is about to be caught doing something he shouldn't. Hot-water pipes run down the wall to one side of the door.* ROMAN *squeezes in behind them and is only about a couple of feet away from her as she walks out and closes the door. Her coat is unbuttoned and her handbag is dangling from a trailing hand. She looks tired. Locking the door mechanically, she walks off along the corridor, unaware of* ROMAN .

She looks and moves in a completely different manner from earlier the same day. Her shoes clack heavily down the stairs. ROMAN *wipes away the sweat on his forehead like a surgeon in an operating theatre. Through the stairwell window he can see his tired wife carelessly throw her handbag into the open car. She has forgotten to switch off the alarm – the car flashes its headlights and starts bleeping its horn. After a while it stops.* HANKA *drives away.* ROMAN *crawls out from behind the pipes, his face ashen . . .*

29

ROMAN *is standing with his overcoat collar turned up in front of the door-keeper's lodge at the hospital. His taxi is pulling away in the background.* ROMAN *looks around – he does not want to be caught by his friends from the hospital. He glances over towards the courtyard from which they are most likely to appear and moves into the shadows.* HANKA *drives towards him from the opposite direction. She pulls up alongside him and winds down the car-window. She is natural, happy and smiling, different again from how she was not so long ago in the stairwell on Dobra Street.*

HANKA: Am I late? Have you been waiting long?

(ROMAN *looks at her and cannot understand the total and rapid change.*)

Do you want to drive?

(*She makes a move as if to get out of the driver's seat.*)

ROMAN: No.

(*He walks around the front of the car and climbs into the passenger seat. He is unable to disguise the traces of what he has just experienced. Her welcoming smile slowly vanishes from her face.*)

HANKA: Something wrong?

(ROMAN *replies in the negative.* HANKA *turns towards him and delicately places her hand against his cheek.*)

Had a bad day?

(ROMAN *freezes under her touch. He cannot come to terms with the thought that only a short while earlier, perhaps with a similar gesture, she . . .*)

Was it an operation? Tell me.

ROMAN: Yes.

HANKA: Someone died?

ROMAN: Yes.

(ROMAN *is thinking about her hands touching his face.* HANKA *is stroking him gently and compassionately.*)

Take your hand off me.

(HANKA *stops stroking him but does not remove her hand.*)

HANKA: Who was it?

(ROMAN *explodes.*)

ROMAN: Don't touch me!

(*A small group of doctors and the consultant are walking away from the hospital towards the car.*)

Let's go.

(HANKA *looks at him, finding his behaviour incomprehensible. There is only one thing* ROMAN *wants – to get away as quickly as possible.*)

I'm sorry. Please, let's go.

(*The car moves off.*)

[261]

30

HANKA *wakes. It is night-time. Still with her eyes closed, she feels the empty space on the pillow beside her and sits up.*

HANKA: Roman?

> (*She gets up and throws on her dressing-gown. She notices a narrow strip of light beneath the bathroom door and pulls at the handle:* ROMAN *is sitting in the bath.*)
>
> Roman . . .

ROMAN: I couldn't sleep.

> (*An opened packet of cigarettes and a small, ladies' lighter lie on top of the washing-machine.* ROMAN *meets her gaze.*)
>
> I couldn't find my own.

HANKA: No problem.

ROMAN: Tell me something – were you ever any good at physics?

HANKA: Why?

ROMAN: A body immersed in liquid loses a proportion of its weight equal to – what? I can't remember how it goes after that.

HANKA: A body immersed in liquid loses a proportion of its weight equal to the amount of water it displaces – I think that's right. Come back to bed.

ROMAN: That must be right.

> (HANKA *returns to the bedroom.* ROMAN *shuts the bathroom door after she has gone and slides the bolt across. He pulls her handbag out from the corner behind the bath and replaces the cigarettes and the lighter. He stubs out the cigarette under a stream of tap-water in the sink.* HANKA *calls out loudly so that he can hear her.*)

HANKA: Roman!

> (ROMAN *also speaks loudly.*)

ROMAN: Yes?

HANKA: Is everything OK?

ROMAN: Everything's fine.

> (*It is now day-time.* HANKA *is sitting in the large sitting room, listening to the noises emerging from the little room which* ROMAN *has turned into a workshop – the banging of a hammer against soft metal. She goes over to the television set; a children's cartoon*

is showing. HANKA *slowly turns up the volume and picks up the telephone.* ROMAN *is planishing the rivets connecting two strips of tin. He stops suddenly, listens for a moment, then pulls out his earplug from the cupboard and attaches it to the telephone standing beside him. He puts the earphone in his ear and hears the ringing tone. A male voice answers after a while, a voice he recognizes.*)

MARIUSZ: (*Voice over*) Hello.

HANKA: (*Voice over*) It's me.

MARIUSZ: (*Voice over*) Hanka – good morning.

HANKA: (*Voice over*) I have to see you.

MARIUSZ: (*Voice over*) I've been waiting all week for you to say that.

(ROMAN's *face crumples into the expression of misery we know already from the house on Dobra Street. This time he looks even more unhappy.*)

HANKA: (*Voice over*) Well, now I want to.

MARIUSZ: (*Voice over*) I've been missing you.

HANKA: (*Voice over*) Good. Can you make Thursday?

MARIUSZ: (*Voice over*) I can make any day.

HANKA: (*Voice over*) Thursday. At six.

MARIUSZ: (*Voice over*) Hanka – is something –

HANKA: (*Voice over*) At six.

(*We can hear* HANKA *putting down the receiver.* ROMAN *immediately dismantles his equipment and starts banging the rivets linking the two pieces of tin with his hammer.*)
What are you making?

ROMAN: Something for the battery – not long before it's winter.

HANKA: I've still got a jar full of berries from the lakes – do you fancy something to eat? Pierogi* or something? Are you hungry?

ROMAN: No, but I will if you're making something.

---

* Pierogi – little dumplings, a staple of the Polish diet, often filled with meat or cheese.

31

HANKA *is waiting for* MARIUSZ *in the flat on Dobra Street. She is sitting at the large old table in the kitchen and looking through some old photographs she has taken down out of a box: her with her mother in Zakopane, her with a teddy-bear, also in Zakopane, several old identity-card photographs, her as a smiling young girl on a beach holding hands with her parents. She is interrupted by the sound of the front doorbell. A smiling* MARIUSZ *walks in and unzips his jacket.*

HANKA: Don't bother. I don't have much time.

> (MARIUSZ *follows her into the room and wants to put his arms around her.* HANKA *does not resist, but displays no passion or warmth.*)

MARIUSZ: I've been desperate to see you.

> (HANKA *slips out of his grasp and sits down.* MARIUSZ *puts his hand on her knee and, looking her square in the eyes, slowly starts to slide it up her thigh.* HANKA *stops him midway.*)

HANKA: No.

> (*He withdraws his hand.*)

MARIUSZ: No, OK.

HANKA: I mean generally 'no'. This is the last time we see each other.

MARIUSZ: Hanka —

HANKA: That's all I wanted to tell you. Now go.

> (*The camera slowly tracks towards a part of the room which at first sight contains nothing remarkable. There is a forty-centimetre gap between the cupboard and the wall in a space concealed behind the open door. In that space, his head forced to one side by the lack of room, is* ROMAN.)

MARIUSZ: I don't have to go to bed with you, but don't throw me out.

HANKA: I'm not throwing you out. But just go.

MARIUSZ: I love you. We never discussed it before –

HANKA: And we're not going to now either.

MARIUSZ: Has he found out?

HANKA: No, he hasn't found out and he's not going to find out. Now zip up your coat and go.

(HANKA *gets to her feet.*)

MARIUSZ: Have I done something wrong? You can't suddenly
just –

HANKA: You haven't done anything wrong. Don't take it
personally.

(MARIUSZ *looks at her as if she has done him a gross injustice.*
HANKA *pulls the zip on his coat up for him.*)

You're looking great.

(MARIUSZ *does not know how to deal with this new development
and stands with a hang-dog expression on his face.*)

MARIUSZ: Hanka –

HANKA: You'll be all right. You can pick up your physics again.
Or any of the other girls on the course.

(*She shoves him gently towards the hallway.* MARIUSZ *looks as
if he still wants to say or do something, but* HANKA *gives him no
opportunity. She closes the door behind him. She leans back
against it for a few moments, doubtless surprised or taken aback
by his declaration of love, which she had not expected.* HANKA
*waits for a while until he has properly left the building, then
switches the light off in the living room and shuts the door on her
way out. Only then does she notice something which she initially
finds impossible to believe. She takes another step forward, but
then stops with her hand still on the door handle, feeling as if she
has just looked in the mirror and seen someone else's face reflected
in it. Still incapable of believing what she has seen, she goes back
into the room and takes a step towards the gap between the
cupboard and the wall. It is dark. She switches on the overhead
light and takes another step forward. She can see* ROMAN's *face
right in front of her. They look at each other for a long while.*
ROMAN *is standing stiffly in his uncomfortable and humiliating
position.*)

Come out of there (*Then more loudly.*) Come out of there!

(ROMAN *does not move.*)

What do you think you're playing at? I suppose you wanted
to see us rolling around on the bed together? Well you
should have come a week earlier, you would have seen
everything.

(ROMAN *speaks softly, barely moving his lips.*)

[265]

ROMAN: I did.

HANKA: You did?

ROMAN: I was on the stairs outside. I know everything.

(*The front doorbell rings out unnaturally loudly against the background of silence.* HANKA *freezes, as does* ROMAN, *for reasons which are obvious.*)

Answer it.

(HANKA *walks to the front door and opens it.* MARIUSZ *is standing there with a serious expression on his face and looks as if he has taken a decision of the gravest importance.*)

MARIUSZ: I want you to marry me. Get a divorce and marry me.

(*Without saying a word, almost as if no one is standing there at all,* HANKA *shuts the door.* ROMAN *extricates himself from behind the cupboard, his dark sweater covered in white flakes of plaster.* HANKA *comes back into the room and suddenly clasps herself to the dirty jumper.*)

HANKA: Hug me. If you still want to.

(*She does not feel him lift his arms around her. Quite the opposite.* ROMAN *collapses weakly on to the floor and remains sitting there.* HANKA *kneels down beside him. This gesture has no symbolic meaning – she simply wants to be near him.*)

This is the most important thing I've ever asked of you: put your arms around me.

(*She gazes intensely into his eyes.* ROMAN *slowly raises his arms and touches her shoulders.*)

ROMAN: I haven't got the strength.

(HANKA *clings to his body, crying uncontrollably like a child.* ROMAN *caresses her and tries to calm her down. The crying dies away.* HANKA *speaks into his jumper, so indistinctly that* ROMAN *initially cannot even catch what she is saying.*)

HANKA: You're right, we should –

ROMAN: Yes.

HANKA: We should have a child, adopt one. There are so many children with no one to love them. You were right.

ROMAN: It's too late.

HANKA: But you've not leaving me just . . . just because I slept with –

ROMAN: No.

[266]

HANKA: I'll look after it, if you can find it in yourself to forgive me. You put your arms around me, didn't you?

ROMAN: Yes.

HANKA: I never knew – I never thought you would be so upset.

ROMAN: I didn't think so either. I don't have the right to be jealous.

HANKA: You do. And I – you were right. I'll tell you everything from now on, so you don't have to –

ROMAN: I got a spare key cut.

HANKA: Well, you won't have to in future. You'll see.

ROMAN: I think we should have a break from one another. For a while.

HANKA: Yes. You go off somewhere. I'll look after the child. I'll go and see a lawyer.

ROMAN: No, you go somewhere. I don't want that physics student –

HANKA: OK. I'll go off somewhere then.

(HANKA *smiles a slight, tentative smile. She does not know how* ROMAN *will react, but he manages a slight smile with the corners of his eyes.*)

You're right. I'll go.

32

ROMAN *is collecting a pair of well-made, recently sharpened skis from the ski-shop. He runs his finger along the edges to check the keenness and nods to the* OWNER, *who is clearly pleased with his work. The shop is full of labels with boots, bindings, skis and other equipment. The tools are all neatly arranged in whole sets, all with red handle-grips. The boots fit perfectly into the newly fastened ski bindings.*

OWNER: Not too small?

ROMAN: They're for the wife.

OWNER: That's different, then. Women need smaller skis.

33

HANKA *is filling in a stack of tickets and suddenly hears a voice above her.*

MARIUSZ: Excuse me, I was wondering how much a ticket to Melbourne costs.

(HANKA *looks up. She tries not to raise her voice.*)

HANKA: Go away.

MARIUSZ: I only wanted to ask how much a ticket to Melbourne costs.

(HANKA *is keen to avoid a slanging match. She looks around and recognizes the young man to whom she gave the scarf and umbrella.*)

HANKA: Janusz!

(HANKA *turns to* MARIUSZ *and loudly announces in an official tone of voice.*)

My colleague here will give you all the information you want. He deals with that part of the world. Excuse me.

(*Evening. The bureau is already closed for the day.* ROMAN *knocks on the plate-glass window.* HANKA *prepares to leave the office and* JANUSZ, *the same man we met earlier, closes the door behind her and locks it with the security lock.* HANKA *notices the skis in the car. She runs her fingers along the edges, as* ROMAN *had done previously.*)

HANKA: Fantastic.

ROMAN: I booked a couchette for Thursday. Is everything OK?

HANKA: Everything's fine. I fixed an appointment with the lawyer for tomorrow.

34

HANKA *walks out of the door marked 'Lawyers' Co-operative'. She stops in front of a shop selling women's dresses and notices a figure in a lurid jacket standing reflected in the glass next to her.*

MARIUSZ: Hello.

HANKA: Hi. Still not in Melbourne yet?

MARIUSZ: That time, I – I was being serious. You probably
 thought I was fooling around.

HANKA: No, I didn't.

MARIUSZ: I love you.

HANKA: Listen. I needed someone to go to bed with. You're not
 bad, but you're not as fantastic as you obviously think you
 are. I've slept with others better. And I don't need you any
 more. Got it?

MARIUSZ: I don't believe you.

HANKA: Take my word for it. I've swapped you for someone else.

MARIUSZ: Don't say that. Those aren't your words, it's not you
 talking.

HANKA: It's me, it's me – really. And you've still got quite a lot to
 learn.

35

ROMAN *zips up his sports bag. The skis and ski-sticks are already
standing in their holder.*

HANKA: . . . Apparently it all takes quite a long time. More
 difficult if we want a boy, but easier if it's a girl. The lawyer
 says we can rely on total discretion. Only he advised us to
 move flat so that she doesn't find out accidentally from
 talking to the neighbours. That's not a problem, is it?

ROMAN: No, of course not. How long does all this take?

HANKA: For a girl? Several months – there are a lot of girls,
 everyone seems to want boys. The only thing you have to
 sort out is a certificate testifying you're sterile.

ROMAN: Mikolaj can arrange all that.
 (ROMAN *puts the bag down to one side.* HANKA *grasps his hand.*)

HANKA: Roman, this is what you want, isn't it?

ROMAN: Yes.

HANKA: Do you want me to ring from Zakopane? Every day?

ROMAN: No.

HANKA: You do trust me, don't you?

ROMAN: Yes.

36

ROMAN *hands* HANKA *the ski bag through the carriage-window.*
HANKA: It's only for ten days.
ROMAN: It'll do you good.
HANKA: Roman . . .
  (*She is leaning out of the window and is quite close to him now.*)
  I know I'm always telling you this – but I love you. I really
  mean it. I mean it more than ever.

37

ROMAN *pours some milk out of a bottle into a saucepan. He notices
little* ANIA *through the window (the one from the seventh story) playing
around in the yard outside.* ANIA *has sat her dollies on the bench and is
talking to them.* ROMAN *opens the window slightly so that he can hear
the subject of her conversation, but from this distance he can hear
nothing. He stands, still holding the saucepan. The telephone rings.
There is silence on the other end of the line.*
ROMAN: Hello.
  (ROMAN *hears or perhaps imagines he can hear the receiver being
  put down. He goes over to the window and shuts it forcefully.*)

38

ROMAN *pulls up outside the shops and parks the car. There is little
movement at this time of day.* ROMAN *takes out a string shopping bag
and locks the car. Suddenly he freezes, his hand still on the door-
handle.* MARIUSZ *has stepped out of a shop in his bright jacket and is
carrying a load of shopping.* ROMAN *cannot take his eyes off him.*
MARIUSZ *walks over to his small Fiat – fastened to the roof-rack are a
pair of skis.*

39

ROMAN *has already changed into his white overcoat and trousers. He is walking along the corridor with the hospital* CONSULTANT.

ROMAN: I was . . .

CONSULTANT: Yes?

ROMAN: I was wondering if it was possible – to put me down for fewer operations.

CONSULTANT: Fewer? You've only got three today.

ROMAN: I mean, in general.

CONSULTANT: Upset about the young girl? What was her name – Ola?

ROMAN: Ola Jarek. Yes –

CONSULTANT: No one could have predicted she would –

ROMAN: I know. But I'd still like fewer operations.

CONSULTANT: Ever thought about taking appendixes out for a change?

(*Roman stops, astonished at the joke.*)

ROMAN: You know something, maybe that's the answer.

40

ROMAN *is mindlessly watching a documentary with the volume turned down. For the nth time that day he walks over to the telephone and mechanically dials a number. The signal is engaged.* ROMAN *immediately puts down the receiver – it has clearly been engaged for some time. He puts out the bottle for the milkman, comes back and dials the number again. This time, to his surprise, he gets a ringing tone and someone picks up the receiver. It is a* WOMAN's *voice.*

WOMAN: (*Voice over*) Hello?

ROMAN: Good mor— . . . good evening. I'm sorry, I've been having trouble getting through. Could I speak to Mariusz?

WOMAN: (*Voice over*) He's not here. Who's calling?

ROMAN: A friend – from his physics class.

WOMAN: (*Voice over*) He's gone skiing. To Zakopane. Any mess—

41

HANKA *is standing at the back of a long queue for a cable-car ticket.
The queue has spilt out of the small building. The weather is beautiful:
the ground lies covered in snow and the sun is blazing hot. Skiers are
leaning back against the upright skis they have dug deep into the snow
and sunning themselves.* MARIUSZ *appears behind* HANKA *carrying
his skis. He studies her for a while –* HANKA's *face is lifted towards the
sun.* MARIUSZ *takes two reserve tickets out of his pocket and wards off
the sun with his hand.*

MARIUSZ: The 9.45 – it's yours.
    (HANKA *looks down initially at the ticket and only then turns
    around.*)
HANKA: What – what are you doing here?
MARIUSZ: They told me where you were at the office, so I drove
    down. I don't – I didn't believe you when you said –
    (HANKA *looks at him for a second before her expression changes
    to the one we know from one of the first few scenes. She stares
    intently ahead almost as if into space.*)
    Hanka –
HANKA: Hold these for a moment. I've forgotten something.
    (*She gives him the skis and, skidding slightly on the frozen steps
    in her ski boots, runs off towards a taxi.*)

42

Still in her skiing outfit, HANKA *dials a long-distance phone number.*
HANKA: Is that the hospital?
VOICE: (*Over*) Yes.
HANKA: I'm calling from Zakopane – the name's Hanna Nycz. Is
    my husband there?
VOICE: (*Over*) The doctor called to say he wouldn't be in today.
    Can you hear me all right?
HANKA: Yes. I hear you. I have a message, it's very important. If
    he rings again, would you tell him I'm on my way home – on
    the first available bus or train. Hello?

VOICE: (*Over*) I heard you. That's fine, I'll pass it on.

43

ROMAN *is sitting by the table in his overcoat: he has just finished writing a short note. He folds it, tucks it into an envelope and throws it carelessly on to the table before leaving the flat.*

44

At the bus-station, HANKA *desperately tries to squeeze her way to the front of the queue waiting to get on the bus to Warsaw. She pushes her way up the steps.*

HANKA: Have you got a seat? I've got to –

(*She looks so determined that the driver, without saying a word, points to the empty seat right next to him.*)

45

ROMAN *gets into his car outside the block. He heads south, crossing into the lane marked with a huge sign: 'Krakow'. It begins to rain and so he switches on the windscreen wipers. He also switches on the radio, finds a station and turns the volume up loudly. The car is travelling fast, the radio is blaring, and the highway can be seen curving gently to the right up ahead. The car reaches the bend but instead of following the curve ploughs straight ahead, leaping off the highway into a concrete factory wall. Silence. A young man on a bicycle with a small trailer loaded down with luggage is approaching in the opposite direction. He looks over towards the car and slows down, his hair wet on account of the rain. The wall was not as thick as one might have imagined and the car has smashed clean through it, landing virtually in one piece on the other side. The slight drizzle falls into the car through the smashed front windscreen.* ROMAN *is hanging over his seat-belt, thrown forward over the crumpled steering wheel. Drops of rain stream down his bloodied face. The sagging fingers of one hand*

*slowly unbend. He half opens an eye and sits back in the driving seat.
Feeling his way blindly, he reaches over and turns the music down. He
can see the rain collecting on the smashed windscreen and opens his
mouth to catch a drop.*

It is getting dark and is still raining. HANKA's *bus passes the police
car standing on the hard-shoulder. The young man is holding his
bicycle not far away.* HANKA's *eyes are half closed, but even if she
had been looking she would not have been able, in the rain and
increasing darkness, to make out the small group of people loading the
remains of the Mazda on to a large rescue truck. Neither would she
have seen the young man get on his bicycle and disappear into the
darkness.*

46

HANKA *enters the flat, still in her ski boots and jacket. She switches on
the light. The flat is quiet and empty. She notices the envelope on the
table and reaches for it, in order to learn her fate.*

47

ROMAN, *with a bandage around his head and a plaster-cast on his
chest, is lying in the room adjoining the smallish, badly equipped
operating theatre in a small-town hospital. A young* NURSE *walks
over and leans over him.*

NURSE: Can you hear me?

(ROMAN *signals with his eyes that he can.*)

Your wife isn't in the hotel in Zakopane. She left for Warsaw
first thing this morning.

(ROMAN's *face betrays the hint of a smile.*)

ROMAN: Could you – ring Warsaw? 37–20–65.

(*The telephone rings.* HANKA, *still in her skiing outfit, senses that
this call will confirm her worst forebodings and that it is all too
late. She clasps her hands together to prevent herself from picking
up the receiver.*

The NURSE *carries the phone over and holds it as near to*

as possible. The ringing tone continues, uninterrrupted.)
NURSE: No one there?
(ROMAN *does not pay any attention to her and eventually hears
the receiver being picked up and the weak, hoarse voice of his
wife.*)
HANKA: (*Voice over*) Hello?
ROMAN: Hanka . . .

DECALOGUE TEN

The cast and crew of *Decalogue Ten* included:

JERZY	Jerzy Stuhr
ARTUR	Zbigniew Zamachowski
SHOP OWNER	Henry Bista

Director of Photography	Jacek Blawut
Cameraman	Jerzy Rudzinski
Producer	Ryszard Chutkowski
Composer	Zbigniew Preisner
Artistic Director	Halina Dobrowolska
Sound	Nikodem Wolk-Laniewski
Lighting	Jerzy Tomczuk
Film Editor	Ewa Smal
Production Managers	Pawel Mantorski
	Wlodzimierz Bendych
Costume Designers	Malgorzata Obloza
	Hanna Cwiklo
Director	Krzysztof Kieślowski

Still: Jerzy Stuhr as Jerzy and Zbigniew Zamachowski as Artur

I

It is early spring. Patches of snow still lie on the ground, but the sun is already beating its way along the dried-out pathways surrounding the block of flats. Mothers are walking along wheeling their prams. An obituary notice announcing the funeral of one of the tenants has been stuck to the glass window of a stairwell entrance.

A small one-room flat. One of the walls is taken up by metal cabinets secured with heavy padlocks. There are no carpets, rugs or plants. Only the cabinets, one large table, a bed by the window, and a stool instead of a bedside table. There is also an aquarium: large, red fish are floating stomach upwards on the surface of the water.

2

The cemetery is flat and deserted. We are witnesses to a formal funeral. Neither the intricate procedures of this ceremony, nor the extent to which it has become a mechanized ritual, are of interest to us. A short, corpulent man wearing a grey suit is making a speech. He has it prepared on a scrap of paper, but knows so well what he intends to say that he does not take advantage of it. We will be referring to him as the GOVERNOR. *Not without reason, as we shall see.*

GOVERNOR: . . . he sacrificed his family, his professional and perhaps even his emotional life for a noble passion. Who can say today how much this passion may have cost him? If Root – which is what we used to call him in the Union after his wartime code-name – thought there was a chance of acquiring an important addition to his collection, nothing could stop him. Considerations of time, distance and expense were meaningless to him – he dropped everything in pursuit of his dream and, I would not hesitate to use this word in assembled company, his desire.

(Two men stand nearest the grave. One is dressed with an elegance typical of a white-collar worker and it is obvious that although he has grafted hard to get where he is today, there is still

quite a way to go. The other, a few years his junior, is the exact
opposite. Wearing a green, military jacket and high lace-up
boots, his long, fair hair falling around a loosely tied scarf, he has
a lively and intelligent gaze which at present appears a little
absent. They are the sons of the deceased and are the only
relatives present. The stand out from the rest of the mourners
because of their position virtually right over the grave and because
they look a good deal younger. They do not appear like lost,
suddenly deserted sons, despite the occasion. Concluding his
speech, the GOVERNOR *addresses them.*)

GOVERNOR: In bidding farewell to our outstanding colleague, the
winner of eleven international gold medals and participant in
so many exhibitions, I would like to express my deepest
condolences to the family and to offer my support and
assistance if it may ever be required. On behalf of the Board
of the Polish Philatelic Association, on behalf of friends and
competitors, and finally, on my own behalf, I bow my head
in respect. Farewell.

(*The grave-diggers, who have been waiting impatiently for the*
speech to end, now get to work. A queue of mourners forms in
front of the two sons to pay their final respects.)

3

ARTUR *and* JERZY *have difficulty finding their bearings among the*
identical blocks on the estate.

JERZY: I was here – several years ago – it's on the seventh floor.
That much I remember.

(*They stand, bewildered.* ARTUR *spots the obituary notice fixed*
to a front entrance. They make their way towards that block of
flats.)

4

There are four keys, three locks and one padlock. The two brothers try
fitting the keys into the locks. Without doubt, the padlock is the easiest.

As they open it, a metal bar falls away. They are not so sure what to do with the remaining keys.

ARTUR: Look, metal . . .
    (*Indeed, the door is reinforced with a thick solid metal sheet. They play around with the keys.*)

JERZY: Dad used to open them by himself. I saw him.
    (ARTUR *discovers a fourth lock at the very top of the door, just under the embrasure: this resolves the problem of the fourth key, which looks like a long nail, but has a hidden set of teeth which flick out only after it has been turned in the lock. It is not surprising that it would not fit any of the other locks. The key easily slides into the top lock, which has a small and barely visible hole, after which there is a clicking sound: it is now open. There are three locks left, but everything is now much simpler. One opens to the left, as is normal, the other, in order to confuse intruders, to the right. The third is a flat Yale key. After several attempts, the door-handle finally releases, setting off a shrill alarm bell. The brothers quickly close the door, but the alarm bell continues to wail. A* NEIGHBOUR *in slippers and wearing a smart shirt and tie runs down from the floor above.*)

NEIGHBOUR: Gentlemen?

JERZY: We're family.
    (*They are forced to shout – the alarm bell drowns everything. The* NEIGHBOUR *runs into the flat. A small mirror in the tiny hallway hangs on a nail which turns out to be the alarm switch. The wailing stops. The* NEIGHBOUR *returns to the front door and blocks the entrance.*)

NEIGHBOUR: Identity cards, please.
    (JERZY *takes out his ID card. The* NEIGHBOUR *inspects it closely.*)

ARTUR: I don't usually carry mine – I'm his brother.

JERZY: Yes, he's my brother.
    (*The* NEIGHBOUR *compares the ID photograph with* JERZY'S *face and decides that it more or less fits. So too do the first name and surname of the father.*)

NEIGHBOUR: You should always carry your ID. This one is rather old, you should get a new one.
    (*He returns the card and offers his hand.*)

My deepest condolences.

JERZY: Thank you.

(*The* NEIGHBOUR *walks up to the mezzanine, glancing over his shoulder once more. The brothers open the door with a degree of trepidation.*)

5

JERZY: Christ!

(*We are familiar with the flat. The room with the metal cabinets, the narrow bed covered with a blanket, the stool, the kitchen with an old fridge and salt kept in a glass jar, the bathroom coated in acrylic paint. The brothers walk around the tiny flat in shocked disgust and stand over the aquarium with the dead fish.*)

Starved to death. They should be thrown out.

(*They attempt to lift the aquarium, but it is too heavy.*)

Go and get a ladle.

(ARTUR *returns from the kitchen with a ladle. He catches the fish and pulls them out. All goes well: only one stubbornly refuses to be caught, but is finally scooped up.* ARTUR *carries the dripping ladle to the toilet, empties it, pulls the chain and flushes the fish away.* JERZY, *who is standing in the middle of the room, wrinkles his nose.*)

It stinks in here.

ARTUR: It stinks, you're right.

(*He goes over to the window and twists the handle, but the window refuses to budge.* JERZY *tries the doors on to the balcony, without success. He eventually discovers some nails in the window-frame.*)

JERZY: Nailed up like a coffin.

ARTUR: Why?

JERZY: Why the alarm? Why the padlocks? Didn't you know the old man?

ARTUR: Not really.

JERZY: What did he do for fresh air?

(*A large air-conditioner is built into one of the windows.* ARTUR *puts his ear to it.*)

ARTUR: (*In English*) Air-conditioning. It even works.

(JERZY *looks at the thermostat in the air-conditioner.*)

JERZY: This regulates the temperature. And the humidity.

(*From the bunch of keys we saw earlier, they find some to fit the padlocks to the cabinets and open them, pulling back the metal flaps which bar the doors. The cabinets are full of neatly stacked albums; philatelic accessories, such as magnifying glasses, tweezers, etc. lie on a separate shelf. Catalogues and philatelic journals from all over the world stand on a shelf next to them. The eleven gold medals which their father won at international exhibitions have been stored in a special place.*)

We'll have to sell all this. Know anything about stamps? Anything at all?

(ARTUR *shakes his head: he doesn't have a clue.*)

ARTUR: What will you do with the money – fridge, is it, or a new TV set?

JERZY: I've already got them. Maybe a video. If there's enough.

(ARTUR *shrugs his shoulders.*)

ARTUR: And I'll waste the lot. Right down to the last penny – whatever it's worth. (*He makes an obvious drinking gesture.*) I could do with a drink. Dad wouldn't have anything in the flat, I suppose.

(JERZY *opens the fridge and finds a bottle with a tiny bit of vodka left at the bottom.*)

JERZY: Not for me. I've still got some business to see to.

(ARTUR *pours out the drink fairly, trying not to spill any.*)

ARTUR: Not even half a measure each – well, here's to Dad. Well?

(JERZY *raises his glass, but drinks only half of it, cautiously. ARTUR knocks it back and nods his head with relish – it is cold. They sit down.*)

How much do you reckon it's all worth?

JERZY: Stamps are valuable these days. I haven't a clue, maybe two hundred thousand, maybe even half a million.

(*He finishes off the rest of his vodka. He takes several albums out of the cabinet and recites, while throwing them one after the other on to the table.*)

The wasted life of our mother. Poor food. Patches on our trousers.

[283]

ARTUR: Don't.

JERZY: Did you know they had nothing to bury him in? I had to give him my suit.

(ARTUR *opens an album at random and picks a page.*)

ARTUR: What drives people to want to possess something at all costs? You should know. You like material things.

JERZY: Me? I like my creature comforts but the things themselves mean nothing. As for Dad, I never understood him.

(ARTUR *smiles.*)

ARTUR: Well, you're not looking too bad for it. I haven't seen you for two years.

JERZY: And?

ARTUR: You haven't changed a bit. You've even got the same suit on.

JERZY: No, it's a new one. I just like the colour. Is it really two years?

ARTUR: You gave me a reference in January – actually, it's more than two years. I still owe you twenty grand. I'll be able to pay you back now. What have you been up to?

JERZY: I spent some time in Libya, on construction work. Interested?

ARTUR: Not especially.

JERZY: I earned a fair bit. Moved flat. I'm supposed to go back there again, then I'll buy a car. You're right, it's boring.

(ARTUR *studies him intrigued. He had not expected this hint of bitterness from his brother.*)

ARTUR: Do you feel any older?

JERZY: No, I have all I want – for what it's worth. My little boy – do you remember him? He doesn't give a damn about all that. Goes around boasting instead that you're his uncle. He has a photo with your autograph on it – it's the height of cool in class apparently.

(ARTUR *smiles modestly.*)

ARTUR: I thought I only counted with the young ladies.

JERZY: Boys too.

ARTUR: I'll give you a record for him. He'll be the first to have it – it's a demo copy.

(JERZY *nods.* ARTUR *smiles. They are enjoying each other's company.*)

[284]

Just like old times, eh? How about it, then? Another drink?

(JERZY *looks at his watch and makes a calculation.*)

JERZY: OK. Will you go?

(ARTUR *puts on his jacket and checks to see whether he has any money. He leaves the room, but turns around at the door.*)

ARTUR: Until seven, OK? Then you've got to kick me out. We're playing at the Riviera tonight at eight.

(*As* JERZY *starts to examine the contents of a corner cupboard there is a ring at the doorbell.*)

JERZY: Come in!

(*The doorbell rings again.* JERZY *opens the door – a man of indeterminate age is standing there.*)

Yes?

(*The man bows politely.*)

MAN: Bromski's the name.

JERZY: Please.

BROMSKI: May I?

(JERZY *lets him pass through inside. The man offers his hand: it is sweaty.* BROMSKI *smiles, evidently under the impression that it is an agreeable smile.*)

Are you –?

JERZY: Yes.

BROMSKI: I have a small matter to discuss with you.

(JERZY *shuts the door, checking to see whether* ARTUR *is on his way back. He shows the man into the room.* BROMSKI *regards the scattered albums with interest.*)

Selling up, gentlemen?

JERZY: You said you had a matter to discuss.

BROMSKI: Ah yes. I realize this may not be the most opportune moment, but this matter –

JERZY: Fire away.

(*The man smiles every so often: perhaps he has a nervous twitch.*)

BROMSKI: I was a friend of your father's. Perhaps you saw me today. I was at the cemetery.

JERZY: What exactly is this business about?

(*The man reaches for his wallet, takes out a scrap of paper and unfolds it, but then immediately folds it back again.*)

BROMSKI: It's all a little embarrassing – but your father . . . you

[285]

see . . . this is . . . the deadline passes in a few days' time. He
owed me 220,000 zlotys.
(*He gives the scrap of paper to* JERZY, *who reads it. The
signature is indeed that of his father.*)
JERZY: I didn't know.
BROMSKI: I am aware that the funeral costs –
JERZY: Indeed.
BROMSKI: Precisely. If you would permit, I could perhaps . . .
find something of equivalent value here. It would make
things a lot less troublesome.
(*He points towards the albums spread out on the table.* JERZY
*stands between him and the table. He writes a telephone number
on the back of the scrap of paper and gives it to* BROMSKI.)
JERZY: Please give me a ring in five days' time. I'll try to get the
money.
BROMSKI: Very kind of you, otherwise I would have been forced
to consult a lawyer. Do I understand that you have no
intention at present of getting rid of the collection? Because
if you required any advice, or consultation, I would be –
(ARTUR *enters the room, triumphantly clutching a bottle.*)
I understand. Of course, you have your reasons. In such a
situation, I would myself –
(*A moment of embarrassed silence. Finally the man bows and
leaves.*)
JERZY: Dad owed that guy 220,000. He's the first one to have
turned up. For the time being.
(ARTUR *puts the bottle down on the table, looks at the things
which* JERZY *has taken out of the corner cupboard, and goes over
to the newspaper cuttings.*)
He collected cuttings about you.
ARTUR: I thought he didn't even know my first name.
JERZY: Look, I wouldn't mind the fridge and the bed with the
mattress. They'd be handy on the allotment. The rest is
yours – agreed?
(ARTUR *looks through the cuttings. The publication dates and
names of the papers have been scrupulously noted at the top of
each one.* JERZY *is not sure whether* ARTUR *has accepted his
division of the spoils.*)

[286]

Agreed?

ARTUR: Agreed, agreed. Did you ever wonder why there's such an age difference between us?

JERZY: I was born before '49, you in '56. In between time he was in prison.

ARTUR: Of course. I hadn't thought about it that way. (*He opens the bottle and pours out a measure each.*) Did he ever tell you anything about it?

JERZY: I was too small. And somehow later there was never any opportunity. He was in the Home Army, with some high rank or other. I remember the day he came back from prison. We were all tanned, but he was ever so pale. Mum started preparing the welcome home meal at least a week beforehand. Borrowed a table-cloth, worked miracles with the food, borrowed some knives and forks – you know, really went to town, made up the table especially. He stood at the table, looked at it and said: 'So, all the time I've been away you've been living like kings.' And went to his room and never came out. I used to see him from time to time after that – he used to smile a lot. Sometime around '58 he got a letter from an old comrade-in-arms. He came into the kitchen, steamed off the stamp and then just stared at it, examining it really closely. Just stood there, staring . . .

ARTUR: And that's when it all began?

JERZY: Presumably. He knew nothing about stamps before that. But from then on he lost interest in everyone else: Mum, me, then you . . .

ARTUR: Nice story about the table-cloth, though. Bit out of fashion these days, but maybe I could write a song about it.

JERZY: What is in fashion these days?

ARTUR: Stupidity. I remember – you got a bicycle, a blue bicycle.

JERZY: Dad inherited it. His brother had left for America before the war and died there. Mum got a watch and I got the bicycle – he spent the rest. Mum never told me how much he got, but it was several thousand dollars at least. I had no shoes on my feet, but had a bicycle. Mum sold her watch to buy food, and he started collecting stamps. He couldn't have cared less about anything else . . .

[287]

(ARTUR *raises the glass.*)

ARTUR: I'm beginning to take to the bloke.

JERZY: Who?

ARTUR: The old man. Kicking the bucket like that with so little fuss – no pills, no booze, no injections . . .

(*They drink up.*)

JERZY: Who knows if it wasn't for the best.

ARTUR: Listen. What are we going to do with the flat? I'm registered, but I never actually lived here.

JERZY: It's owned by the state. I don't know if anything can be done with it. Buy it, sell it – do you want to live here?

ARTUR: No way.

(ARTUR *fills up the glasses again. They drink.* JERZY *winces.*)

JERZY: Poison.

ARTUR: You get used to it. One more, to Dad. Hell, I hardly even knew him. You never appreciate what you've got until it's not there any more.

JERZY: Right now all we've got is a 220-grand debt.

(*He reaches for the nearest albums and looks through them.*) I've heard about a stamp market. I think it's in a school somewhere on Krajowa Rada Narodowa Street. Maybe you could try there?

(*The stamps are arranged in isolated groups with huge gaps between each one. A single stamp, sometimes even several on one page, according to a system incomprehensible to the uninitiated.* JERZY *passes the albums to* ARTUR.)

ARTUR: Does your boy collect stamps?

JERZY: Not seriously. He likes ones with aeroplanes on them.

(ARTUR *stops at one particular page in the album.*)

ARTUR: Give him these. Three balloons . . . no, Zeppelins. They're bound to be a set. (*He reads out aloud*) Polarfahrt. He'll have something from Grandad.

(*From under the cellophane strip, he pulls out three stamps with three Zeppelins in three different colours: blue, red and brown. The colours are pale and passive, almost as if faded.*) Nice. Some kind of race, or something. From 1931.

6

A taxi pulls up in front of the estate of one-family detached houses.
JERZY gets out. ARTUR leans out behind him. They are not drunk,
although perhaps speaking a little loudly on account of the rumbling
engine of the taxi.
ARTUR: Here?
JERZY: Here.
ARTUR: Rather nice. Tell the little one I have that record for him.
JERZY: He isn't so little any more.
(ARTUR *gets back into the taxi.*)
ARTUR: To the Riviera. (*As the taxi moves off, he winds down the*
window.) Glad we bumped into each other again.

7

JERZY *stands in the kitchen doorway. His* WIFE *was attractive once*
upon a time, but her features have now become drawn on account of
the day-to-day struggle for survival. She looks at JERZY *with definite*
anger: as usual, he is late and has failed to arrange what he had
promised.
JERZY: I'm sorry . . .
(*His* WIFE *does not react.*)
I didn't have time. We'll go tomorrow. I got chatting with
Artur after the funeral.
WIFE: The surgery is closed tomorrow.
JERZY: Well the day after tomorrow then. I'll phone. I'm really
sorry, but you know . . .
WIFE: I'm saying nothing.
JERZY: Obviously not. Piotrek!
(JERZY *turns and goes to his son's room.*)
Do you remember Grandad?
PIOTREK: A little.
JERZY: I've brought something for you from Grandad – some
stamps to remember him by.
(JERZY *rummages through the wallet and pulls out the three*

[289]

Zeppelins. He gives them to PIOTREK, *who lays them out on top of his exercise book and examines them.*)

PIOTREK: Nice.

JERZY: Grandad's dead, did you know? He was buried today.

(*The boy looks at him. His eyes glaze over.* JERZY *is surprised.*) Are you crying?

PIOTREK: No, I've cried already. Mum told me at lunch.

(JERZY *closes his eyes.*)

It's sad about Grandad, isn't it?

JERZY: Artur's going to give you a record of his. Brand new, no one else has got it yet.

(*The boy nods.*)

Has your tooth been hurting?

PIOTREK: No, not really.

JERZY: I'm sorry I didn't make it . . .

PIOTREK: Mum was furious. She's been screaming all day.

8

A colourfully painted minibus with a huge yellow 'City Live' logo in English on it is being driven around the Marszalkowska roundabout. Four long-haired youths and young teenage girls are seated inside. ARTUR *is sitting at the window, eating an apple. Musical equipment, speakers and cables lie scattered around the bus.*

GIRL: You shouldn't eat apples. They're not good for you. You can get cancer.

ARTUR: You mean from smoking.

(*He points to the cigarette which is dangling from the* GIRL'*s mouth. She shakes her head.*)

GIRL: No, from apples.

(*The long-haired* DRIVER *stops the bus on Grzybowska Street, just in front of the school.*)

DRIVER: Here?

(ARTUR *grabs his bag.*)

GIRL: Want me to come along?

ARTUR: I'll be back in an hour. Set up the equipment and try to do something with the mike so it doesn't crackle.

9

The school which houses the largest stamp club in Warsaw. ARTUR, *carrying his several albums and bag, is clearly out of place. He looks curiously at the people examining the albums and stamps in various parts of the hall.* ARTUR *notices people approaching one man in particular, whom they draw aside and consult for advice.*

   ARTUR *gives him his albums.*

ARTUR: I wanted to find out how much these might be worth. How to sell them and so on.

   (*The* EXPERT *glances through the first album and immediately returns them all back.*)

EXPERT: Are you Root's son?

   (ARTUR *nods.*)

   This is only a fragment of his collection.

ARTUR: I'm willing to sell the whole lot.

EXPERT: Would you be so kind as to wait a moment?

   (*He disappears.* ARTUR *sits on the window-sill and looks around: a group of young boys are rummaging through a box full of cheap postage stamps. The* EXPERT *returns after a while, accompanied by the* GOVERNOR. *He is the short corpulent man in a grey suit who made the speech at the funeral.*)

   The Governor would like to meet you.

GOVERNOR: There are two of you, aren't there?

ARTUR: Yes, two.

GOVERNOR: Would it be possible to come and visit you both some time at your father's flat?

   (ARTUR *finds the whole situation a little bizarre.*)

ARTUR: Of course, if that's what you'd prefer.

GOVERNOR: I know the address.

10

The metal cabinets in the flat are open. The albums which JERZY *and* ARTUR *earlier took out of the cabinets have now been replaced. The* GOVERNOR *paces around impatiently, apparently unable to keep still.*

It is hard to imagine how he managed to control himself for so long during the funeral speech.

GOVERNOR: So, gentlemen, what are your plans?

JERZY: We are looking to sell them. We need the money.

GOVERNOR: If it is no great secret – which ones in particular?

(ARTUR *looks as if he is about to reply.* JERZY *cuts him short.*)

JERZY: We have them. You can take our word for it.

(*The* GOVERNOR *reaches for a metal box which is standing in one of the cabinets. He opens it with one of the keys from the large bunch we saw earlier. The box – which, one should add, is not the only one of its kind in the cabinet – contains two large albums. The* GOVERNOR *opens the album he has just pulled out at a random page and shows* JERZY *a stamp from it. There is no hesitation – it appears he is more than familiar with the collection.*)

GOVERNOR: With this one alone, you could buy a small Polish Fiat. With two you could buy a Volkswagen. The whole set would be enough for a decent flat.

(ARTUR *looks at his brother.* JERZY *swallows in amazement. It is the first time someone competent has been able to tell them anything about their father's collection.*)

JERZY: How much – how much are they worth? More or less?

(JERZY *points to the albums, cabinets, boxes, everything.*)

GOVERNOR: Tens of millions. Nobody in Poland would be able to buy this collection – they simply wouldn't have the money. You would have to sell it off gradually on the Western market through a professional intermediary, but legally this could be done only through a Government agency. Through illegal traders, you could probably sell them off individually for about 50 million zlotys. But it would throw the market into chaos for several months.

(*The* GOVERNOR *halts in mid-flow. He clearly enjoys and has a talent for making little speeches. He pauses only to check if he has had the intended effect and then continues.*)

Your father invested his whole life in this collection. I spoke about it at the cemetery, but I am not certain whether you quite understood me. If you are not convinced by what I say about the material value of this collection, you may like to consider another aspect: it would be criminal to squander

away thirty years of a person's life, even if it was only the life of
a father whom you didn't really know. He did not do all this
for money, gentlemen. He did it for love.

(*The* GOVERNOR *has clearly concluded his speech and is awaiting
applause; the conclusion, especially, was rather well put. But no
applause is forthcoming. Both brothers stand stock-still. The*
GOVERNOR *therefore reaches again into the cabinet and takes out
a few books lying on one of the shelves.*)

You have here some catalogues, gentlemen. Here are the
prices: in Poland, abroad, and the number of examples
available on the market. You do not need to be an expert to
understand them. All that is required is a bit of time and
patience. I sincerely hope that in memory of your father you
will find both. Well, goodbye, gentlemen. If you – if you need
any help, I am at your disposal. What I said at the cemetery is
true. I was a good friend of your father's, and now, well,
goodbye.

(*The* GOVERNOR *takes his leave. The silence is broken by the
sound of the door closing.*)

ARTUR: Holy shit.

JERZY: Yes. Surprise, surprise.

II

JERZY *enters the house and immediately spots* PIOTREK, *who is closing
a door to one of the rooms. He puts his finger to his lips.* JERZY *looks at
him inquiringly.* PIOTREK *goes up to his father.*

PIOTREK: Have you been at work?

JERZY: This morning? Yes, I was, then I left. I met up with Artur.

　　　(JERZY *takes a brand new 'City Live' record out of his briefcase
　　　and gives it to* PIOTREK. *His son smiles at the record, but continues.*)

PIOTREK: Mum called. She was trying to get hold of you – right
　　　now she's asleep.

JERZY: What for?

　　　(PIOTREK *does not know.*)

PIOTREK: I put a blanket over her.

　　　(JERZY *takes off his coat.* PIOTREK *stands by his bedroom door*

[293]

*and beckons to his father. He is holding the new record in his hand
and is thrilled to discover on the sleeve a dedication and the
autographs of all the members of the band.)*
Are these really their autographs? All of them?
JERZY: Seems so. Look, Artur's written something. Just here:
'For Piotrek – hope this cheers you up.' Great, isn't it?
(It is obvious from PIOTREK's *expression.)*
How are the Zeppelins?
*(*PIOTREK *takes him into his room. A huge pile of stamps lies on
the table.* PIOTREK *smiles, pleased with himself.)*
PIOTREK: I traded them in. Look how many I got in exchange.
*(*JERZY *looks at the colourful mess and his smile vanishes instantly.)*
JERZY: Who with?

12

*Several young boys are standing in front of a stamp shop on
Swietokrzyska Street.* PIOTREK *points out one of them to his father
from inside the Skoda, which is parked neaby on the pavement. It is a*
BOY *in wire-rim glasses.* JERZY *gets out of the car.*
JERZY: Stay there and don't move.
(He approaches the BOY, *who appears cocky and self-assured.)*
I'd like to make you an offer.
(The BOY *responds immediately, clearly street-wise.)*
BOY: We are here to serve you.
JERZY: Come over here. No fuss.
(He nods for the BOY *to follow him. There is an archway leading
into a courtyard around the corner on Czackiego Street.* JERZY
goes through, lets the BOY *pass, and then blocks the way so that
there is no escape. The* BOY *becomes nervous.)*
BOY: What's going on?
*(*JERZY *goes right up to him. The* BOY *warns him.)*
Watch it, or I'll thump you.
*(But there is no room for manoeuvre. He is already right up against
the wall.)*
JERZY: You took a young kid for a ride.
BOY: I've got a living to earn.

JERZY: He was my son.

BOY: Nowadays just about everyone's got parents.

(*JERZY suddenly grabs the* BOY *by the nose and grips it firmly between two fingers, bringing tears to the* BOY'*s eyes.*)

JERZY: The set of Zeppelins – hand them over.

(*The* BOY *says nothing.* JERZY *gives his nose a twist and grips it even more tightly. It starts to bleed.*)

BOY: I sold them.

JERZY: For how much?

BOY: Forty grand.

JERZY: Who to?

(*The* BOY *says nothing.* JERZY *gives the nose a further twist – any further and it would be practically upside-down. Tears mingled with blood are streaming down the* BOY'*s face. He moves his head, probably wanting to say something, but finds it impossible.* JERZY *loosens his grip.*)

BOY: A shop. On Wspolna Street.

JERZY: If you're lying, you'll be sorry.

(*The* BOY *catches his breath with difficulty and holds his nose – blood is streaming out from between his fingers.*)

BOY: Please don't tell on me. He'd – he'd kill me.

JERZY: So would I if I had half the chance.

(*He massages his aching fingers.*)

13

In the small shop on Wspolna Street, the doorbell rings automatically when the door is opened. The OWNER *likes to think of himself as a bit of a ladies' man: he is wearing an elegant necktie, a bracelet with his blood-type engraved on it, etc.*

JERZY: I'm afraid I have a rather unpleasant matter to discuss with you.

OWNER: I'm very sorry to hear that.

(*He listens carefully.*)

JERZY: A kid from Swietokrzyska Street sold you some stamps for forty thousand zlotys. He ripped off my son for some rubbish in exchange.

[295]

(*The* OWNER *is clearly surprised.*)

OWNER: I'm afraid I have no idea what you are talking about.

JERZY: I see.

OWNER: A misunderstanding perhaps?

JERZY: Perhaps.

OWNER: Such things happen.

JERZY: Yes – and if I were looking to buy a set of three German Zeppelins, Polarfahrt, dated 1931, you wouldn't know anything about them either I suppose?

OWNER: That can be discussed.

(*He reaches under the counter and takes out the three stamps, which have been placed in a special cellophane wrapping.*)

Are these the ones you had in mind?

JERZY: Ah, yes.

OWNER: They are for sale.

JERZY: How much?

OWNER: Not expensive: 190,000 zlotys. One is slightly damaged, probably the result of some unprofessional handling recently. See, just here.

(*He points to a torn corner.*)

JERZY: I am afraid I am going to have to call the police.

OWNER: Be my guest. By all means.

(*He reaches up to a high shelf and brings down a telephone. Next to it he places a small tin with a slit in it and a label: 'Phone-call: 5 zlotys'. The* OWNER *is surprised to see that* JERZY *makes no move to phone. He points at the sticker with the emergency phone numbers on the front for ambulance, fire and police.*)

These are the numbers: 997 or 21–89–09 for the local police station. Are you going to make the call?

(JERZY *stands with the receiver in his hand but makes no move to dial: his bluff has been called. The* OWNER *rummages among some papers and pulls out a receipt.*)

This is the receipt for the purchase. The set was sold to me by a gentleman who was leaving the country – look, here is the description of the stamps, with the damage I mentioned. I paid him 168,000 zlotys. On the wall here, just above your head is my licence for the shop.

(*He points to the licence. It is carefully framed and has a large*

number of official-looking rubber stamps on it.)
Perhaps it is for the best that valuable stamps remain in the
country and are not smuggled abroad. I am sure you will
agree. Also a question of patriotism, wouldn't you say?

14

Jerzy's WIFE *sits in the corner of a settee, knitting.* JERZY *shuffles
around the room in his overcoat.*
WIFE: Are you going out?
JERZY: I've arranged to see Artur.
  (JERZY *feels uneasy about what he has to say. He shuffles around
  a little longer.*)
  Piotrek, leave us, please.
WIFE: No, stay here.
JERZY: We won't be able to buy the furniture after all.
WIFE: Ooooo . . . and can we be told why not?
JERZY: I have to fork out some money on account of father's
  death.
WIFE: You said we'd come into money, not end up spending any.
  Didn't your father collect something or other? You said . . .
  but that was when at least you had something to say for
  yourself . . . wasn't it stamps?
JERZY: Yes, it was stamps.
WIFE: I heard they were worth something.
JERZY: They are.
  (*The* WIFE *carries on with her knitting.* JERZY *stands by the
  window, silent.*)
WIFE: I thought you were in a hurry.
JERZY: I am.
WIFE: Well, what are you waiting for? Get going.

15

*Artur's band is playing in a large hall. Male and female fans sway to
the rhythm.* ARTUR *is singing and screaming into the microphone.*

ARTUR: Kill, kill, kill
Screw who you will
Lust and crave
Pervert and deprave
Every day of the week
Every day of the week
On Sunday hit mother
Hit father, hit brother
Hit sister, the weakest
And steal from the meekest
'Cos everything's yours
Yeah, everything's yours

(JERZY *approaches the platform, feeling out of place. He pushes his way through the flashing lights and people. As he gets closer, he makes a sign to* ARTUR. ARTUR *points with his eyes to where* JERZY *should wait for him.* JERZY *goes backstage to the dressing room. He hears how the hall explodes with screams of ecstasy.* ARTUR *appears, sweating. They go out on to the terrace.*)

JERZY: You'll catch a cold.

(ARTUR *makes a disdainful gesture with his hand.*)

ARTUR: I already have.

JERZY: The bloke rang about the money. I've arranged to meet him on Sunday.

ARTUR: What, the 220 grand?

JERZY: Yes, I've got 90,000 put aside for the furniture for Piotrek's room. I told them it'll have to be put off for the time being.

ARTUR: And the wife?

JERZY: She suspects I've got a bit on the side. Now that I am not going with them to the country on Sunday, she'll virtually be certain.

ARTUR: Maybe I should deal with him?

JERZY: He's a sneaky bastard, he might pull the wool over your eyes. So what shall we do? Have you got any cash?

ARTUR: Zilch. You know how it is: easy come easy go. I could sell the amp.

JERZY: What will you play on?

ARTUR: You don't play on an amp. It's worth about 60,000. But what about the rest?

[298]

(*There is a moment's silence. They look at each other.*)

JERZY: Well?

ARTUR: The stamps? For some reason . . . I'm not too keen on doing anything with them straight away.

JERZY: Neither am I.

(JERZY *smiles with relief.* ARTUR *smiles as well. Night on a cold terrace: the two brothers have made a silent pact.*)

ARTUR: Let's leave them where they are.

(*A* MEMBER *of Artur's band appears on the terrace.*)

MEMBER OF BAND: Hey, we're on.

(*He disappears.*)

ARTUR: Ninety and sixty, that's one-hundred and fifty. That leaves seventy. We'll borrow it somehow. OK?

16

JERZY *puts the luggage on the roof-rack of the Skoda and says goodbye to* PIOTREK. *His* WIFE *emerges from the house.*

WIFE: There's nothing left to eat in the fridge. I am taking everything to the country.

JERZY: I'll buy what I need.

WIFE: Don't be alarmed, but I've locked up all the cupboards and chests of drawers. I don't want anyone poking around.

JERZY: No one's going to.

WIFE: I've also hidden my cosmetics.

(*His* WIFE *has said her piece and so gets into the car. She fastens her seat-belt straight away, refusing any assistance from* JERZY *in this tricky operation. The car moves off.*)

17

A taxi draws up before the block on our estate. ARTUR *gets out, pulls out a large, heavy sack and looks up. It is already late. There are few lights on in the block, but* ARTUR *notices the light is on in his father's flat. Somebody must be there. He leaves the sack at the foot of the stairwell entrance and finds a quite thick, young branch in the bushes*

*growing around the block. He makes a long, stout stick out of it,
swishes it around in the air a few times, then disappears through the
entrance doors with the sack over his shoulder.*

18

ARTUR *tries to open the door as quietly as possible. He enters, holding
the stick above his head.* JERZY *is sitting at the table, looking at the
stamps. He looks up.*

ARTUR: I was worried in case someone was poking round.
  (*He dumps his sack on the floor.* JERZY *looks at it in surprise.*)
  What the hell are you doing here?
JERZY: Just looking.
ARTUR: I had no idea.
JERZY: I was here yesterday as well.
ARTUR: What time?
JERZY: Before lunch.
ARTUR: We must have just missed each other. I came just before
  noon.
JERZY: I'd left by then.
ARTUR: Look, I'll be staying here on and off.
  (*He gets up and empties the contents of the sack on to the bed.
  Shirts, T-shirts, trainers, socks and bed-linen come tumbling
  out.*)
JERZY: Have they thrown you out?
ARTUR: No. I was just worried about all this stuff here. It's not
  safe – anyone could get in, just like you've done. Somebody
  ought to be here. In any case, I'm registered.
JERZY: Fair enough, I'd feel happier about it.
  (ARTUR *unpacks.*)
  Guess what I've found.
  (*He shows his brother two stamps in a special album with a page
  to themselves.*)
  The only set of its kind in Poland. But incomplete.
  (*He shows* ARTUR *the photograph of the whole set printed in the
  catalogue.*)
  Blue, yellow – the pink one's missing. Ever seen this before?

(JERZY *now shows him a thick pad full of carefully written notes.
He finds the page with the heading 'Mercury 1851'.*)
'Pink Austrian Mercury 1851, hidden after the war by Z.,
traced by K.B.R., stolen during the renowned robbery of '65,
turned up briefly in Krakow at J.'s, sold (or traded) in '68
before J.'s departure from Poland, J. asked in Denmark said
he didn't remember the name of the buyer, knew only that he
travels regularly to Krakow and was recommended to him by
K.W., who died in '71. News from K.B.R. – it is in Poland,
somewhere in the south, M.W., perhaps? Any chance? Tip-
off: not for money.' Half the notebook is taken up with stories
like this one. Numbers of some sort or another . . . it's all very
hard to follow. I've been reading it for hours.

ARTUR: Pink Austrian Mercury . . . it must have looked beautiful
next to these other two.

(*It is now night-time. The two sit facing each other across the table
with a magnifying glass and tweezers, surrounded by albums and
catalogues. They exchange their father's notes. JERZY points to the
open album. There is an empty page*).
It doesn't feel the same without them. Wonderful name that –
Zeppelin.

JERZY: The little idiot. I suppose he meant well.

ARTUR: I'll work on it.

(*Dawn. ARTUR stretches out on the balcony, feeling rather cold
after the sleepless night. He leans out over the balcony and tenses.
He calls JERZY. They lean over the balcony together and look up
towards the rest of the block above them, silhouetted against the
brightening sky.*)

ARTUR: Anyone could shin down a rope from up there. It's only
three floors – they'd be in in no time.

JERZY: We need bars.

ARTUR: One on the balcony, another across the window. Dad
nailed them up, but one blow would easily smash the glass. No
problem.

JERZY: You know something? I feel as if all my other problems
have ceased to matter. They've simply vanished, completely.

ARTUR: Must feel good.

[301]

JERZY: It does. Very.

ARTUR: Maybe they never existed at all. Maybe it's all in the
mind: you don't want them – they're not there.

JERZY: Write a song about it.

ARTUR: After I've finished telling people to sin. I've got an idea.
Let's find a stamp. Worth about 100,000. Officially, so
there's some record of it.

(*They return to the flat and look through the catalogues.*)

19

The little stamp shop on Wspolna Street. The OWNER, *today in a
different necktie, emerges from behind a curtain. A polite, welcoming
smile.* ARTUR, *unshaven, with his long hair and green jacket, checks
to see they are alone. He puts his bag on the counter and takes out his
wallet. He places a stamp before the* OWNER.

ARTUR: I've heard good reports about you. That you know about
these things.

OWNER: A little, naturally.

ARTUR: I came across this little something the other day. Is it
worth much?

(*The* OWNER *reaches for the catalogue and turns the pages. He
talks to* ARTUR *without raising his eyes.* ARTUR *notices that the*
OWNER *has long ago found what he was looking for.*)

OWNER: Where did you find it?

ARTUR: At home.

OWNER: Your own home?

ARTUR: Not exactly.

OWNER: It's worth 15,000 zlotys. I'll buy it for three thousand.

ARTUR: Let's say five.

OWNER: Four. It's stolen.

ARTUR: OK, it's a deal.

(*The* OWNER *reaches into the cash register and takes out 4,000
zlotys.* ARTUR *counts it, but is watching the man all the time and
whisks the stamp off the counter just as he is about to make a
move towards it.*)

OWNER: What are you . . . ?

(ARTUR *seats himself on a small chair. He brushes a speck of imaginary dust off the counter and takes out a tape-recorder from the bag standing on it. He rewinds the tape and stops it.*)

ARTUR: Shall I switch it on? Let's see if it's recorded anything . . .

OWNER: What do you want?

(ARTUR *points towards the licence which the owner had so willingly showed* JERZY *the other day.*)

ARTUR: A licence like that must be worth its weight in gold nowadays.

OWNER: All right. Now what do you want?

ARTUR: The three stamps with the Zeppelins. German, year 1931. I'll give you 4,000 zlotys and a brand-new tape-cassette. BASF. There's a few minutes' recording on it, but it lasts for ninety minutes.

OWNER: Very clever. I knew there was something fishy about you when you walked in.

ARTUR: You should have followed your nose.

OWNER: Someone else was here the other day . . .

ARTUR: That was my brother.

OWNER: He wasn't quite so smart.

ARTUR: He didn't have all the details then. He didn't know about you.

OWNER: Are you interested in the money or the stamps?

ARTUR: The stamps.

OWNER: I see. Are you the sons of . . .?

ARTUR: Yes.

OWNER: I see.

(*He takes out a metal box, similar to the ones in the father's cabinets, and opens it. He takes out three stamps wrapped in delicate cellophane. He flashes a friendly smile before handing them over to* ARTUR.)

I know this is a personal matter, but do you intend to dispose of your father's collection, or keep it?

ARTUR: We're hanging on to it. (*In English*) 'For keeps', as they say in English.

(*The* OWNER *smiles once more. He has taken a liking to* ARTUR.)

OWNER: Do you know anything about stamps?

[303]

ARTUR: As you can see, we're only beginners.

(*The* OWNER *hands* ARTUR *the stamps and quickly takes the 4,000 zlotys and the cassette.*)

OWNER: It is not inconceivable that I may have a proposition to make you.

ARTUR: We're open-minded. It's in vogue these days.

20

Bars have already been fitted on the balcony and across the windows. ARTUR *has made himself at home in his father's flat: we can see a guitar, scattered sheets of music and equipment. He himself is sitting face to face with a large dog, pushing a piece of sausage towards its nose.*

ARTUR: Not from the right hand. No!

(*He says this as the dog begins to move his nose closer. The dog turns his head away, feigning complete disinterest.* ARTUR *transfers the sausage to his left hand. The dog wolfs it down in seconds.* ARTUR *pats him on the head – the dog is visibly pleased with himself. There are footsteps on the stairs.*)

Who's there?

(*The dog pricks up his ears and gives a deep, throaty growl.* ARTUR *gives a command.*)

Go get!

(*The dog is at the door in a flash. He barks loudly, snarling ferociously.*)

Enough. Heel!

(*The dog calms down as the noises in the corridor cease. He returns to the room and sits by the metal cabinets. Breathing heavily, his large tongue hanging out of his jaws, he looks deeply into* ARTUR *'s eyes.*)

21

JERZY *walks around his own house, moves across the terrace and unlocks the door before going into the room which is separated from the*

*rest of the building. He takes off his coat, throws it on to the bed and
goes in to his son's room.*

JERZY: Has Artur called?

PIOTREK: I haven't taken any calls.

JERZY: Is Mum angry?

PIOTREK: No. She says things are more relaxed now. Look what
she bought me.

> (PIOTREK *points to a pair of attractive blue braces. He
> demonstrates how to clip them on.*)

Great, aren't they?

JERZY: Great. What about school?

PIOTREK: I got a better grade for Russian.

JERZY: How much better?

PIOTREK: Top marks. Maths isn't so good . . .

JERZY: I can give you a hand.

PIOTREK: Mum says she can arrange a private tutor. She says
you're unreliable.

JERZY: Well, don't rely on me then.

> (*He leaves the room, slightly ruffled. He knocks at the door to the
> room where his* WIFE *is sitting.*)

Mind if I use the phone?

WIFE: Please yourself.

> (JERZY *dials a number. His* WIFE *holds up the palm of her hand
> so that* JERZY *cannot avoid noticing it. He looks puzzled.*)

JERZY: What's up?

WIFE: Look, the finger . . .

JERZY: The wedding-ring? Where's the wedding-ring? Have you
lost it?

WIFE: I sold it.

JERZY: Why?

WIFE: How else was I going to pay for the renovating?

JERZY: I have to go over there. To see Artur. No one's answering.

WIFE: End of conversation then.

JERZY: I'm sorry.

22

JERZY *tries to open the door to his father's flat, but the key, which he thought he had mastered by now, does not appear to fit. The threatening, muffled growling of a dog can be heard from behind the door.*

ARTUR: Who's there?

JERZY: It's me, Jurek!

(ARTUR *draws back the bolts. The dog is frothing at the mouth.*) Take that brute away.

(ARTUR *can be heard pulling the snarling animal away from the door. The dog is now barking from the back of the flat.*)

ARTUR: I've shut him in the bathroom.

JERZY: What the hell is going on in here? The key doesn't fit the lock.

ARTUR: I've changed it. I was advised to change the locks from time to time. Here, this is your new one.

JERZY: Who advised you?

ARTUR: Just friends who know about these things.

JERZY: You could have bloody well told me. I couldn't get hold of you. I was trying to get through all afternoon on the phone.

ARTUR: What's the problem? I went out shopping and then took the dog for a walk.

JERZY: It's nothing. I spent a few hours in the library. We ought to replace the fish in the tank. Guess why Dad used to keep them in here?

(*He takes out a pad which he has clearly been using to make notes in the library.*)

'Fish are the best indicators of air purity in a given space. They grow and live healthily only if the air is free of substances damaging to printed matter, books, stamps etc.' I translated this myself from a Czech monthly.

ARTUR: Clever old you.

(*The dog is still growling from inside the bathroom.*)

JERZY: Is he always like this?

ARTUR: Only when locked up. Shall I let him out? I'm worried he might go for you.

JERZY: You'll have to do something about him. He has to be
taught to recognize me.

(ARTUR *leaves the room and puts the dog on a small leash in the
bathroom. He cautiously brings him back into the room. The dog
curls his lips to reveal a huge set of fangs.*)

ARTUR: He's one of us, boy. One of us. Look.

(*He ties the leash around the door-handle and goes up to* JERZY.
*He puts his arms around him demonstratively, draws him close
and kisses him.*)

Look boy, it's Jurek. He's my brother, he's one of us. Dear
old Jurek.

(*The dog calms down slightly, but still eyes* JERZY *suspiciously.*)

There's a good dog . . .

(*He unties the leash from the door-handle. The dog does not
move.*)

Try stroking him. Go on . . .

(JERZY *stretches out his hand. The dog immediately bares his
teeth and tenses.*)

He'll get used to you. Stay the night, maybe he'll get over it.
I brought a folding bed. I hate having to sleep two to a bed,
even when it's girls.

(JERZY *sees the music sheets which* ARTUR *has been working on
spread out on the table.*)

JERZY: Composing something?

ARTUR: Trying. It's not coming. I can't concentrate. I took the
dog out and ran into the bloke who Dad was in debt to. He
was hanging around here.

JERZY: But we paid him off.

ARTUR: He said he had friends.

JERZY: Does the dog have to be taken out? Couldn't you just
make a sand-box for him?

ARTUR: He's a big dog. He has to have a run at least once a day.

JERZY: Perhaps we should get another one. One for me, one for
you. That way we could take them out in turns.

ARTUR: Maybe we'll have to.

(*The telephone rings.*)

Hello?

23

*A charming back room in the small stamp shop on Wspolna Street.
The* OWNER *has poured coffee into tiny cups. Because there is so little
space, the guests have been given small armchairs, while the* OWNER
*perches on a window-sill. He smiles and affectedly offers round the
sugar.*

OWNER: Have you by any chance come across the small matter of
the pink Austrian Mercury?

(JERZY *is still offended from their last meeting.*)

JERZY: We have. You seem to be very well informed.

OWNER: We stamp-collectors tend to know one another. Are you
aware of how much it is worth?

ARTUR: We know that there is one in Poland.

OWNER: Yes. And I know who has it.

(*The brothers look at each other.* ARTUR *even takes out the
match from his mouth which he has been chewing.*)

ARTUR: We're a bit low on money. My brother has sold his car,
but . . .

OWNER: Money is not the problem in this particular case,
gentlemen.

JERZY: So what is?

OWNER: This is a problem of . . . I would have to know how
badly you really wanted it.

ARTUR: Pretty badly.

JERZY: Pretty badly.

OWNER: You see, gentlemen, I would like us to meet again to
discuss this matter. But for this to be profitable you would
both need to have a medical check-up.

JERZY: A check-up?

OWNER: Blood-group, sedimentation, a urine test . . .

JERZY: Do you intend to treat us for a disease? Or sell us the
stamp?

OWNER: The stamp is not for sale. And only I know who has it.
Your father was unable to track it down for years, even
though he wanted it desperately. Therefore, if you also want
it badly . . .

ARTUR: A check-up can be arranged, it's no great problem.
OWNER: That is what I thought.

24

A green park, full of people. Maybe someone is playing the piano in the shade of Chopin's silver weeping willow. ARTUR *taps out the rhythm lightly with his foot, as we have seen him do before. The* OWNER *looks through the results of the medical check-up.* JERZY *is anxious.* ARTUR *waits with a smile to see what will happen next.*

OWNER: Yes, as I said, it is not a question of money. The person who owns the pink Austrian Mercury lives in Tarnow.
    (*The brothers look at each other. Everything tallies with their father's notes: Tarnow is in the south of Poland.*)
JERZY: And what does he want?
OWNER: He wants a set in exchange. It is a small one, consisting of only two stamps. They are currently in the possession of a serious collector who lives in Szczecin.
JERZY: A serious collector?
OWNER: Good question. He is after a certain tiny stamp, quite undistinguished, which . . .
ARTUR: Which we have. But what does our blood-group have to do with it?
OWNER: Which, gentlemen, you do not have.
JERZY: So who does?
OWNER: As it happens, I do.
ARTUR: OK, let's quit playing games.
OWNER: All right. I am coming to the point. Only you fit the bill.
    (*He points to* JERZY, *who is so surprised he virtually falls over backwards.*)
ARTUR: Why him?
OWNER: Only he has the appropriate blood-group. You see, gentlemen, the stamp is worth about one million zlotys.
JERZY: 880,000, to be precise.
OWNER: Exactly. Roughly one million zlotys. However, it is not for sale. Each successive link in the chain prefers an exchange, and a very specific one at that.

[309]

JERZY: And what is your preference? Blood?

OWNER: Actually, no. A kidney. My daughter is sixteen and extremely ill. Being on a dialysis machine for the rest of her life is out of the question. I am looking for someone who is prepared to . . . your father, you see, was too old.

(ARTUR *looks at* JERZY *and grins.*)

ARTUR: Too bad. Shame my blood-group isn't the right one for your daughter.

OWNER: No, yours is not.

(*He looks at* JERZY *again.*)

25

The dog lies at the foot of the cabinets, but his eyes follow JERZY, *who is agitated.*

JERZY: Bloody hell . . . am I supposed to give up one of my kidneys for the sake of a stamp?

ARTUR: For the sake of a pink Austrian Mercury, dated 1851. But you're right. You have a family, a son . . .

JERZY: After all, we're talking about a part of a human being, a part of me.

ARTUR: True. But I wouldn't hesitate for a second if it was me. What the hell do I need a kidney for anyway – I've got two, after all. I know a bloke who's been running around for twenty years with only one kidney and he gets off with women all the time. No problems, touch wood.

JERZY: To hell with it.

ARTUR: Anyway, look at it like this: you're saving the life of a girl. A young girl. Very noble gesture.

JERZY: Artur . . .

ARTUR: I'm not twisting your arm. It's your kidney.

JERZY: But our stamp.

ARTUR: Sit!

(*The dog gets up and sits down. He looks at* ARTUR *and* JERZY, *then reluctantly, after stretching himself out, lies down again. He is panting, his tongue hanging out.* JERZY, *keeping a close eye on the dog, crouches on the floor by the window. Large, red goldfish are again swimming in the aquarium.* JERZY *reaches for a packet of fish food and sprinkles some into the water. The fish swim up to the surface and eagerly throw themselves at it.*)

JERZY: Catch 22 . . . Greedy little devils. Look.

ARTUR: It's only natural. They want to live.

26

Artur's band are rehearsing in a gym hall. ARTUR *gives the cue for the various instruments to come in. If such a band played with a conductor, then* ARTUR *would be fulfilling the role. A young* LAD, *whom we have not yet encountered, is standing at the microphone. The music reaches the point at which the lead singer is supposed to come in.*

ARTUR: Now!

(The LAD *misses his cue.)*

Wakey, wakey.

(The group plays, the LAD *starts to sing, but he is unsure of himself and sluggish.)*

LAD: I don't know. Don't know who
　　But I want nothing from you
　　And give nothing in return.

(They break-off in mid-bar.)

GUITARIST: It's not right.

ARTUR: No – but he'll get the hang of it.

GUITARIST: Why can't you come with us? The venues are great.

ARTUR: I can't make it. Maybe after the holidays, or some other
　　time.

27

JERZY *makes his way over to his room from the veranda. The doors are locked. He knocks, then bangs. His* WIFE *appears at the window.*

WIFE: What?

JERZY: I want to come in.

(After a while the key grates in the lock. He pushes it, but as it half-opens he can see two suitcases and a hold-all. His WIFE *is*

standing next to them. She is holding a piece of paper in her hands.)

WIFE: I've filed for a divorce. This is a copy.

(*She opens the door wider. Taking advantage of* JERZY's *stunned amazement as he reads the document, she carries the suitcases and hold-alls out of the house and dumps them on the veranda.*)

If you want the rest of your stuff, you'll have to call. But only after the hearing. This should keep you going in the meantime.

(*She slams the door shut. The noise jolts* JERZY *out of his daze. He bangs the door with his fists. The door opens slightly – this time it is on a chain.*)

Anything else?

JERZY: We have to talk . . . I have to decide . . . what . . .

WIFE: Hold on a minute.

(*She disappears and returns to hand him a small card.*)

This is the number of my lawyer. If you want to tell me anything before the divorce, ring him. He'll pass it on.

(PIOTREK's *face is glued to the window. He tries to make out his father in the dark. He says nothing – obviously he is afraid of his mother.*)

JERZY: Kiss my arse!

28

JERZY *is sitting on his suitcases. The dog no longer reacts suspiciously to his presence.* ARTUR *unfolds the spare bed, which barely fits into the room.*

JERZY: I've made up my mind.

(ARTUR *smiles and offers* JERZY *his hand.* JERZY *grasps it.* ARTUR *clasps him and they embrace in brotherly fashion.*)

ARTUR: What good are kidneys for, anyway? Can you pickle them?

JERZY: No. Maybe they're good for stew.

ARTUR: One kidney stew please, waiter. Hey, I'm impressed.

29

ARTUR *sits in a hospital corridor. It is already late.* ARTUR's *eyes follow everyone who passes. He rises to his feet on seeing a young* NURSE.

ARTUR: Excuse me . . .

NURSE: Yes.

ARTUR: I'm waiting for . . .

NURSE: Are you the one . . . from City Live?

> (ARTUR *smiles modestly.*)

ARTUR: I am he.

NURSE: Oh Jesus . . .

ARTUR: My brother's having an operation. They're removing a kidney.

NURSE: They've finished. Everything's fine. Can I – touch you?

ARTUR: Of course. Are you really sure everything's all right?

> (*Shyly and delicately, almost as if she were blind, the* NURSE *touches* ARTUR's *face.*)

NURSE: Everything is fine. You know, you're really quite nice in the flesh. I imagined you to be quite different. We can wait together if you like.

30

ARTUR *helps* JERZY *down the hospital steps.* JERZY *is pale and weak, but otherwise behaves normally. On the other hand,* ARTUR's *expression is altered: clearly something has happened.*

ARTUR: How are you feeling?

JERZY: Fine, I don't feel any different. As if nothing has happened. Have you got the stamp?

> (ARTUR *reaches into his wallet. They stop. He takes out the stamp, this time professionally wrapped: a beautiful, pink Austrian Mercury.*)

Jesus, there it is. How long have you had it?

ARTUR: Well – well, a week already.

JERZY: Why didn't you show it to me? I couldn't stop thinking about it.

ARTUR: Jurek, I couldn't.

(JERZY *looks at his brother and notices the strange expression on his face.*)

JERZY: What's up?

ARTUR: While you were having the operation and I was sitting in the hospital . . . Jurek, we were burgled.

JERZY: What?

ARTUR: We were robbed. They stole the lot.

(ARTUR, *with tears in his eyes, rests his head on his brother's shoulder.*)

31

The dog is lying on the bed and not paying the two brothers the slightest attention. There is no hint of its previous threatening energy. JERZY *is inspecting the flat. The bars across the balcony have been bent back and sawn through. Precise, circular holes have been cut in the glass window and the padlocks have also been sawn through on the cabinets. Sheets of paper are lying scattered everywhere.* JERZY *is staring at the dog.*

JERZY: And the brute?

ARTUR: They locked him in the bathroom.

JERZY: I said you should have put him down. Get down!

(*The dog crawls off the bed with its tail between its legs and patters up to the window. Following him with his eyes,* JERZY *notices the fish in the aquarium: they are again floating upside down in the water.*)

They're dead.

ARTUR: I forgot to tell you. It doesn't make any difference what the air's like now anyway.

JERZY: What the hell were you doing in the hospital anyway? Did you think they couldn't manage without you or something?

(ARTUR *lowers his head.*)

What are the police doing about it?

(*The front doorbell.*)

ARTUR: Come in.

(A police officer in plain clothes enters the flat. He is young and athletic. He greets ARTUR, *and then looks at* JERZY.)

OFFICER: And you are . . .?

ARTUR: He's my brother. He came out today.

OFFICER: How do you feel?

JERZY: How do you think I feel? Have you any idea how much all this was worth?

OFFICER: A pretty good idea. I will have to ask you to accompany me to the station.

JERZY: Gladly. Have you checked up on the guy who sold my brother the dog? Who could have locked him in the bathroom?

(The dog, sensing that they are talking about him, raises his head. He falls sleep again with a slight grumble.)

OFFICER: We have already checked it out. You are on the wrong track: the dog was trained by a former colleague of ours. I'll leave you our number.

(He takes out a visiting card and hands it to JERZY.)

While we are on the subject . . . your brother wasn't sure . . . the alarm-system by the windows and the balcony door had been disconnected. From the inside. Do you happen to know anything about it?

(The officer pulls over a chair and shows JERZY *a piece of wire which is hanging from a box under the ceiling.* ARTUR *looks questioningly at* JERZY.)

JERZY: I disconnected it while I was putting in the bars. So that we could open the windows. I thought the bars would be sufficient.

OFFICER: I see. Your brother wasn't sure. I will be in touch. Or you can contact us.

ARTUR: You never told me about the alarm.

JERZY: I forgot to mention it. But surely we must have talked about . . .

ARTUR: I don't remember.

(ARTUR continues to look questioningly, JERZY *shrugs his shoulders.)*

This is all we have left.

(He takes the stamp out of his wallet.)

[315]

Solomon would have commanded us to tear it in two and give it to the one of us who didn't agree to it in the first place. But that was a long time ago . . .

(*He gives the stamp to* JERZY.)

You have it, it was your kidney. I don't want it anyway.

(*He gets up and puts on his jacket. The situation is now reversed.* JERZY *watches* ARTUR *attentively, with suspicion.*)

JERZY: Where are you off to?

ARTUR: I'll be back in the evening. I've arranged to meet someone down the pub.

(JERZY *waits until he has left, then goes over to the telephone and dials a number.*)

JERZY: Hello. Is that the police station? I would like to speak to Officer . . .

32

The OFFICER *joins* JERZY, *who has been waiting for him in the café.*

OFFICER: You wanted to see me.

JERZY: Hello.

OFFICER: I'm listening.

JERZY: You see, officer, I'm not really quite sure how to say this . . .

OFFICER: I quite understand.

JERZY: You may consider this a bit low of me . . .

OFFICER: Don't worry about what I might think.

JERZY: Would you like a drink?

OFFICER: No, thank you.

JERZY: I was thinking that perhaps you ought to consider checking up on my brother.

(*The* OFFICER *doesn't react. He listens attentively.*)

That dog – nobody else could go near it. Yet someone locked it up in the bathroom. He says he sat in the corridor during my operation . . .

OFFICER: He did. And later on, he was lying down in the nurses' off-duty room.

JERZY: I am not saying it was him – but he had so many different

friends, played at so many concerts . . .
OFFICER: Thank you. You have been most helpful.

33

The OFFICER *leaves the café and gets into a waiting car. The car
moves off. It turns left into Jasna Street, then parks in the busy lot in
front of the Atlantic Cinema. The* OFFICER *goes into a coffee bar at
the back of the Central Department Store.*

34

The OFFICER *is looking for someone in the bar. He smiles and goes up
to the bar-counter.* ARTUR *is sitting there.*
OFFICER: You wanted to see me . . .
ARTUR: Hello. I'm crazy, right?
OFFICER: No, why?
ARTUR: After so many hours together I suddenly want to meet in
a café . . .
OFFICER: Discretion. I'm used to it.
ARTUR: Precisely. We kept talking and all the time something
kept running through my mind – I didn't really know how to
tell you.
OFFICER: Now perhaps?
ARTUR: Maybe I'm wrong. In fact I'm sure this is wrong. I – I'm
worried that Jerzy, my brother, may have had something to
do with it. That alarm-system – why didn't he tell me he had
disconnected it? He agreed to the kidney operation, knowing
that he would be lying in hospital. On top of which . . . but
it's all so confusing. I gave him the stamp, which was the
cause of everything, and he wasn't even pleased.
OFFICER: You have been most helpful.
ARTUR: That's what they say in the films.
OFFICER: But so you have. Thank you.

35

After leaving the café, JERZY *walks towards Marszalkowska Street. On the other side of the road, he sees the kid in the glasses whose nose he had nearly wrenched off. He stops in front of the main post office, hesitates for a moment and then goes in. As usual, the place is busy.* JERZY *finds the window where they take letters. A presentation pack with a few stamps in it is sellotaped to the glass window which divides the customers from the assistants.* JERZY *approaches slowly and examines the ordinary Polish stamps which have recently come into circulation. He waits until the assistant,* TOMEK (*whom you may remember from the sixth story*), *has finished stamping a pile of registered envelopes.*

JERZY: Have any stamps . . . been issued recently?

TOMEK: Them. (*He points to the presentation pack.*) Royal Castle for ten zlotys plus the PRON set for six, twenty-five and sixty zlotys.

(TOMEK *is polite. Who knows why?*)

JERZY: All together that's . . .

TOMEK: One hundred and one.

(JERZY *takes out his wallet and finds fifty zlotys. He rummages through his pockets and finds some small change. He scrupulously counts each coin. Somebody walks past and he looks up to see* ARTUR *standing in front of him. He is staring at the same presentation pack. After a while, he turns round. The brothers look at each other, surprised and uneasy.*)

JERZY: I didn't expect you here.

ARTUR: Neither did I. Are you buying them?

JERZY: I'm thirty-five short.

(ARTUR *reaches into his pocket. He takes out some change and counts it.*)

ARTUR: Here, take forty.

(*He gives everything he has to* JERZY.)

13270810R00190

Made in the USA
San Bernardino, CA
15 July 2014